M T W T F S

8:

9:

10

11:

Using the *Teach Yourself in 24 Hours* Series

Welcome to the *Teach Yourself in 24 Hours* series! You're probably thinking, "What, they want me to stay up all night and learn this stuff?" Well, no, not exactly. This series introduces a new way to teach you about exciting new products: 24 one-hour lessons, designed to keep your interest and keep you learning. Because the learning process is broken into small units, you will not be overwhelmed by the complexity of some of the new technologies that are emerging in today's market. Each hourly lesson has a number of special items, some old, some new, to help you along.

12:

10 Minutes

The first 10 minutes of each hour lists the topics and skills that you will learn about by the time you finish the hour. You will know exactly what the hour will bring with no surprises.

1:

20 Minutes

2:

Twenty minutes into the lesson, you will have been introduced to many of the newest features of the software application. In the constantly evolving computer arena, knowing everything a program can do will aid you enormously now and in the future.

3:

30 Minutes

Before 30 minutes have passed, you will have learned at least one useful task. Many of these tasks take advantage of the newest features of the application. These tasks use a hands-on approach, telling you exactly which menus and commands you need to use to accomplish the goal. This approach is found in each lesson of the *24 Hours* series.

4

5:

40 Minutes

You will see after 40 minutes that many of the tools you have come to expect from the *Teach Yourself* series are found in the *24 Hours* series as well. Notes and Tips offer special tricks of the trade to make your work faster and more productive. Warnings help you avoid those nasty time-consuming errors.

50 Minutes

By the time you're 50 minutes in, you'll probably run across terms you haven't seen before. Never before has technology thrown so many new words and acronyms into the language. This *Teach Yourself* series will fully explain any confusing or difficult terms.

60 Minutes

At the end of the hour, you may still have questions that need answered. You know the kind—questions on skills or tasks that come up every day for you, but that weren't directly addressed during the lesson. That's where the Q&A section can help. By answering the most frequently asked questions about the topics discussed in the hour, Q&A not only answers your specific question, it provides a succinct review of all that you have learned in the hour.

Teach Yourself WINDOWS® CE in 24 Hours

Teach Yourself WINDOWS® CE in 24 Hours

David Hayden

SAMS PUBLISHING

201 West 103rd Street
Indianapolis, Indiana 46290

This book is dedicated to my son, Brent David Hayden, and in loving memory of Doris Viers.

Copyright © 1997 by Sams Publishing

FIRST EDITION

International Standard Book Number: 0-672-31065-1

Library of Congress Catalog Card Number: 97-65463

2000 99 98 97 4 3 2 1

Interpretation of the printing code: the rightmost double-digit number is the year of the book's printing; the rightmost single-digit, the number of the book's printing. For example, a printing code of 97-1 shows that the first printing of the book occurred in 1997.

Composed in AGaramond and MCPdigital by Macmillan Computer Publishing

Printed in the United States of America

Trademarks

Publisher and President Richard K. Swadley
Publishing Manager Dean Miller
Director of Editorial Services Cindy Morrow
Director of Marketing Kelli S. Spencer
Assistant Marketing Managers Kristina Perry, Rachel Wolfe

Acquisitions Editor
Kim Spilker

Development Editor
Brian-Kent Proffitt

Production and Copy Editor
Heather Stith

Indexer
Johnna VanHoose

Technical Reviewer
Valda Hilley

Editorial Coordinator
Katie Wise

Technical Edit Coordinator
Lynette Quinn

Resource Coordinator
Deborah Frisby

Editorial Assistants
Carol Ackerman
Andi Richter
Rhonda Tinch-Mize

Cover Designer
Tim Amrhein

Book Designer
Gary Adair

Copy Writer
David Reichwein

Production Team Supervisors
Brad Chinn
Charlotte Clapp

Production
Cynthia Davis
Michael Dietsch
Paula Lowell
Carl Pierce

Overview

Contents

Acknowledgments

The following people have been instrumental in making this book a reality:

Raymond and Sharon Schilling, Kimberly Allen, Alex Tsakiris, Mike Hollowell, and Rhadd Hunt.

About the Author

David Hayden is a renowned 10-year veteran in the handheld PC industry. Currently he is Marketing Manager for the Consumer Division of Compaq Computer Corporation where he has launched the PC Companion, a Windows CE-based handheld computer, in addition to the first Presario and Armada notebook PCs. He was the product manager for Lucid Corporation, the developer of the spreadsheet built into the Casio Boss electronic organizer. As President of Dallas-based Palmtop Resources, he provided consulting services for companies developing and using handheld computers. David also operated the first handheld PC forum on CompuServe and has written numerous articles on handheld computers.

Tell Us What You Think!

As a reader, you are the most important critic and commentator of our books. We value your opinion and want to know what we're doing right, what we could do better, what areas you'd like to see us publish in, and any other words of wisdom you're willing to pass our way. You can help us make strong books that meet your needs and give you the computer guidance you require.

Do you have access to CompuServe or the World Wide Web? Then check out our CompuServe forum by typing `GO SAMS` at any prompt. If you prefer the World Wide Web, check out our site at `http://www.mcp.com`.

Just a Minute

> If you have a technical question about this book, call the technical support line at 317-581-3833.

As the publishing manager of the group that created this book, I welcome your comments. You can fax, e-mail, or write me directly to let me know what you did or didn't like about this book—as well as what we can do to make our books stronger. Here's the information:

Fax: 317-581-4669

E-mail: `opsys_mgr@sams.samspublishing.com`

Mail: Dean Miller
Sams Publishing
201 W. 103rd Street
Indianapolis, IN 46290

Introduction

In 1987, Sharp released the Wizard and it changed the way many people worked. Although this first pocket-sized "electronic organizer" was very limited by today's standards (it offered simple address book and scheduling functionality), it provided a glimpse of things to come. Many products followed, providing bits and pieces of the puzzle. Products such as the Poqet PC were the first to put true PC functionality in a pocket-sized device. The USR Palm Pilot pioneered one-button data synchronization with PCs. The Hewlett Packard Palmtop PCs provided popular applications such as Lotus 1-2-3 and Quicken. Smith Corona's HandiFax offered on-the-fly faxing. No one product combined all of these features into one device. Until now.

With Microsoft's introduction of Windows CE and support from major hardware manufacturers such as Compaq, Casio, and Hewlett Packard, the PC companion or handheld PC (HPC), as Microsoft refers to these devices, was born. The Microsoft Windows CE platform is a Windows 95-like operating system with traditional information manager applications such as an address book, appointment scheduler, task manager, calculator, and world clock. These applications just scratch the surface, though. Microsoft Pocket Word and Pocket Excel provide the basic functionality of their desktop counterparts. Windows CE provides very rich communications capabilities far beyond basic e-mail. Pocket Internet Explorer allows you to browse the Web from virtually anywhere, and other communications options let you access a remote computer from wherever you are.

Microsoft Windows CE almost never saw the light of day. In 1993, Microsoft began an ambitious project known as WinPad. WinPad was to be an operating system designed specifically for PDAs (Personal Digital Assistants) that included scheduling and applications and handwriting recognition similar to that found on the Apple Newton. Several hardware manufacturers, such as Sharp, pledged their support for WinPad. Before the product was completed, Microsoft cancelled the project, saying that "the technology was not ready for prime-time." A couple of years later in 1995, Bill Gates, CEO of Microsoft, decided to develop an operating system, code-named Pegasus, that was to become Windows CE (Consumer Electronic). Instead of redesigning WinPad, he decided to build Windows CE from the ground up based on user needs and the state of technology today. On November 17, 1996 at the Treasure Island Hotel in Las Vegas, Microsoft Windows CE was born.

What really defines this new category of Windows CE devices is the integration of all of these features and their seamless connectivity to Microsoft Windows-based PCs. For many older handheld PCs and electronic organizers, connectivity to a desktop or notebook PC seemed to be an afterthought. Although most of them provided an optional cable and software, very few offered synchronization with popular PC applications. Microsoft Windows CE provides synchronization with Schedule+ and other scheduling programs and drag-and-drop file compatibility with Microsoft Word and Excel.

Although Windows CE, and the products that include it, provide impressive functionality, look for improvements in both Windows CE and handheld PCs in the near future. The first release of Windows CE does not include handwriting recognition, faxing, or direct printing capabilities, although several third-party software developers offer utilities to address these limitations. Microsoft may incorporate some or all of these features in subsequent revisions of Windows CE. Hardware improvements such as color screens, more memory, and improved communications options such as faster modems, wireless paging, and cellular communications are sure to appear in future products.

Within 24 hours, you will be writing letters, making appointments, entering contacts into your address book, checking your e-mail, surfing the Net, balancing your checkbook, and even playing Solitaire with Windows CE.

Part I

Getting Started in the Morning

Hour

1 Getting Familiar with Windows CE

2 Getting Started

3 Take Windows CE for a Test Drive

4 Understanding Synchronization

5 Call for Help

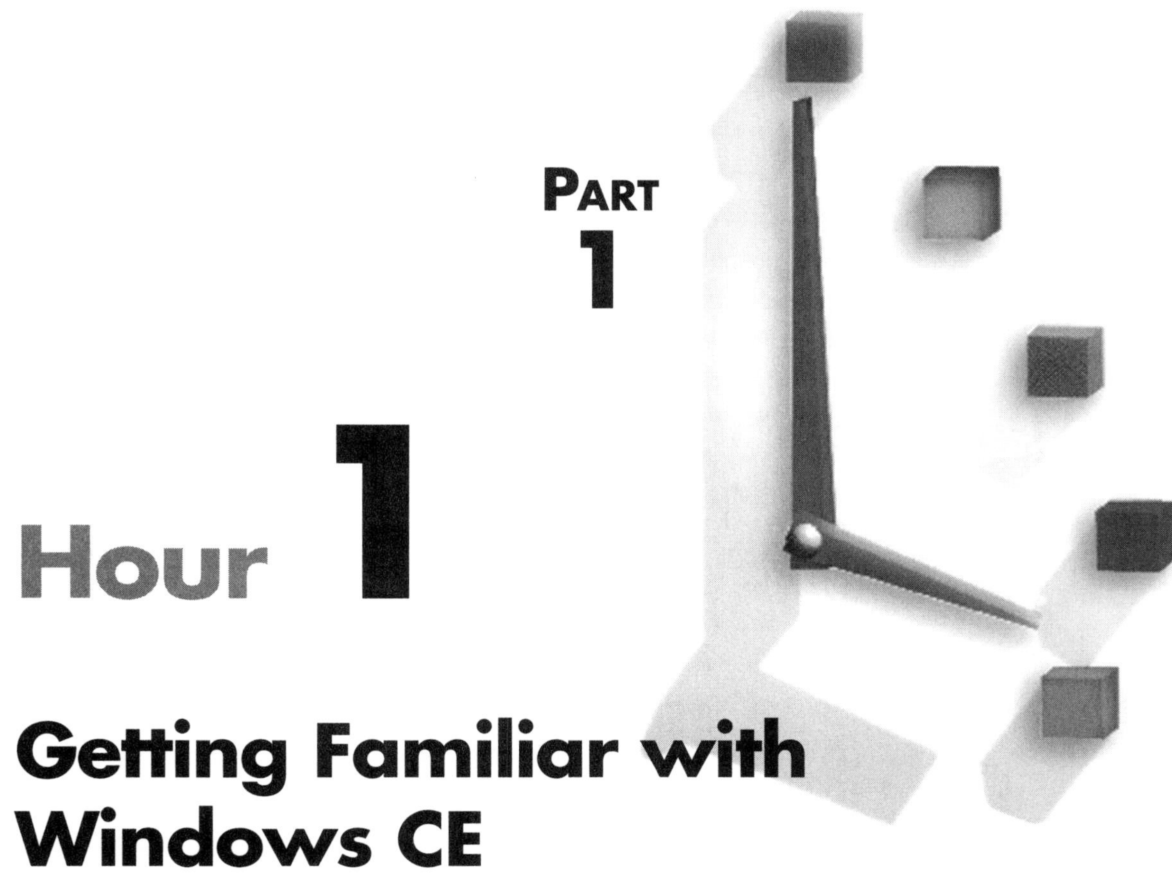

Part 1

Hour 1

Getting Familiar with Windows CE

They said it couldn't be done: a powerful Windows-like operating system built into a one-pound, pocket-sized computer...they were wrong! Welcome to Microsoft Windows CE, a powerful and intuitive operating environment that is a pleasure to learn and use. A handheld personal computer (also known as an HPC) built around Windows CE keeps you organized, in touch, and connected. Windows CE comes with an impressive array of applications, including an electronic calendar, address book, word processor, spreadsheet, and communications applications, to provide computer functionality wherever you go.

In this first hour, while you drink your morning cup of coffee, you will be introduced to Windows CE. You will learn how to use the keyboard or stylus to navigate the system and will become familiar with the user interface. You will understand the similarities and differences between Windows 95 and CE as well as how you can use the built-in applications.

You will learn about the following topics in this hour:

- The key elements of the Windows CE user interface
- How to get around Windows CE efficiently
- The differences between Windows CE and Windows 95
- How to quit Windows CE

Understanding the Windows CE Interface

The Windows CE interface is a very simple graphical design reminiscent of the look and feel of Windows 95. If you have used Windows 95 before, you will feel at home with Windows CE immediately. If you have never used Windows 95, you will learn in the following pages how the graphical elements of the Windows CE interface enhance ease of use and increase efficiency.

Microsoft Windows CE is

- A graphical user interface (GUI) similar to Microsoft Windows 95
- Compatible with Win32 API (Advanced Programmer Interface) so that developers can use industry-standard development tools to create Windows CE programs (Windows CE cannot run Windows 95 programs.)
- A subset of the Microsoft Office suite of applications
- Software that turns your handheld PC (HPC) into a pocket-sized electronic communicator

Why Windows CE?

- Seamless data *synchronization* with your desktop or notebook PC
- Easy to use with familiar Windows 95-like graphical user interface
- Compatibility with popular desktop programs such as Microsoft Word, Excel, and Schedule+
- The capability to check your e-mail with Inbox, surf the Net with Pocket Internet Explorer, and access your company's network remotely with Terminal

In Hour 2, "Getting Started," you will go through the initial setup that you see the first time you turn on your handheld PC (HPC). The first thing you will notice is that Windows CE does not take you through a time-consuming startup procedure as Windows 95 does. Figure 1.1 shows the typical Windows CE screen that most users will see after completing the initial setup. Other than your background picture (referred to as *wallpaper*) most Windows CE HPCs share almost identical functionality whether from Compaq, Hewlett-Packard, or any other manufacturer.

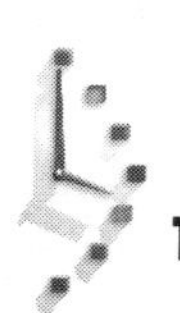

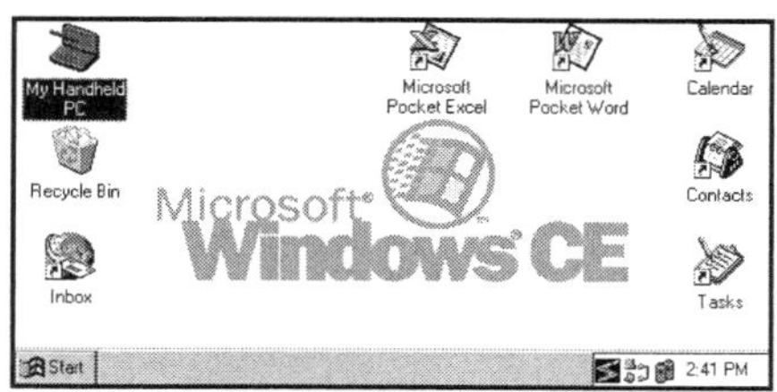

Figure 1.1.
The Windows CE desktop.

What's on My Windows CE Computer?

Windows CE's primary work area is called the desktop. Figure 1.1 contains several icons on the desktop titled My Handheld PC, Recycle Bin, Microsoft Pocket Word, Microsoft Pocket Excel, Calendar, Contacts, Tasks, and Inbox. Don't worry if you are missing an icon; all Windows CE HPCs include each of these applications. Some icons may just be in a different section of your HPC. Also, some HPCs may have an extra icon or two, such as Pocket Internet Explorer.

Each of these icons starts a program or function when you double-tap the icon with the included stylus or your finger. You'll learn to use the stylus later in this hour. If you prefer to use the keyboard, Windows CE offers an abundance of keyboard shortcuts, which are also covered later in this hour.

The My Handheld PC icon allows you to navigate to different folders and programs. You can move through several levels of folders and view files throughout your HPC with a simple point and double-tap. Within My Handheld PC, you can organize files and folders and copy, rename, delete, and create shortcuts to your favorite program. Selecting the My Handheld PC icon opens the Windows CE Explorer view in Figure 1.2.

The Recycle Bin icon is where you drag and drop files and folders that you want to delete. In Hour 6, "Understanding Files and Folders," you will learn more about shortcuts, Windows CE Explorer, and the Recycle Bin.

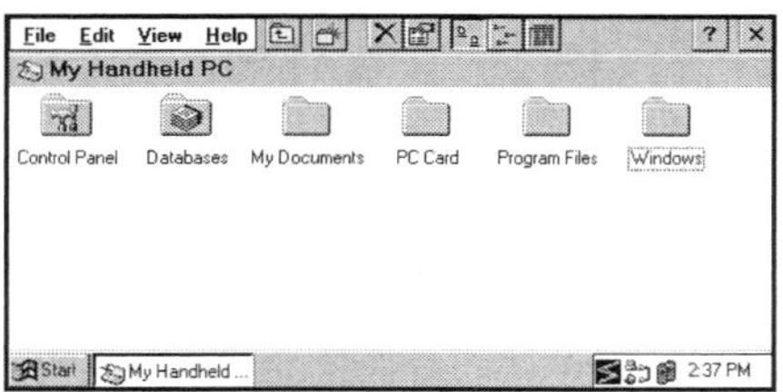

Figure 1.2.
The Windows CE Explorer.

For the first time, powerful word processing that is compatible with the word processor you probably use on your desktop or notebook PC is available in a pocket-size computer. Microsoft Pocket Word, a subset of the best-selling Microsoft Word program, features painless file translation between the pocket and desktop versions of Word through a cable or docking station. You will explore Pocket Word in-depth in Hour 10, "Using Pocket Word." With Pocket Word you can write a letter, compose a memo, or take notes anywhere. In addition to basic editing features, you can also change fonts, alignment, and attributes such as boldface, italics, and underline. You can also create bulleted lists and search for and replace text. An outline view, covered in Hour 11, "Advanced Pocket Word," makes it easy to organize long documents with various levels of detail. Although Windows CE does not directly support printing, you can transfer the document back to your desktop PC to check spelling and print it. Figure 1.3 shows a memo written in Pocket Word. Notice that Pocket Word supports graphics as well as text attributes.

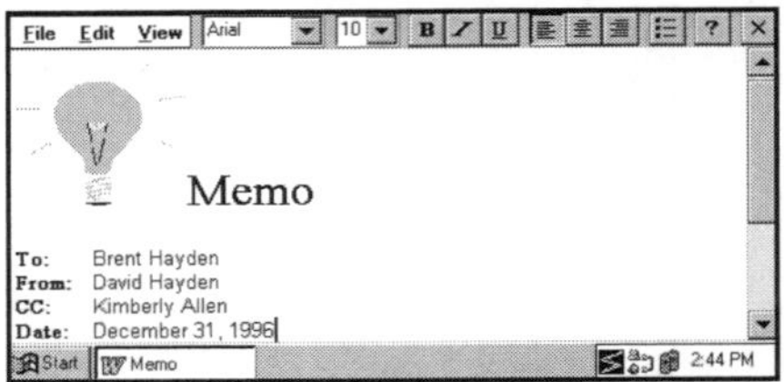

Figure 1.3.
Microsoft Pocket Word.

Microsoft Pocket Excel is a powerful and surprisingly easy-to-use spreadsheet that is based on Microsoft Excel for desktop PCs. Pocket Excel is more than just numbers and financial functions. You can track expenses, balance your checkbook, manage investments, create reports, and prepare an amortization schedule. Figure 1.4 shows a typical Pocket Excel screen. In Hour 12, "Using Pocket Excel," you will learn how to create workbooks, enter and edit data, use functions and formulas, and use other advanced features. After you are finished, you will learn how to transfer your spreadsheet back to your desktop PC for printing or to use the more advanced features found in Microsoft Excel for Windows 95.

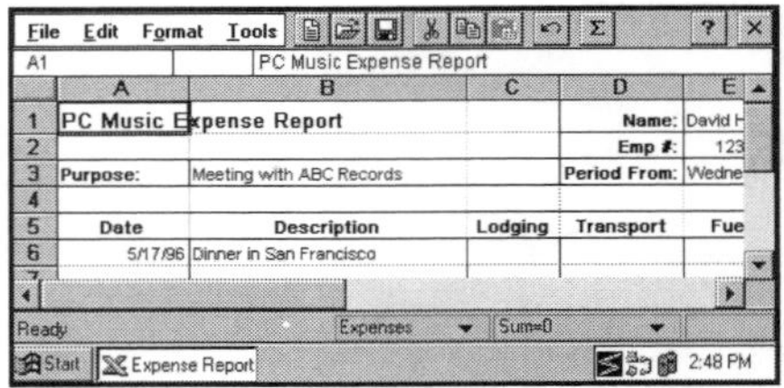

Figure 1.4.
Microsoft Pocket Excel.

Although you may have purchased your HPC primarily for the powerful word processor or spreadsheet, you will probably use Information Manager more than any other program. Information Manager, a subset of Microsoft Schedule+, enables you to keep track of contacts, appointments, and tasks. Although the desktop version of Schedule+ (included on the CD bundled with your HPC) includes these functions in one tightly integrated program, Windows CE splits them into three separate programs: Calendar, Contacts, and Tasks.

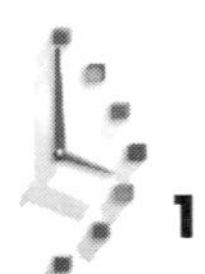

Calendar is a flexible scheduler for managing appointments and events. In Hour 7, "Scheduling with Calendar," you will learn how to view your daily or weekly schedule; enter, edit, and delete appointments; and create recurring appointments. Calendar also enables you to set a variety of alarms to alert you of pending appointments. Figure 1.5 shows a typical Calendar screen.

Figure 1.5.
Calendar's Daily view.

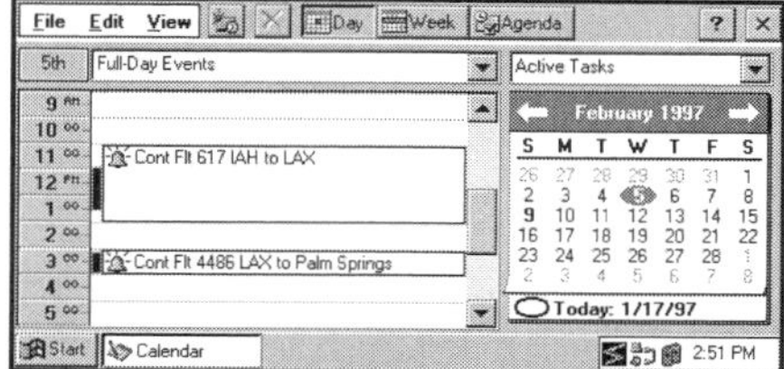

If you are looking for an electronic address book in which you can quickly look up information, Contacts delivers. You will learn how to enter, edit, delete, sort, and view contacts in a variety of formats in Hour 8, "Keep in Touch with Contacts." Figure 1.6 shows an example of a Contact screen.

Figure 1.6.
Contacts' Card view.

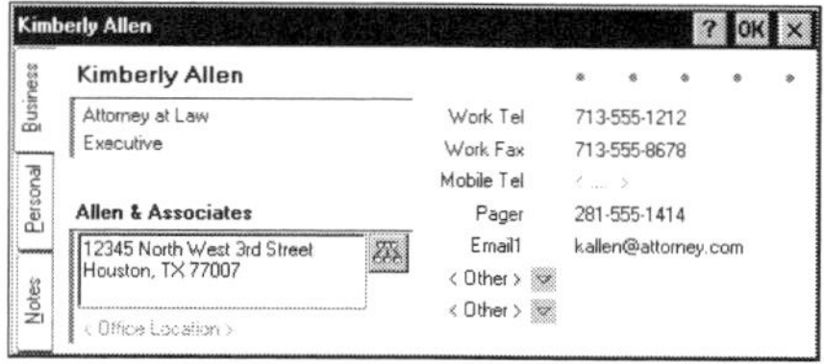

If you stay organized by creating "to-do" lists, you will find Tasks a pleasure to use. Figure 1.7 shows a typical Tasks screen. In Hour 9, "The Task at Hand," you will learn how to create, change, or remove entries in your to-do list. With a touch of the screen, you can mark a task as complete and sort and view tasks in a variety of formats.

Figure 1.7.
Tasks' List view.

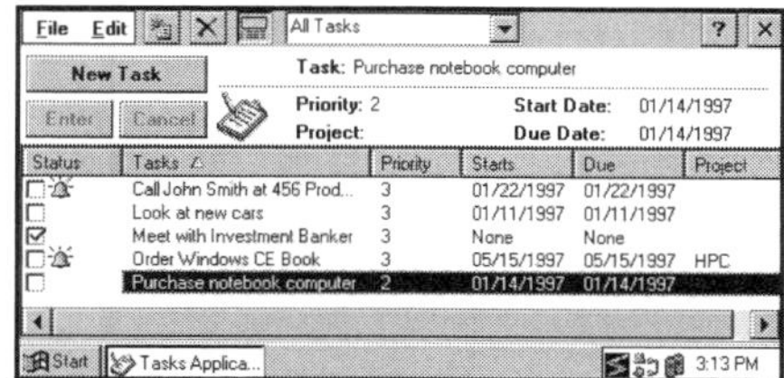

One thing that separates Windows CE HPCs from electronic organizers and other handheld computers is their powerful communications capabilities. The media has always talked about the future of pocket-size e-mail and Internet computers. Windows CE brings the future here today by providing a host of communication features, such as World Wide Web access through Pocket Internet Explorer (as shown in Figure 1.8).

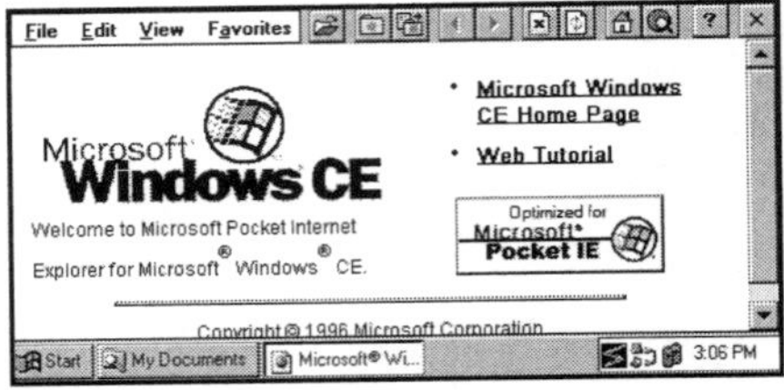

Figure 1.8.
Pocket Internet Explorer.

With Inbox you can send and receive electronic mail messages either while your HPC is attached to your desktop PC (using Microsoft Exchange) or remotely via a modem available for many HPCs. In Hour 15, "Using Inbox for E-mail," you will learn how to set up your HPC for communicating and connect to your e-mail service, and how to compose, send, and retrieve messages. If you have entered e-mail addresses in the Contacts program, you can easily send e-mail messages to those contacts with Inbox. Figure 1.9 shows the Inbox message list.

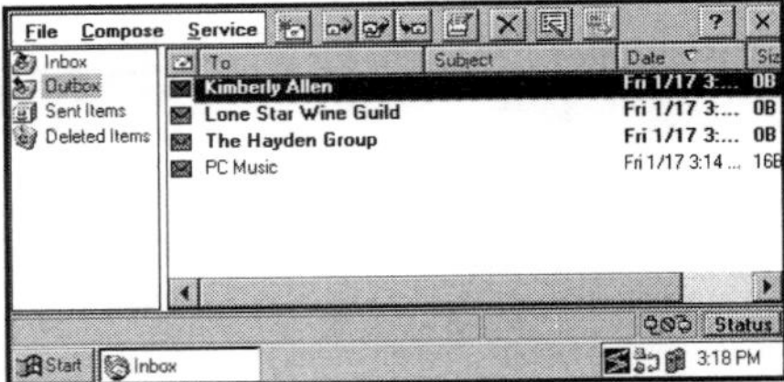

Figure 1.9.
The Inbox message list.

Terminal is another useful communications program that enables you to connect to other online and e-mail services, such as CompuServe, MCI Mail, and electronic bulletin boards. Also, you can remotely access your company's network if it has been configured as a remote access server (RAS). Figure 1.10 shows an example of a Terminal session. You will learn more about Terminal and RAS in Hour 18, "Using Terminal."

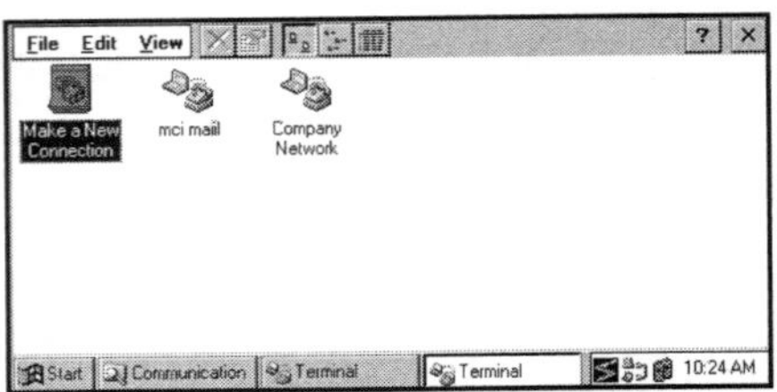

Figure 1.10.
A Terminal session.

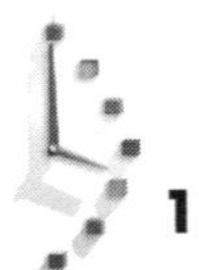

In addition to the applications previously described, Windows CE provides several useful accessory programs. The World Clock accessory enables you to set the date and time for your home city as well as any other city in the world; it also provides useful information such as airport codes, telephone dialing codes, distances, and time zones. In Hour 2 you will learn how to set up and use World Clock. A simple on-screen calculator enables you to perform on-the-fly calculations that can be pasted into documents and spreadsheets. In Hour 13, "Using Calculator," you will explore this program in more depth.

When work time becomes play time, Windows CE provides the popular Solitaire card game, which you will explore in Hour 14, "Take a Break with Solitaire." If that is not enough to stifle your productivity, Microsoft offers an optional Entertainment Pack for Windows CE that includes 10 other simple games.

Windows CE Interface

In the past, most handheld computers and electronic organizers required that you use a tiny keyboard to access features and enter data. Windows CE is the first handheld operating system to combine a stylus-based touch screen, a Windows-like interface, and an industry-standard development platform to assure a wealth of third-party software. Once you learn one program, you are well on your way to learning the others, because all Windows CE programs share a very similar interface.

Because quick and easy access is so important to Windows CE users, Microsoft invested significant resources on usability testing to assure a very simple and straightforward design. You will see the results of Microsoft's efforts when you use commands or functions and they perform exactly as expected. Important to this design are graphical elements that provide access to numerous options.

The taskbar, located along the bottom of the screen, is used primarily to launch and switch between programs. If you want to hide an application from view, tap the program name on the taskbar with the stylus. To display the program, tap the program name on the taskbar again. The lower-right corner of the taskbar displays the time and miniature informational icons that indicate, for example, your battery status. The buttons on the taskbar give you one-touch access to Windows CE programs much like the buttons on a car stereo give you access to your favorite radio stations. The most important button on the taskbar is the Start button, which you will learn more about shortly.

All Windows CE programs have some sort of pull-down menu system. Most programs have an Edit pull-down menu similar to that shown in Figure 1.11 and a File menu. The Edit menu allows you to undo your last action, cut, copy, and paste, and use other options depending on the current program. The File menu provides options to create, open, save, and close files. Several applications, such as Pocket Word and Calendar, have a View menu that enables you to view your data in several formats. Depending on the program, other menus, such as a Help menu, may be available.

Figure 1.11.
The Edit menu.

Scroll bars enable you to easily move around a file if some information is out of view. Although this feature is common in graphical user interfaces (GUIs), it is particularly useful in Windows CE because Windows CE screens are much smaller than a desktop monitor. To use a scroll bar, select the on-screen up or down arrows (typically located on the right side of a window) to move up or down a line at a time. Pocket Excel displays a scroll bar at the bottom of the window so that you can move left and right a column at a time. As you navigate through a document, you will notice that a small bar moves up and down (or left and right) as you scroll around the screen. This bar graphically represents your position within a document.

The toolbar, located near the top of the screen, provides one-touch access to commonly used functions, such as centering or underlining. A recessed button indicates that the option is selected. Every Windows CE program has a unique toolbar.

Using Dialog Boxes

Dialog boxes appear frequently when you use Windows CE programs. These boxes present you with many options in the form of check boxes, command buttons, radio buttons, and drop-down list boxes. Figure 1.12 shows a typical dialog box with these elements.

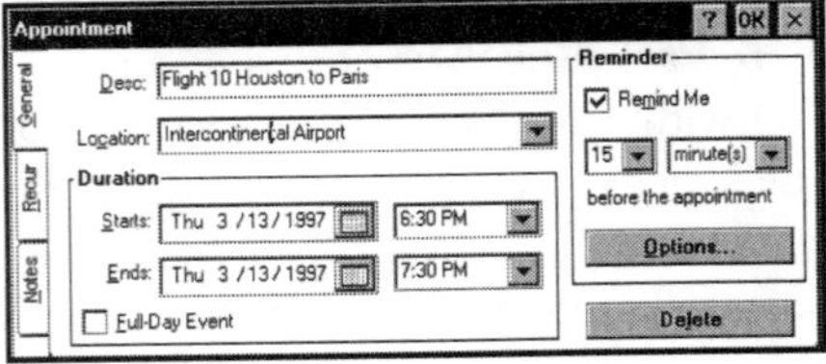

Figure 1.12.
A dialog box.

Check boxes present yes/no options that are marked with a check to signify a yes response and show an empty box to indicate a no response. You have three ways to check and uncheck boxes:

- Tap the check box or text next to the desired box. Check boxes toggle between options, so every time you tap the box, Windows CE will check or uncheck the box depending on the previous selection.

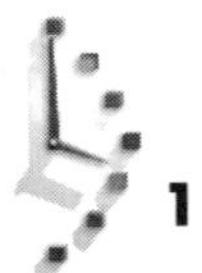

- Press the Tab (forward) or Shift+Tab (backward) keys to move to different check boxes on the screen. When a dotted line surrounds the desired check box text, press the Enter key. Press Enter again to return to the previous setting.
- Press and hold down the Alt key, and then type the underlined letter of the check box text.

Many dialog boxes also contain command buttons that offer access to a variety of options. There are several ways to select a command button:

- Tap the button with the stylus or your finger.
- Press and hold the Alt key, and then type the underlined letter on the button. For example, in Figure 1.13, you would press Alt+O to select the Options command button.

Figure 1.13.
Using the Alt shortcut key.

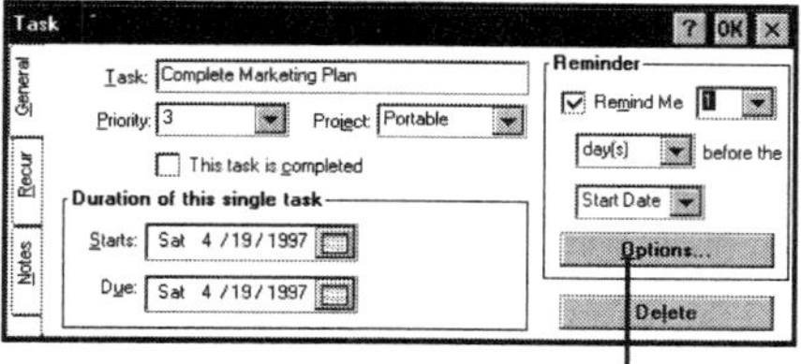

- Press and hold the Tab key to cycle through all on-screen command buttons. A dotted line surrounds the button when it is ready for selection. When the line surrounds the button you want, press the Enter key to execute the command.

In some programs, Windows CE uses radio buttons for options that require more than a yes/no response. Figure 1.14 shows an example of radio buttons. Making a radio button selection is very similar to selecting a command button. Follow one of these three approaches when selecting radio buttons:

- Tap the open circle to the left of the text you want to select with the stylus or your finger.
- Press and hold the Alt key, and then type the underlined letter next to the button.
- Press and hold the Tab key to cycle through all radio buttons. A dotted line surrounds the text next to the current button. When the line surrounds the text of the button you want, press the Enter key to select it.

Drop-down list boxes enable you to select from a list of options without taking up valuable screen space. If a data entry box contains a down arrow to the right of the field, tap the down arrow to display all available options, and select the one you want.

Figure 1.14.
Using radio buttons.

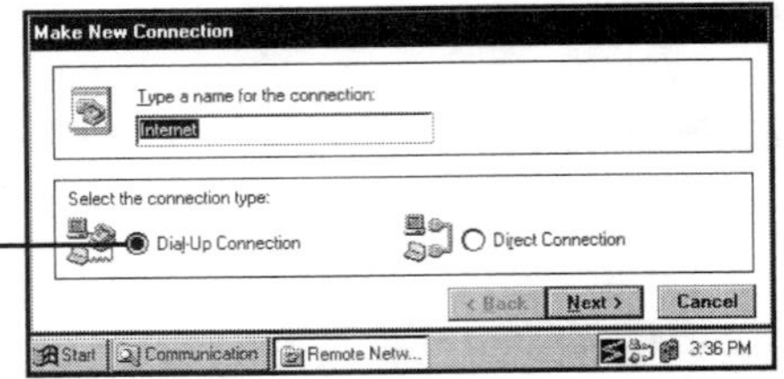

An activated radio button

Using the Stylus as a Mouse

Just as the mouse is the primary way to navigate Microsoft Windows, the stylus is the primary input device for Windows CE. The touch screen is very efficient because you can tap exactly where you want on the screen. Because all Windows CE handheld PCs feature a touch-sensitive screen, you can use your finger or the included stylus to start programs, select features from menus, select text, or do virtually any other action except data entry.

Tapping the screen with the stylus is essentially the same as moving the mouse to point and pressing the left mouse button in Windows 95. To start a program, you will often be required to rapidly tap twice on the screen. As explained in Hour 2, you can change the speed at which you double-tap. A few Windows CE programs support the equivalent of a right mouse-click. For those programs that support this feature, the Windows CE equivalent is to press and hold down the Alt key while tapping an item with the stylus.

JUST A MINUTE

If the stylus does not respond as expected after you initially set up your HPC, press Ctrl+Alt+= to recalibrate your stylus settings.

Using the Start Menu

The most important part of the taskbar is the Start button, which, when selected with the stylus, launches the Start menu. This menu is the Windows CE main menu and enables you to run programs, load documents, change settings, and get help. Selecting one of the options from the menu takes you to the next level so that you can select the program you want to run, the document you plan to use, or the setting you need to change. Figure 1.15 shows an example of the Start menu with multiple programs on the taskbar.

Figure 1.15.
The Windows CE taskbar.

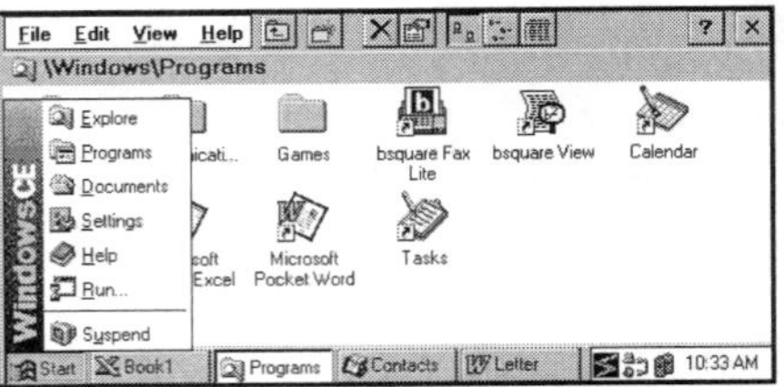

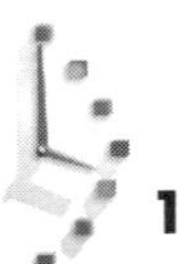

You can access the Start menu in the following ways:

- Tap the Start button with the stylus or your finger.
- Press the Windows key on your HPC keyboard.
- Press the Tab key until a dotted line surrounds the Start button, and then press the Enter key.

Refer to Table 1.1 for a list of the Start menu options and their associated functions. When the Start menu is visible, you have three ways to access the command you want:

- Type the underlined letter of the command.
- Use the stylus or your finger to tap the command.
- Use the up or down arrow key to select the command and press the Enter key.

Table 1.1. Start menu options.

Command	Function
Explore	Starts Windows CE Explorer (same as double-tapping My Handheld PC)
Programs	Displays a list of folders and programs you can open
Documents	Displays a list of the most recently used documents
Settings	Allows you to change your Windows CE configuration (starts Control Panel)
Help	Provides access to Windows CE online help
Run	Loads the Run dialog box so that you can select the program you want to run
Suspend	Turns off your HPC and puts Windows CE in suspend mode

Using the Keyboard

Although the stylus is generally the preferred way to select functions, keyboard shortcuts, once you learn them, can provide the most efficient way to get from point A to point B. Table 1.2 identifies keyboard shortcuts used in conjunction with the Windows key.

Table 1.2. General keyboard shortcuts.

Keyboard shortcut	Function performed
Windows key	Activates the Start menu
Windows key+C	Starts Control Panel
Windows key+E	Starts Explore My Handheld PC
Windows key+H	Starts Windows CE Help
Windows key+I	Reconfigures stylus settings
Windows key+K	Reconfigures keyboard settings
Windows key+R	Displays the Run dialog box
Alt+Tab	Loads Task Manager to switch between programs

Although each Windows CE program uses different keyboard shortcuts, several shortcuts work across most applications. Table 1.3 shows commonly used keyboard shortcuts.

Table 1.3. Program-specific keyboard shortcuts.

Keyboard shortcut	Function performed	Programs supported
Ctrl+Esc	Activates Start menu	All programs
Ctrl+N	Creates a new document or entry	Pocket Word, Pocket Excel, Calendar, Contacts, and Tasks
Ctrl+O	Opens a new document	Pocket Word, Pocket Excel, and Pocket Internet Explorer
Ctrl+S	Saves a document	Pocket Word and Pocket Excel

To type all uppercase letters, turn on Caps Lock by pressing both Shift keys simultaneously. You will notice the letter A in the right corner of the taskbar. To turn off Caps Lock, press both Shift keys again.

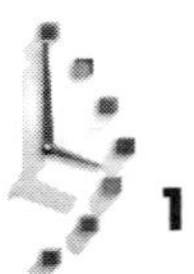

1

Windows CE and Windows 95 Compared

The Windows CE desktop, Start button and menu, taskbar, toolbar, Explorer, and Control Panel all bear a striking resemblance to Windows 95. Despite their similarities, however, there are many differences between Windows CE and Windows 95.

The most obvious difference between Windows 95 and Windows CE is that Windows CE is always open. Unlike Windows 95, which requires a sometimes exhaustive startup routine, Windows CE is ready to go the moment you turn on your HPC.

Another fundamental difference is that unlike Windows 95, Windows CE does not support tiling or overlapping windows. Although Windows CE is a multitasking operating system like Windows 95, you cannot view more than one program or document at a time. You must switch to another program or document through the taskbar or Task Manager (accessed by pressing Alt+Tab).

Windows CE also does not support direct printing, although optional software is available to support this function. To print a file, you must use HPC Explorer on your desktop PC or transfer a file and print from within the desktop versions of Word, Excel, or Schedule+. Refer to Hour 4, "Understanding Synchronization," for an explanation of HPC Explorer.

The following sections analyze several aspects of Windows 95 and Windows CE to provide you with an understanding of these two operating systems.

The Desktop

The familiar My Computer icon on Windows 95 is the counterpart to Windows CE's My Handheld PC and provides very similar functionality. Windows CE does not support floppy disk drives, CD-ROM drives, or direct printing. Therefore, unlike Windows 95, these options are not displayed when you select My Handheld PC. Figures 1.16 and 1.17 show a typical desktop view for Windows CE and Windows 95.

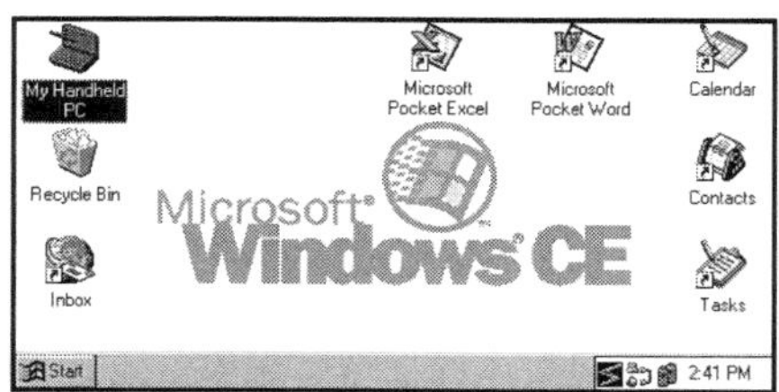

Figure 1.16.
A typical Windows CE desktop view.

Figure 1.17.
A typical Windows 95 desktop view.

The Recycle Bin functions almost identically in Windows 95 and CE. The primary difference is in the amount of space allocated to store recently deleted files. The Recycle Bin in Windows CE, like the one in Windows 95, can be set to a maximum size of 10 percent of available memory. You can adjust the size of Windows CE's Recycle Bin, but given the limited memory on most Windows CE HPCs, it is recommended that you leave it the default size.

Windows CE is compatible with the Windows 95 graphics format (.bmp) for background wallpaper, so you can share wallpaper between the two platforms. When you transfer a .bmp file from your desktop computer, it is converted to a .2bp format. The smaller screen used by most Windows CE handheld PCs is a lower resolution (typically 480 × 214 pixels) than a typical Windows 95 PC (typically 800 × 600 pixels), so you may have to adjust the size of the image depending on the background you choose.

Just like Windows 95, Windows CE supports program shortcuts (icons placed on the desktop that run particular programs when they are selected). Windows CE includes program shortcuts for Pocket Word, Pocket Excel, Contacts, Calendar, Tasks, and Inbox.

File Translation with Pocket Word and Pocket Excel

Microsoft had to make some trade-offs when designing Word and Excel for Windows CE, given the limited memory and storage of the Windows CE HPCs. Given the 80/20 rule, which says that 80 percent of the users use only 20 percent of the features of Microsoft Word and Excel, Microsoft included the most frequently used features of these two applications in their pocket counterparts. In Pocket Word, you lose tables, and in order to check spelling or grammar and print, you must transfer the document back to your desktop PC. Microsoft

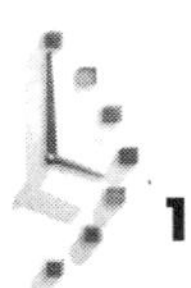

Pocket Excel excludes charting and macros, as well as direct printing. Pocket Excel provides about 100 of the most commonly used Excel functions.

Because of the lack of some features in Pocket Word and Pocket Excel, some formatting and other attributes are changed or removed when files are transferred to the HPC from Windows 95. Tables 1.4 and 1.5 describe the results of transferring Word and Excel documents between Windows 95 and CE.

Table 1.4. Translating documents from Word to Pocket Word.

Conversion attribute	Conversion results
Tables	Text is shown without borders and separated by tabs.
Columns, table of contents, index, fields, color, and numbering	Text is shown, but some formatting may be lost.
Fonts	Closest available font, point size, and shade of gray is used.
Headers, footers, footnotes, annotations, revisions, style sheets, borders, shading, and OLE objects	These items are removed when the file is transferred to the HPC, but the original remains intact. Embedded objects are converted to pictures. Objects not stored in the file are removed.

Just a Minute

In certain situations, complex tabs and some numbered lists and section headings may not be converted properly.

Table 1.5. Translating Excel documents to Pocket Excel.

Conversion attribute	Conversion results
Functions and formulas	Supported functions and formulas are converted. Unsupported functions are removed, and the returned value of the function appears. Arrays and formulas containing an external link or intersection range reference are converted to values.
Names	Names that reference worksheets within a workbook are converted, but names that refer to other workbooks' arrays are not converted.
Fonts, Color	Closest available font, point size, and shade of gray is used.

continues

Table 1.5. continued

Conversion attribute	Conversion results
Format	Custom numeric formats are matched to the closest format supported.
Borders, Patterns	All borders are single line, and patterns are removed.
Alignment	Horizontal, vertical, and wrap text attributes remain the same, but vertical text appears horizontal.
Pivot table data	Data is converted to values.
Protection	If a workbook is password-protected, you cannot convert the file. Instead of using password protection, use the Protect Document option, which is supported.
Charts, drawing objects, pictures, dialog sheets, text boxes, and macros	These attributes are not converted.

Schedule+ and Information Manager

Pocket Word and Pocket Excel support file translation, but Windows CE's Information Manager goes a step further by supporting file synchronization with Schedule+. File synchronization means that you can make changes on both the HPC and desktop computer and stay updated on both systems. In Hour 4 you will cover this feature in more detail.

Quitting Windows CE

Windows CE is a multitasking operating system, which means that you do not have to quit one program before starting another. The amount of memory you have on your HPC will determine how many programs you can run at one time. If you run out of memory, Windows CE will alert you that your memory is very low. You will then have the option of choosing which program you want to quit.

Closing Programs

You can close programs in the following ways:

- Tap the X (referred to as the close button) in the upper-right corner of the screen with the stylus or your finger. If your information has not been saved, Windows CE will ask you whether you want to save the information before it closes the program.

- Open the File menu, and select Exit or Close, depending on the program.
- Press Alt+X or Alt+C, depending on the program.

Shutting Down Windows CE

Unlike Microsoft Windows 95, Windows CE does not require that you go through a shutdown procedure. Windows CE is always active. When you are finished using Windows CE, you can either press the OFF button on your HPC, or select Suspend from the Start menu. When you press the ON button, you will return to exactly the same point where you left off.

Back up often! In case you missed that, back up often! If you have ever fallen victim to major data loss, you know the value of backing up. Unlike Windows 95, Windows CE requires battery power even when the HPC is turned off or data may be lost. Even though all HPCs have a backup battery, data loss is still a risk, so, once again, back up often!

Summary

You are on your way to fully understanding what Windows CE is and how to become productive with it. This hour introduced you to the programs that make up Windows CE and explained the key elements of the user interface so that you have a solid foundation to build on. You also learned the differences between Windows 95 and CE and how to use the stylus and keyboard to get around easily. Now that you're ready, grab another cup of coffee, roll up your sleeves, and let's get started!

Q&A

Q Why did Microsoft develop Windows CE?

A Several years ago Microsoft's founder Bill Gates shared his vision of "information at your fingertips," which he described as accessing information anytime, anywhere. After a few false starts, this vision led to the development of Windows CE, a smaller version of Windows and Office 95.

Q Does tapping the touch screen harder make it more responsive?

A No. The touch-sensitive screen responds just as well to gentle taps.

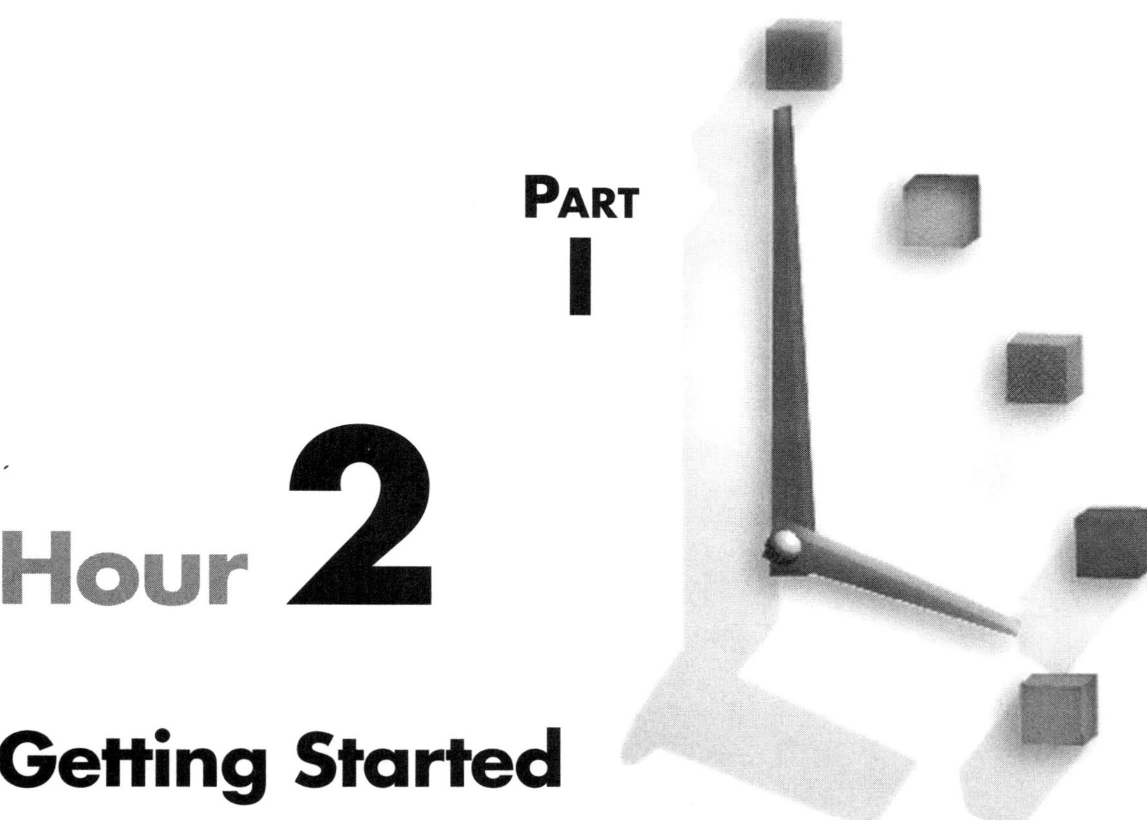

Hour 2

Getting Started

Now that you have seen what you can do with Windows CE, get another cup of coffee and get ready to set up Windows CE. By taking a little time now, you will save yourself a lot of time and aggravation later.

In this hour you will learn how to do the following:

- Set the time and date for your home city
- Add personal information
- Set passwords
- Change the desktop background
- Increase battery life

Setting Up the Touch Screen

The first time you turn on your HPC, you will be prompted for setup information. Each time you complete a screen, tap the Next button to advance to the next section. The first screen is for configuring your HPC's touch screen, a process that Microsoft calls *calibrating*. Calibrating means setting the alignment of the touch-sensitive film that covers the screen. You will be asked to use the stylus that came with your HPC to touch the center of a series of five crosses for several seconds each. To assure accurate settings, be sure to point the stylus at precisely the midpoint of the cross. Keep the stylus positioned in the center of the cross until the cross moves to a new location. After you complete this task, press the Enter key.

If, after continued use of your HPC, you notice that your pointer is not responding as expected, you can readjust the touch screen by following these simple steps:

1. Tap the Start button and select Settings.
2. Double-tap the Stylus icon within Control Panel.
3. Tap the Recalibrate button. (Your screen should look similar to Figure 2.1.)
4. Point and hold the stylus on the center of each cross until the cross stops moving.
5. Press the Enter key when the message `New calibration settings have been measured` appears to save these settings, or press the Esc key to start over.
6. Press the OK button when you're finished.

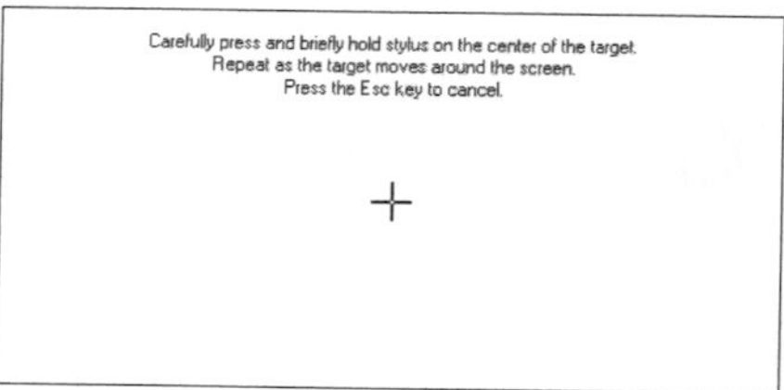

Figure 2.1.
The recalibration screen.

If your HPC is not responding to the stylus, an alternative to the preceding procedure is to press and hold the Ctrl+Alt+= (equal sign) and then follow the preceding steps 3-5.

To set the speed at which Windows CE responds to a double-tap, follow these steps:

1. Tap the Settings option on the Start menu.
2. Double-tap the Stylus icon, and tap the Double-Tap tab.
3. Double-tap the checkerboard pictured in Figure 2.2.
4. Double-tap the icon below the checkerboard to verify your settings, and then tap the OK button.

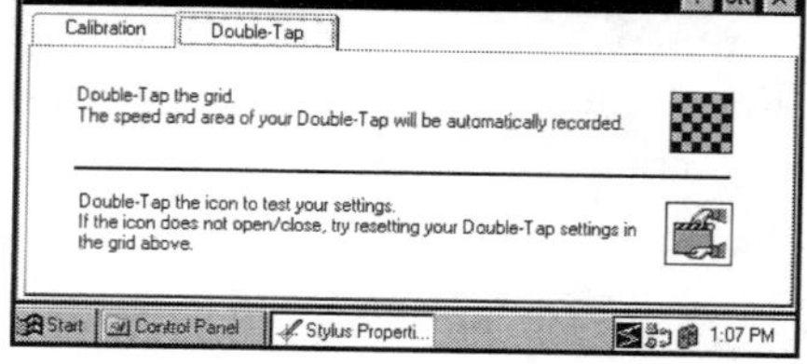

Figure 2.2.
Setting the double-tap speed.

Setting World Clock

After you have completed calibrating the touch screen, you will be prompted to set the World Clock. More than a simple alarm clock, World Clock displays two side-by-side clocks—one for your home city and the other for a city you may be visiting. When you are traveling, one simple tap of the screen changes the date and time to the city where you are.

In addition to date and time, World Clock provides useful information about cities such as area codes, time zones, airport codes, and estimated sunrise and sunset times. Even distances between cities are displayed, a feature that frequent flyers will find useful. World Clock also provides a variety of alarm options.

Starting World Clock

To start World Clock, if you are not already there from the initial setup, follow these simple steps:

1. Tap the Start button.
2. Select Settings from the Start menu.
3. Double-tap the World Clock icon. (Your screen should look similar to Figure 2.3 or Figure 2.4.)

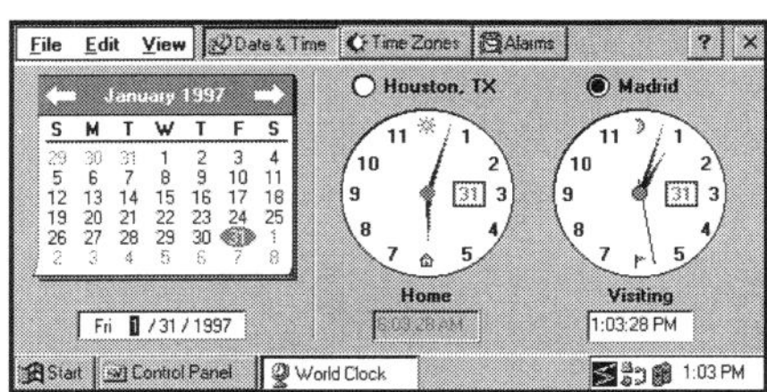

Figure 2.3.
World Clock Date & Time view.

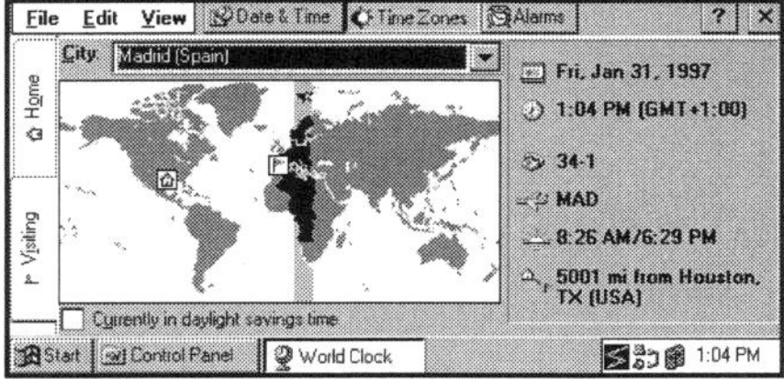

Figure 2.4.
World Clock Time Zones view.

Time Saver

A shortcut to the preceding steps is to double-tap the time display in the lower-right corner of the taskbar.

Setting Home and Visiting Cities

Once you have opened World Clock, you can select or change your home and visiting city by following these steps:

1. Tap the Time Zones button on the toolbar along the top of the World Clock screen.
2. Tap the Home tab on the left of the World Clock screen.
3. Select your city from the list by tapping the drop-down list and selecting the desired city. (If your city is not listed, jump ahead to "Adding a New City.")
4. Make sure the Daylight Savings check box is set correctly (tap the check box to change the setting). Selecting and deselecting the Currently in Daylight Savings Time check box may change the time, so verify that the time is set correctly.
5. To change the visiting city, tap the Visiting tab and repeat steps 3 and 4.
6. Tap the close button and the Yes button in the World Clock dialog box to save changes.

Adding a City

To add a city to World Clock's selection lists, follow these steps:

1. Select the Add City command from World Clock's Edit menu.
2. Select the closest city to the one you want to add from the list by double-tapping it. Your screen should look something like Figure 2.5.
3. Type the name of the new city you want to add in the City Name text box.
4. Change any incorrect information and tap the OK button to add the city.

To make this city your new home or visiting city, follow the directions in the previous section "Setting Home and Visiting Cities."

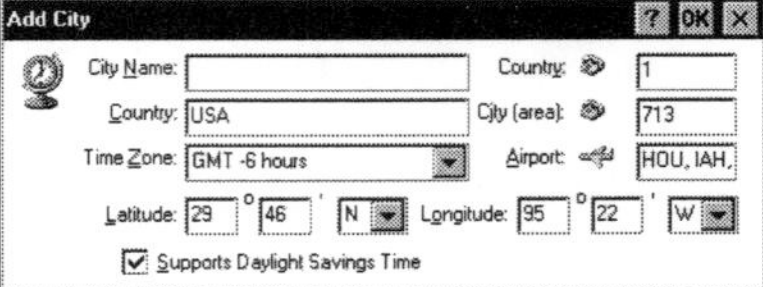

Figure 2.5.
The Add City dialog box.

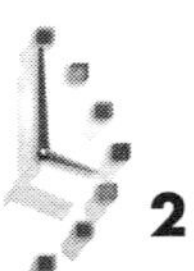

Setting the Date and Time

To set or change the date and time, follow these steps:

1. Tap the Date & Time button from World Clock.
2. Tap the current date from the calendar. If the current month is not displayed, tap on the arrows to the left and right of the month name, and then tap the current date. Verify that you are in the correct year.
3. Tap the Home or Visiting radio button above the clocks, depending on which time you want to change.
4. Enter the current time in the field below the clocks.

Windows CE is quite flexible and accepts just about any time format you enter. Enter a few different times, and you will be surprised at how forgiving Windows CE is. You can separate hour and minutes with a colon or nothing at all. You can specify AM and PM by the two letters or just the first letter (A or P). If you do not specify AM or PM, Windows CE will assume that the time entered is between 8:00 AM and 7:59 PM and will denote it accordingly.

Setting Alarms

Although alarms are primarily attached to appointments or tasks, you may also want to set an alarm for an event or activity not associated with an appointment. You can even use your HPC as a traveling alarm clock. Windows CE allows you to set up to five alarms of this type.

To add a new alarm, follow these steps:

1. Start the World Clock program if it is not already loaded.
2. Tap the Alarm button in the toolbar. (Your screen should look similar to Figure 2.6.)

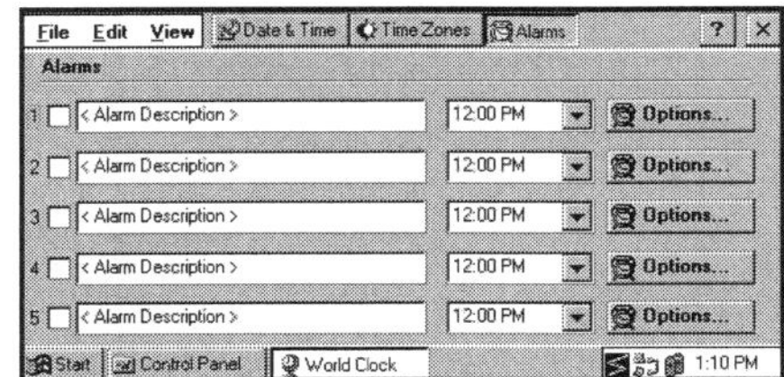

Figure 2.6.
Setting alarms.

3. Tap on the <Alarm Description> field and type a description. A check mark appears in the check box to the left of the description to indicate that the alarm is set.

4. Select a time from the drop-down list or type the desired time in the box.
5. Tap the Options button to change alarm notification defaults, and then tap the OK button.
6. Tap the close button and then the Yes button in the World Clock dialog box to save changes.

Several notification options are available: a flashing light (if your HPC supports this option), an on-screen reminder, and/or a .wav sound. You can set the alarm to sound one of the approximately 20 samples offered or choose a .wav file from the scroll list. You can add to this list of sounds by transferring any standard .wav file from your desktop computer to the Windows folder on your HPC.

Alarms will sound every day unless you disable them. There are two ways to disable an alarm:

- Remove the check mark from the box to the left of the alarm.
- Double-tap the Volume & Sounds icon in the Control Panel, and then tap the check box to the left of Notification to clear the box.

Changing and Adding Owner Information

During the initial setup, enter your name, company name (if applicable), address, and phone numbers. To enter the information, point to each field with the stylus or press the Tab key to move between fields and type in your information.

To add notes, tap the Notes tab and enter any information you want. If you elected to have the owner information displayed at startup, the Notes information will be displayed in a small window of the screen. You can use this feature to display a message such as `Reward if found. Call 214-555-1234.`

To change personal owner information later, first access the screen pictured in Figure 2.7 by double-tapping the Owner icon in the Control Panel, and then make the desired changes.

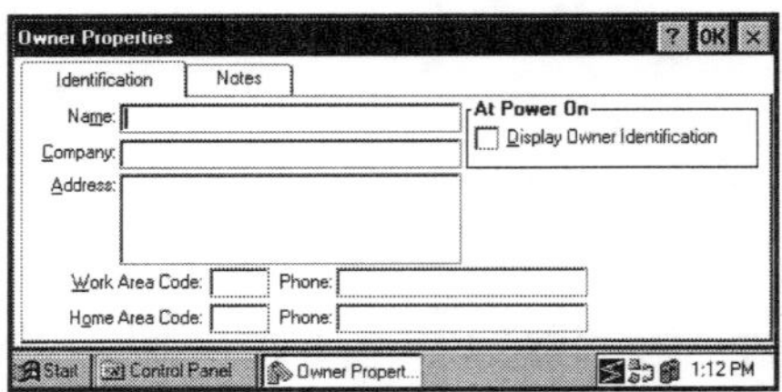

Figure 2.7.
Setting owner properties.

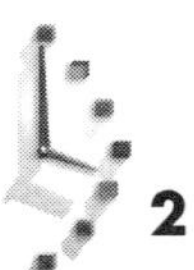

Changing Desktop Background and Adjusting Contrast

The default desktop background depends on which HPC you own. The default background for most HPCs is the Microsoft Windows CE logo (shown in Figure 2.8). You can easily change the default background to one of the eight available backgrounds.

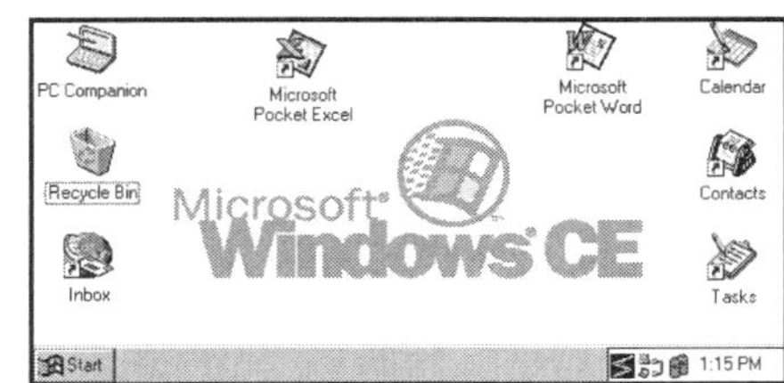

Figure 2.8.
Desktop with Windows CE.

To select your desktop background, follow these steps:

1. Press the Start button and tap Settings from the Start menu.
2. Double-tap the Display icon.
3. Select the background you want from the scroll list at the bottom of the screen or tap the Browse button to search for other background pictures.
4. Tap the Tile Image on Background check box to assure that your entire background is filled with the selected image.
5. Tap the OK button to save changes.

You can also use a background from your desktop PC or even create your own backgrounds using Paint or a similar graphics program. Keep in mind that the maximum display size is 480 × 214 pixels on most HPCs (the Hewlett-Packard HPC being a notable exception), which is in contrast to the 640 × 480 or 800 × 600 pixels typically found on a Windows 95 desktop. Refer to Hour 4, "Understanding Synchronization," for help transferring background images from your desktop PC.

The screen clarity on your HPC is very dependent upon lighting conditions. To adjust the screen contrast, follow these steps:

1. Select Settings from the Start menu.
2. Double-tap the Display icon.
3. Tap the Contrast tab and follow the on-screen instructions (refer to Figure 2.9), which vary from manufacturer to manufacturer. The difference in instructions mainly depends on whether an external contrast control is a feature of your HPC.

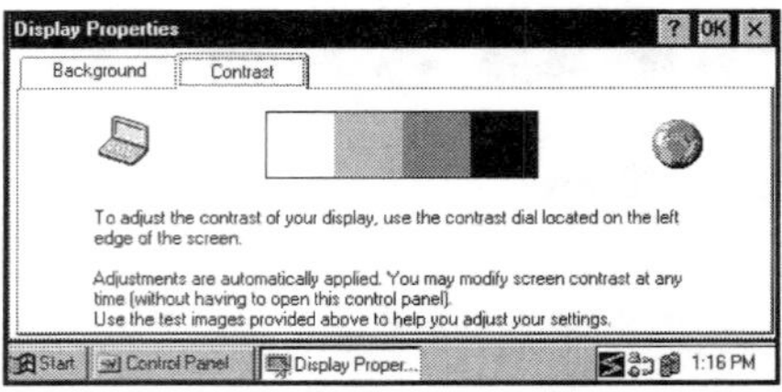

Figure 2.9.
Setting the screen contrast.

Setting Passwords

Windows CE offers protection from prying eyes. You can set a password that must be entered each time your HPC is turned on. To set a password, follow these steps:

1. Tap the Start button, and then tap Settings.
2. Double-tap the Password icon.
3. Enter the password you want; it can be up to eight characters long.
4. Press the Tab key and re-enter the password.
5. Tap the Enable Password Protection check box.
6. Tap the OK button to save changes.

You can change or remove your password by following these steps:

1. Press the Start button, and then tap Settings.
2. Double-tap the Password icon.
3. Type the password you set and press the Enter key. Your screen should look like Figure 2.10.

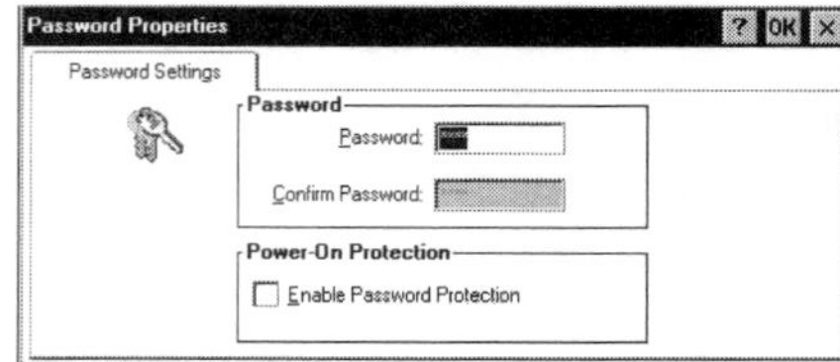

Figure 2.10.
Setting up a password.

4. Tap the Enable Password Protection check box to remove the check. (This will disable the prompt to enter the password that appears each time the HPC is turned on.)
5. Enter a new password in the Password field or press the Backspace key until the field is blank to delete the password.
6. Tap the OK button to save changes.

CAUTION

If you forget your password, you will not be able to get past the password prompt. You will have to completely reset your HPC, which means all your data will be erased. To perform a complete reset, refer to Hour 22, "Fine-tuning and Troubleshooting."

Ways to Increase Battery Life

Although many HPC manufacturers claim battery life up to 40 hours, you may experience substantially less battery life depending on how you use your HPC. Several things can dramatically affect battery life:

- Using PCMCIA cards such as modems
- Extended use of a backlit display (not all HPCs have a backlit display)
- Frequent connection to your desktop PC

To increase battery life, use only low-power consumption modem cards. Using communications with some modems may reduce battery life to as low as five minutes! Typically modems with speeds faster that 14.4Kbps will not be low-power cards. Therefore, you should attach a supported AC adapter or contact your HPC manufacturer for a list of approved low-power modems.

When you first install a modem, you will see the message displayed in Figure 2.11. If you will not be using the modem card in the immediate future, tap the No button to assure that your HPC will not provide battery power to the modem card. When you need to use the modem, remove the card; then reinsert the card and tap the Yes button.

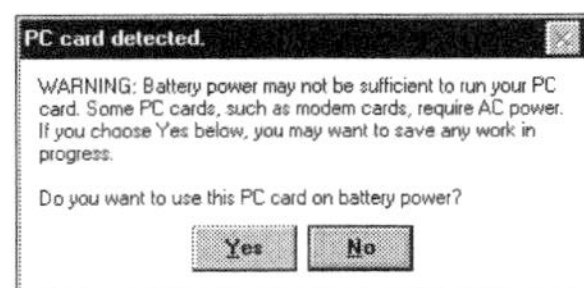

Figure 2.11.
A battery power warning.

Your HPC may have a backlit display button to enhance readability in low lighting conditions. Be prudent when using this feature: It can reduce your battery life by as much as 25 percent!

TIME SAVER

Deactivating alarms and sound can also help conserve batteries.

Additionally, your HPC has an auto-suspend mode that turns off your HPC after a certain period of inactivity. The default is three minutes, but you can change the amount to any time frame from one to five minutes. To change the amount of time, follow these steps:

1. Press the Start button, and then tap Settings.
2. Double-tap the Power icon.
3. Tap the Power Off tab.
4. Select the number of minutes from the drop-down list.
5. Tap the OK button to save your new settings.

As a default, Windows CE assumes you do not want your HPC to turn off automatically after several minutes of inactivity if you are running on AC power. You can override this default by activating the Enable Suspend While on External Power check box.

Because battery life is rapidly drained when the HPC is attached to a desktop PC, you may want to limit the amount of time that your HPC is connected to your desktop or notebook PC. That is not to say that you should limit how often you back up and synchronize your HPC data, but when you are finished with these operations, you should quickly disconnect the cable.

Summary

In this hour you completed the initial setup for Windows CE. You learned to calibrate the touch screen, enter dates and times, and set alarms. You also learned to set passwords, enter personal owner information, and choose your desktop background. Additionally, you should now have a better understanding of ways to increase battery life.

Q&A

Q In World Clock, how do you check the distance between two cities without changing the time?

A Tap the Time Zones tab from World Clock and set your Home City to one city and the Visiting City to the other. The distance between the two cities is displayed. Tap the close button to exit World Clock without saving changes.

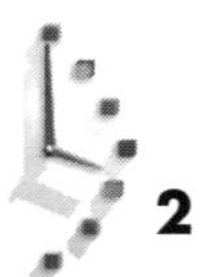

Q Does Windows CE support handwriting recognition?

A Although handwriting recognition is not part of the first release of Windows CE, several third-party software developers, including ART and CIC, have handwriting recognition software that you can easily add to it. Microsoft chose not to include handwriting recognition in the first version of Windows CE, citing that this feature was not fully developed.

PART

I

Hour 3

Take Windows CE for a Test Drive

Now that you have set up Windows CE, it's time to take it for a spin. You better start with a big breakfast, because you will be busy in this hour learning how to do the following:

- Enter appointments
- Add contacts to your address book
- Create a to-do list
- Write a short memo
- Fill in an amortization schedule
- Delve into the Internet

Information Manager

Information Manager in Windows CE, which consists of Calendar, Contacts, and Tasks, is the nerve center of the HPC. Delivering Microsoft's vision of "information at your fingertips," Information Manager provides easy and quick access to contacts, appointments, and tasks. The number of appointments and tasks you can enter is dependent on the amount of memory in your HPC and how you have configured the split between program memory and storage memory.

Using Contacts

For the first part of the tour, add a contact to your address book by following these steps:

1. Double-tap the Contacts icon on the desktop.
2. Tap the New Card icon on the toolbar, and you will see a screen similar to Figure 3.1.

Figure 3.1.
A new contact card.

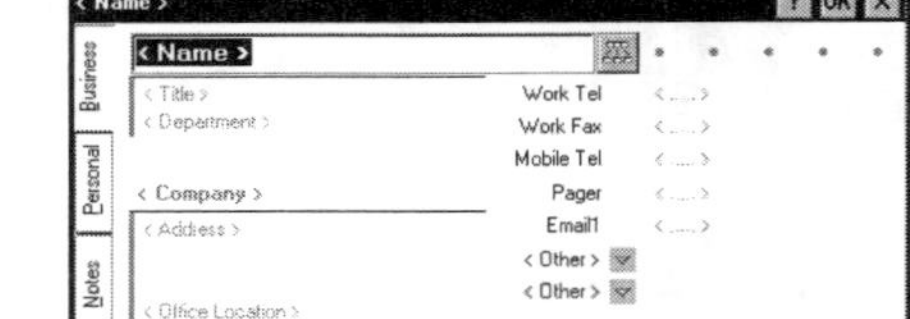

3. Type **`John Smith`** and then press the Tab key. (If you make a mistake typing, press the Backspace key to erase the previous character.)
4. Press the Tab key to skip the Title field.
5. Press the Tab key again to skip the Department field.
6. Type **`The Smith Agency`** in the Company field and press the Tab key.
7. Type **`123 First Ave.`** and then press the Enter key.
8. Type **`Dallas, Texas 75230`** and press the Tab key twice.
9. Type **`214-555-5986`** in the Work Tel field and press the Tab key four times.
10. In the Email1 field, type **`johnsmith@aol.net`**.
11. Tap the Personal tab on the left of the screen.
12. Tap on the Home Tel field and type **`214-555-6234`**.
13. Tap the Notes tab on the left of the screen and press the Tab key.
14. Type **`Children are Brent and Amanda`**.

15. Tap the Business tab to return to the main screen.
16. Tap the OK button.

You are now in the Contact List view where you can see a one-line summary of each of your contacts. Enter several other contacts, following the previous instructions, and your screen should look something like Figure 3.2. To see more than a one-line summary of a contact, double-tap the desired contact to see the detail.

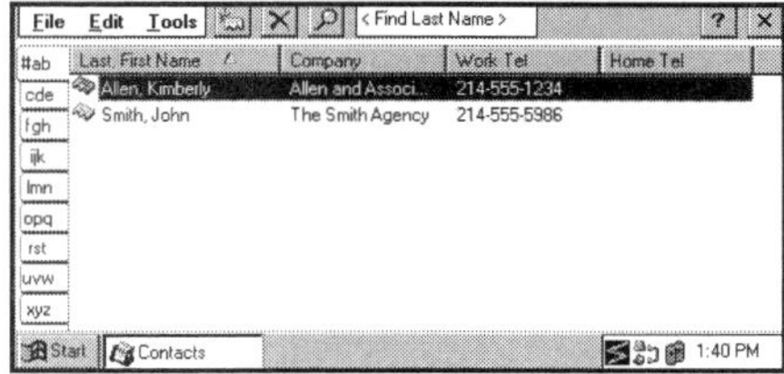

Figure 3.2.
Contact List view.

3

To search for and modify a contact, follow this example:

1. Tap the magnifying glass icon in the toolbar.
2. Type a word to search for, **`dallas`** for example, and then tap the Find Next button. Notice that it is not necessary to capitalize letters when performing a search.
3. If you entered the first contact correctly, your screen should look something like Figure 3.3.

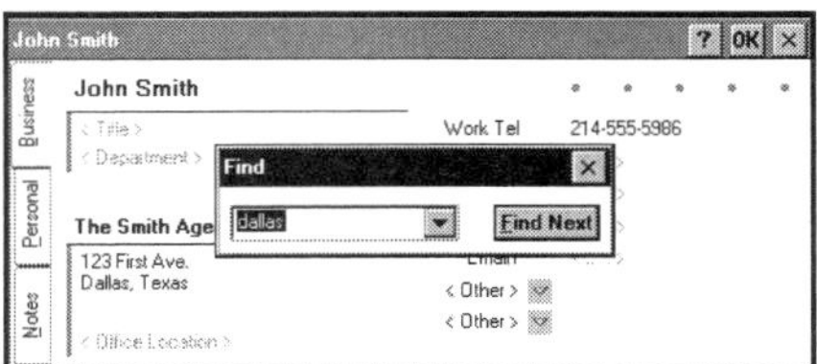

Figure 3.3.
Finding Dallas.

4. Tap the close button in the Find dialog box to view the Contact screen.
5. Tap the Mobile Tel field, and type **`214-555-1099`**.
6. Tap the OK button to return to the Contact List view.

Using Calendar

Now that you know how to add a contact to the electronic address book, try your hand at entering an appointment. Start by selecting Programs from the Start menu and double-tapping the Calendar icon. Your screen should look something like Figure 3.4.

Figure 3.4.
The opening Calendar screen.

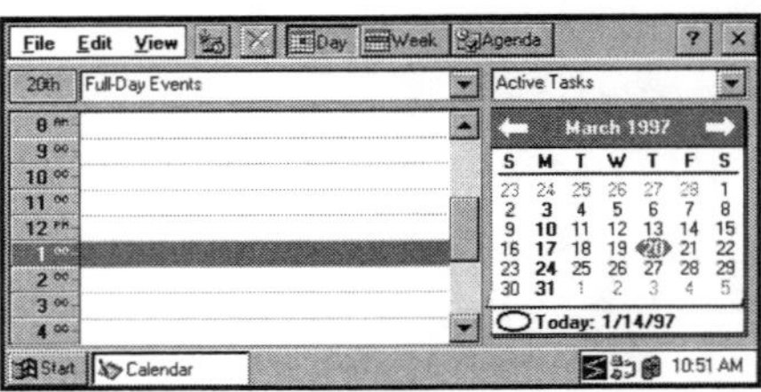

Follow these steps to enter an appointment in the appointment book:

1. Tap the New Card icon in the toolbar.
2. Type **`AA Flight 10 - Houston to Chicago`**, and then press the Tab key.
3. Type **`Houston Intercontinental`** in the Location field.
4. Tap the calendar icon to the right of the Starts field, and double-tap the desired day.
5. Tap the down arrow key of the Time drop-down list, and then tap the up or down arrow until the time nearest to the current time is visible. Tap that time.
6. On the Reminder section of the screen, tap the scroll list that defaults to 15 and change it to 1 by tapping it.
7. Tap the OK button to save the appointment.

If you entered the appointment correctly and your HPC is turned on, an alarm will sound and display a message, such as the one shown in Figure 3.5. On some HPCs, an external LED display will flash to inform you that you have an appointment, even if the HPC is closed and turned off.

Figure 3.5.
A Calendar reminder.

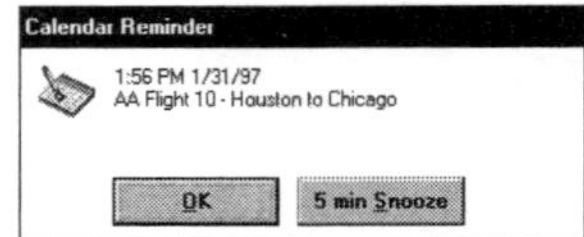

To practice using Calendar, enter a couple of other types of appointments: a full-day event and a recurring appointment. Follow these steps to enter a full-day event:

1. Make sure that you are in the new Appointment screen, which is shown in Figure 3.6.

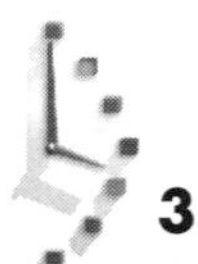

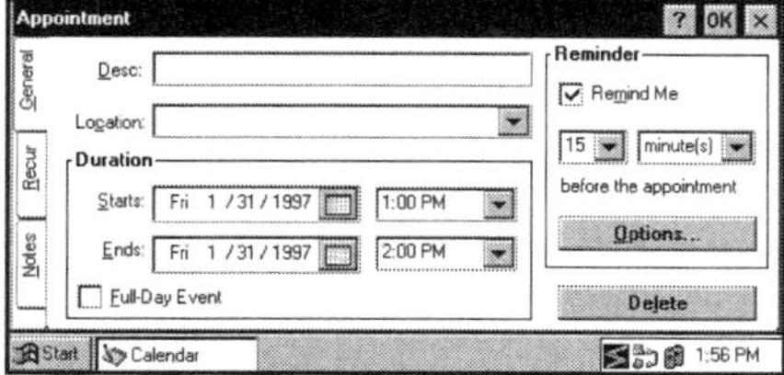

Figure 3.6.
The new Appointment screen.

2. Tap the calendar icon to the right of the Starts field.
3. Double-tap a day of your choice.
4. Type **`Office Closed`** in the Desc. field, and then tap the Full-Day Event check box.
5. Tap the OK button to save this full-day event.

To enter a recurring appointment, follow these steps:

1. Tap the New Appointment icon in the toolbar.
2. Type **`My Birthday`** in the Desc. field.
3. Tap the Recur tab to the left of the screen to enter a repeating appointment. Your screen should look similar to Figure 3.7.

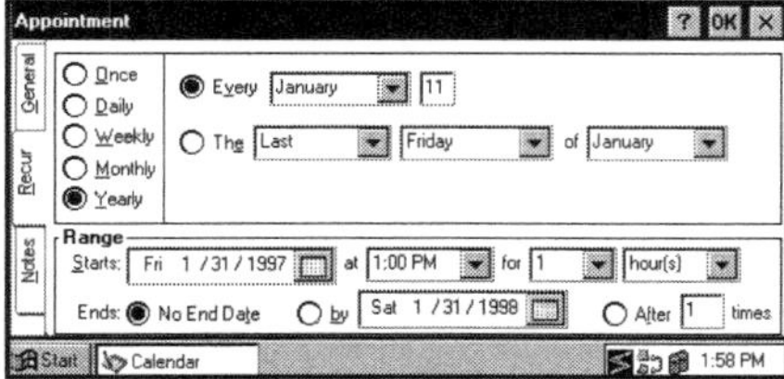

Figure 3.7.
The Recur tab of the Appointment screen.

4. Tap the Yearly radio button to select it.
5. Change the month and day to the right of the Every radio button to your birthday.
6. Tap the OK button to save this recurring appointment.

Calendar allows you to view your schedule in a variety of formats. By default, you are presented with a daily view. A small monthly calendar on the right half of the screen identifies days with appointments in boldface, today's date with an open circle, and the currently selected date with a closed circle. Tap the Week button in the toolbar to see a weekly view of your schedule.

Using Tasks

The final component of Information Manager is the Tasks program. Follow these steps to create a to-do list:

1. Tap the Programs button in the taskbar and double-tap the Tasks icon.
2. Tap the New Task button in the toolbar.
3. Type **`Work on project plan`** in the Task field, and then press the Tab key.
4. Tap the Priority drop-down list, and then press the up arrow on the keyboard until 1 is highlighted in the Priority field. (Alternatively, simply press the 1 key on your keyboard.)
5. Press the Tab key and type **`Pegasus`** in the Project field. Then tap the OK button.
6. Tap the New Task button in the toolbar again to add another task.
7. Type **`Analyze material cost`** in the Task field.
8. Tap the down arrow to the right of the Project field and select `Pegasus`. Then tap the OK button.
9. To add one more task, tap the New Task button again.
10. Type **`Pick up laundry`**.
11. Tap the Project field and type **`Personal`**, and then press the Enter key. Your screen should look something like Figure 3.8.

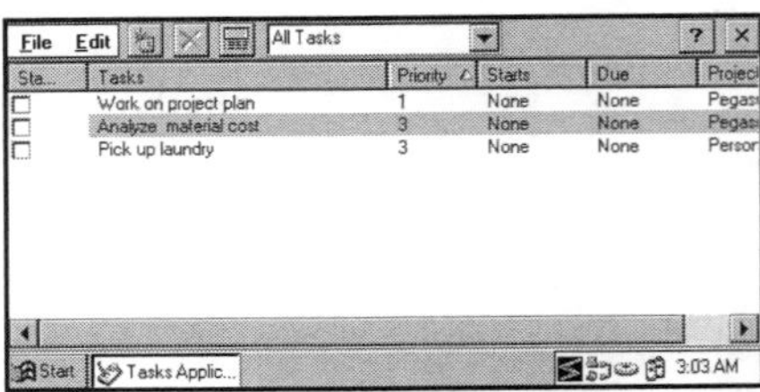

Figure 3.8.
Adding a new task.

You can display the tasks you enter in several ways, and the tasks appear in several areas of Information Manager. Experiment with these different views by following these steps:

1. Tap the drop-down list in the toolbar and select Pegasus. Notice that only tasks with Pegasus entered in the Project field are displayed.
2. Tap the check box to the left of `Work on project plan` to mark it as completed.
3. Tap the drop-down list in the toolbar again and select Completed Tasks.
4. Select All Tasks from the drop-down list.
5. Tap the Calendar button in the taskbar to switch to Calendar.
6. Tap the Agenda button in the toolbar to show all uncompleted tasks.

7. Tap the close button in the upper-right corner to close Calendar.
8. Tap the close button to exit the Tasks program. Information Manager data is saved automatically when you exit Information Manager.

Pocket Word

If you thought word processing with powerful outlining, graphics, and text attributes such as boldface, italics, and underline was not possible on a pocket-size computer, think again. Microsoft Pocket Word offers all these features plus a lot more. To explore what you can do with Pocket Word, start by double-tapping the Microsoft Pocket Word icon. When you have started Pocket Word, enter the following paragraph:

`Now is the time for all good men to come to the aid of their country. Ask not what your country can do for you, but what you can do for your country. The only thing we have to fear is fear itself.`

Press the Enter key twice when finished. Follow these steps to see what Pocket Word can do:

1. Press and hold the Ctrl and Home keys to move to the beginning of the document. On some HPCs, you may have to press another key, such as the Alt or Fn key, at the same time. Refer to the manual that came with your HPC.
2. Type **`Famous Quotes`**, and then press the Enter key twice.
3. Press the up arrow key twice to move to the top line. Your flashing cursor should be just to the left of the *F* in Famous.
4. Tap the Center button in the toolbar.
5. Hold down the Shift key while pressing the End key to highlight the Famous Quotes text. On some HPCs, you may have to press another key, such as the Alt or Fn key, at the same time. Refer to the manual that came with your HPC.
6. Press the B button in the toolbar to make the title boldface. Notice that the B button is recessed to indicate that the text is boldface. To return the text to normal, tap the B button again while the text is highlighted.
7. Tap the font size drop-down list in the toolbar, which by default is set to 10. Tap 12 to change the font size of the highlighted text to 12 points.
8. Press the down arrow key until the flashing cursor is on the second blank line below the paragraph you typed. Then press the Enter key.
9. Press the Bullet button on the toolbar.
10. Type **`John F. Kennedy`** and then press the Enter key.
11. Type **`Ronald Reagan`** and then press the Enter key.
12. Type **`Martin Luther King`** and then press the Enter key twice.

Now that you know how to enter text, move around in a document, center text, and change text attributes, experiment with a few other features:

1. Select Replace from the Edit menu. (Press and hold Alt+E on the keyboard or tap the word Edit to access the Edit menu.)
2. Type **`country`** in the Find What field and press the Tab key.
3. Type **`nation`** in the Replace With field and tap the Find button.
4. Tap the Replace All button.
5. Tap the OK button. Notice that every occurrence of the word *country* has been replaced with *nation*, as shown in Figure 3.9.

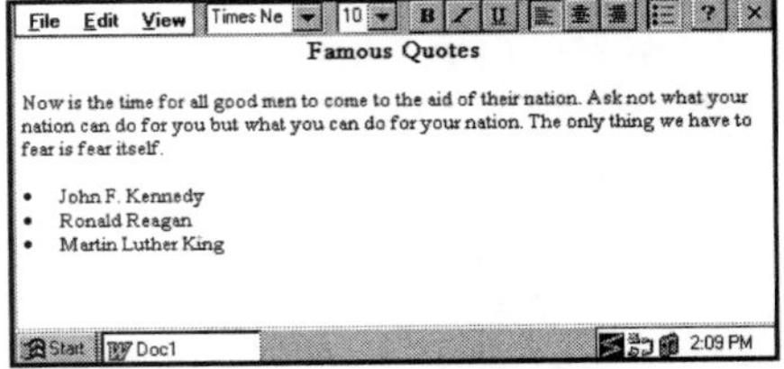

Figure 3.9.
Replacing items in Pocket Word.

6. Double-tap the word *good* on the first line to select it, and then tap the Underline button in the toolbar to underline that word.
7. Double-tap the word *itself*, and tap the Italic button in the toolbar to make that word italic.
8. Select Save from the File menu (or press Ctrl+S).
9. Type **`sample`** in the Name field and press the Enter key.

If you want to explore more of Pocket Word, you may want to jump ahead to Hour 10, "Using Pocket Word."

Pocket Excel

Pocket Excel, a subset of Microsoft Excel for Windows 95, is a powerful spreadsheet program that provides access to a variety of financial applications. To get a feel for what this program can do, follow these steps to create a sample amortization schedule for a loan:

1. Close all programs by tapping the close button in the upper-right corner until you are back to the desktop.
2. Double-tap the Microsoft Pocket Excel icon.
3. Tap the File menu and then select Open.

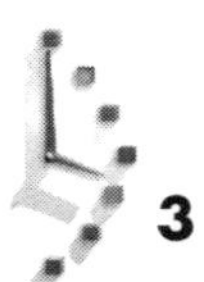

4. Double-tap Amortize from the list to load it. Your screen should look something like Figure 3.10.

Figure 3.10.
Loading a new Pocket Excel spreadsheet.

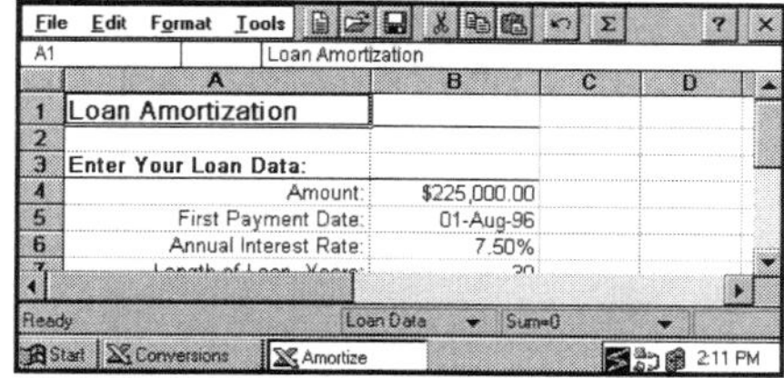

5. To visualize how the Pocket Excel screen is a small window to a giant worksheet, try out the scroll bars. Tap the down arrow in the vertical scroll bar until you see the end of the worksheet. Your screen should look something like Figure 3.11. Tap the up arrow in the vertical scroll bar until you can see the beginning of the worksheet again.

Figure 3.11.
Pocket Excel scroll bars.

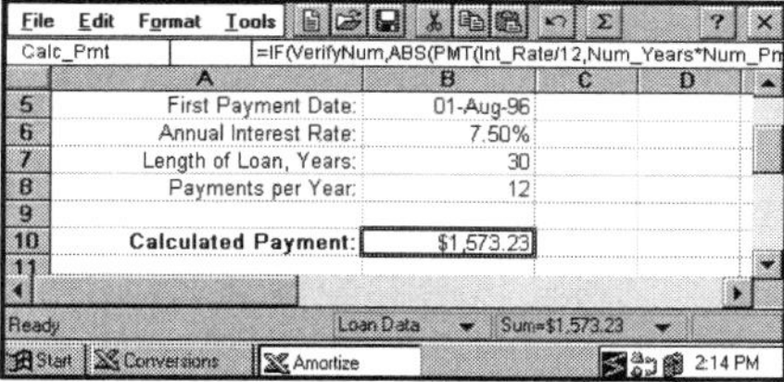

6. Tap the field to the right of Amount and type **`30000`**. Then press the Enter key.
7. Change the date to **`1/1/97`**, and then press the Enter key.
8. For the Interest Rate, type **`.06`**, and then press the Enter key.
9. Type **`5`** for the number of years, and then press the Enter key three times. The calculated payment should be $579.98.
10. To see the effect of changing the number of years to three, press the up arrow three times, type the number **`3`**, and press the Enter key. Notice that the calculated payment is now $912.66.
11. Exit Pocket Excel by tapping the close button and tapping the No button to close the spreadsheet without saving changes.

Refer to Hour 12, "Using Pocket Excel," to explore Pocket Excel in more depth.

Pocket Internet Explorer

By default, Pocket Internet Explorer is not installed on your HPC, although it is included with your Windows CE Desktop Software CD. If you have not already installed the CD, refer to the next hour for instructions on installing HPC Explorer.

In this test drive, you will not log on to the Internet, which requires several steps covered in Hour 16, "Surfing the Net," but you will get a feel for how Pocket Internet Explorer works. Follow these steps:

1. Start Pocket Internet Explorer. Your screen should look something like Figure 3.12.

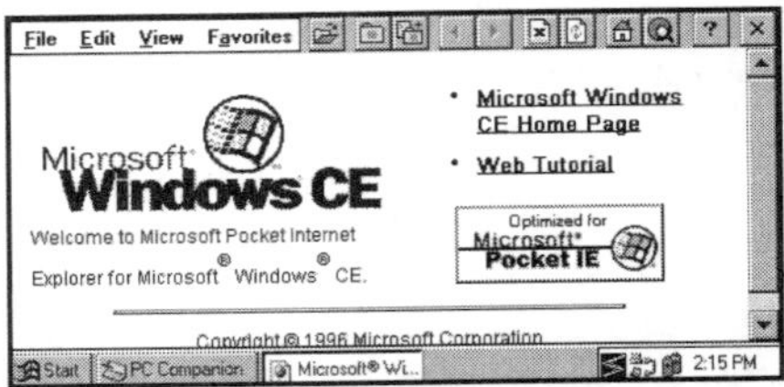

Figure 3.12.
The Web in the palm of your hand.

2. Tap the File menu and press the right arrow four times slowly, noticing the options available from the other menus and returning full circle to the File menu.
3. Tap Open to display the Open Internet Address dialog box. This dialog box is where you type in an Internet address, commonly referred to as a *URL* (Uniform Resource Locator), when you are online. Addresses generally start with `http://www.` and end in `.com`. A good example of a common Web address is `http://www.microsoft.com`.
4. Tap the close button to shut the Open Internet Address dialog box.
5. Tap the close button again to exit Pocket Internet Explorer.

You will explore Pocket Internet Explorer in more depth in Hour 16.

Getting Help

Windows CE features a help system that is available in most programs by tapping the ? in the upper-right corner of the screen. Because this system is context-sensitive, whenever you tap the Help button you are presented with several help topics specific to the program loaded. For example, when you tap the Help button in Pocket Word, you have a list of help topics such as Tips for Using Pocket Word and Formatting with Pocket Word, as shown in Figure 3.13. For more information on the Windows CE help system, refer to Hour 5, "Call for Help."

Figure 3.13.
Windows CE help.

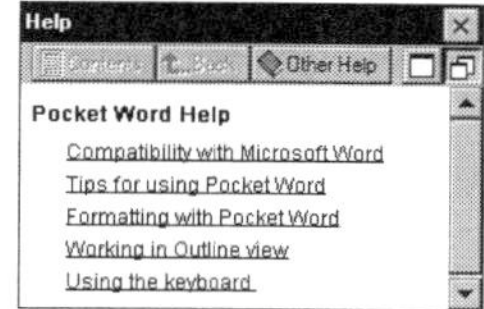

Summary

In this hour, you took Windows CE for a test drive. You got a taste for what you can do with the Information Manager, Pocket Word, Pocket Excel, and Pocket Internet Explorer. All of these applications will be covered in more depth in subsequent hours. You should now be able to understand how your HPC and Windows CE can change the way you work.

Q&A

Q Does Windows CE have a self-running demo mode?

A No, but you can access a hands-on demonstration on Microsoft's Web site at `www.microsoft.com`.

Q Is Windows CE available on any platform other than handheld PCs?

A Yes. Windows CE is Microsoft's scaled-down version of Microsoft Windows and Office. Subnotebook computers, telephones, and other consumer electronics are being built around the Windows CE platform.

PART
I

Hour 4

Understanding Synchronization

What separates HPCs built around Windows CE from the many electronic organizers and handheld computers of the past is their seamless synchronization with desktop PCs. Windows CE enables you to make changes on both your desktop PC and handheld PC and automatically update both computers with the most current information. Additionally, when you are working with Word documents and Excel sheets, file transfers are a simple matter of dragging and dropping files between the two computers. In this hour, you will learn how synchronization works with Windows CE by covering the following topics:

- Installing HPC Explorer
- Synchronizing with Schedule+
- Using Backup and Restore
- Troubleshooting
- Transferring files
- Printing

Installing HPC Explorer

The Windows CE CD that comes with your HPC contains HPC Explorer. HPC Explorer is the software for your desktop PC that facilitates the connection between your computer and HPC. This software creates a partnership between the two that is updated every time they are connected. This partnership not only assures consistent information on both systems, but also provides a backup mechanism for your HPC data in case your data becomes corrupted or your HPC is lost or stolen.

HPC Explorer also synchronizes data between your HPC's Information Manager and Microsoft Schedule+ for desktop PCs. A special Windows 95 version of Schedule+ is included on the Windows CE CD. Even if you already own Schedule+, install this version to assure compatibility with your HPC. If you use Microsoft Word or Excel, you will be able to share documents and spreadsheets with the pocket versions of these applications. If you use Office 97's Microsoft Outlook, Microsoft has announced plans to add Windows CE support for Outlook.

In addition to synchronizing data and sharing documents, HPC Explorer provides a window on your desktop computer of the files and folders on your HPC. Although you cannot run Windows CE programs on your desktop PC, you can copy, rename, move, and delete files.

To install HPC Explorer on your desktop computer, follow these steps:

1. Attach the cable (or docking station) to your HPC and then to the back of your desktop or notebook PC.
2. Insert the Windows CE CD into your computer's CD-ROM drive. Depending on which version of Windows 95 you own and how it is configured, the HPC Explorer installation screen should look like Figure 4.1. If the HPC Explorer installation screen does not appear, refer to the troubleshooting section later in this hour.

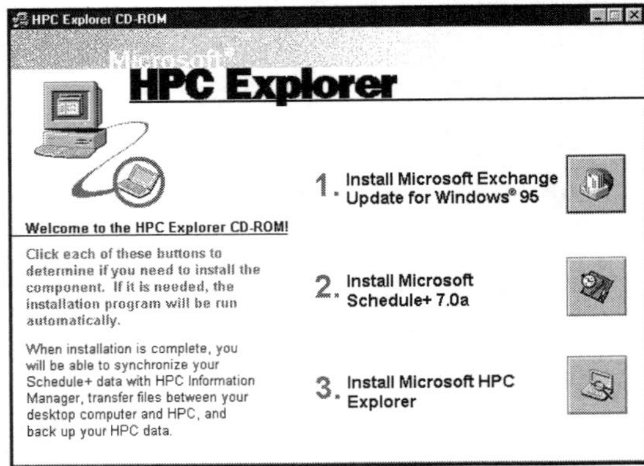

Figure 4.1.
The HPC Explorer installation screen.

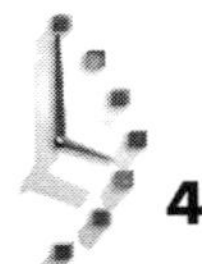

3. Click on the Install Microsoft HPC Explorer icon.
4. Click the Next button to continue and the Yes button to accept the terms of the license agreement.
5. Enter your name and your company name (if applicable), and then click the Next button.
6. Make sure there is a check mark by each of the three components, as shown in Figure 4.2, and click the Next button.
7. Install Microsoft Exchange and Schedule+ by clicking on the appropriate icons and following the on-screen instructions.

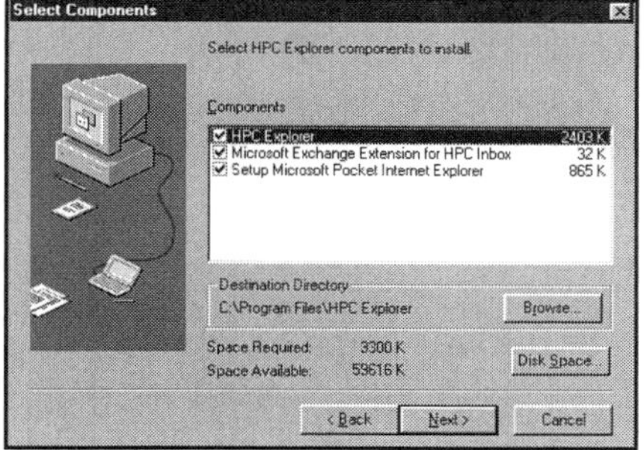

Figure 4.2.
Selecting the components of HPC Explorer.

8. Select the folder to install HPC Explorer in and click the Next button until the installation process begins. The default installation folder is `C:\Program Files\HPC Explorer`.
9. When the Setup Communications dialog box appears, make sure the cable between the HPC and the desktop or laptop computer is connected and click the Next button.
10. Click the Finish button.

The Communications Properties dialog box shown in Figure 4.3 appears on-screen and automatically configures the communications port on your desktop computer and attempts to connect to your HPC. A drop-down list provides the option to change the port your HPC's cable is attached to and identifies the current status of the connection. Consult your desktop computer's user information about the designation of its communications ports if there seems to be a problem.

When you have finished configuring the ports, HPC Explorer loads and connects with the HPC. Your screen should look like Figure 4.4 while this connection is being established.

Once the connection between your desktop and HPC is successful, you will hear a short musical tone, and then Windows CE will create the bond between the two, referred to as the *partnership*. When the partnership setup is complete, your screen should look similar to Figure 4.5.

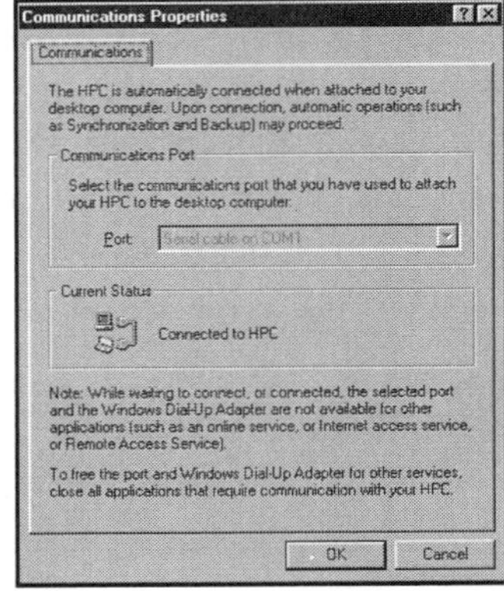

Figure 4.3.
The Communications Properties dialog box.

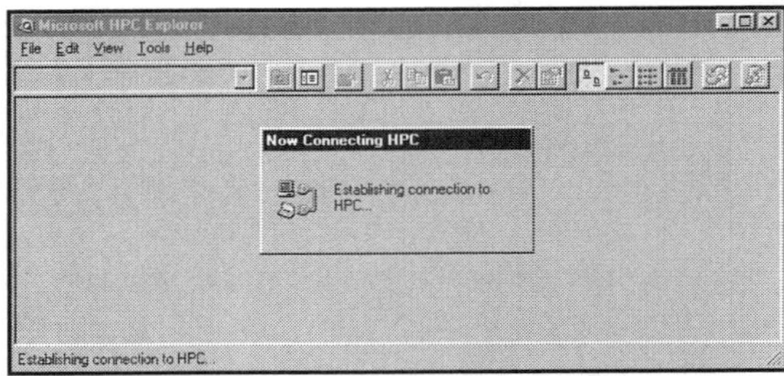

Figure 4.4.
Starting the connection.

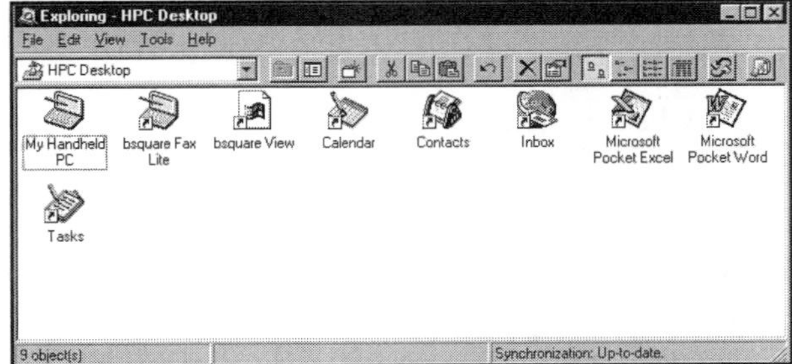

Figure 4.5.
Connection complete.

Synchronizing with Schedule+

The concept behind synchronization is that even if changes are made on both your desktop computer and HPC, both are updated with the most current information. Once the connection between your HPC and desktop computer is established and the partnership is

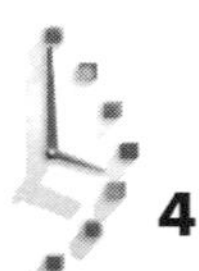

created, synchronization is automatic. There are several issues that you should be aware of to assure accurate synchronization of your data.

The first time you install HPC Explorer you are asked whether you want to create a new Schedule+ data file or use an existing one. This file will be the master file shared between Windows 95 and CE. The synchronization process begins with a Synchronization in Progress dialog box. If any duplicates are found, you will be given the option to remove or keep all.

Resolving Conflicts

What if you entered an appointment on your HPC that was at the same time as another appointment that your secretary entered on your desktop PC? During the synchronization process, Windows CE will inform you of any conflicts between Calendar, Contacts, or Tasks on your HPC and Schedule+ on your desktop computer by displaying a Resolve Conflict dialog box.

This dialog box provides you with several ways of handling a conflict:

- Replace the HPC data with the desktop data
- Replace desktop data with HPC data
- Leave data out-of-date

Select the option you want from the drop-down list.

By default conflicts are resolved manually, although you can set up your system to handle them automatically by following these steps on your desktop computer:

1. Select Synchronization Manager from the Tools menu of HPC Explorer.
2. Click the General tab and select the Don't Prompt Me, And Always radio button. Choose one of the three options from the corresponding drop-down list box as a default.
3. Click the OK button to save changes.

Manual or Automatic Synchronization

When the synchronization process is complete, you will be asked if you want to synchronize automatically every time the computers are connected. Although you might think that you would always want automatic synchronization, there may be circumstances in which you would prefer manual synchronization.

One reason for using manual synchronization is to speed up the connection between your desktop computer and HPC. When synchronization is set to automatic, the synchronization process begins automatically when the computers are attached. Depending on the amount of changes made since the last time the data was synchronized, this process could take several minutes. If you are primarily connecting to transfer Pocket Word or Excel documents, you may want to set synchronization to manual.

To set synchronization to manual, follow these steps on your desktop computer:

1. From the Tools menu of HPC Explorer, select Synchronization Manager.
2. Click the check box entitled Automatically Synchronize Upon Connecting to remove the check mark.
3. Click the OK button to save changes.

When synchronization is set to manual, you can synchronize at any time by selecting Synchronize Now from the Tools menu of HPC Explorer.

Backup and Restore

Synchronization and drag-and-drop file transfer assure that specific data and files are updated on both your desktop computer and HPC. However, you should also back up other files to your desktop computer to protect against complete data loss in case the HPC is lost or stolen. You can quickly restore your HPC to exactly the way it was at your last backup.

Backing up data is quick and easy. You are given the option to back up your data during the installation of HPC Explorer. You also can back up your data anytime by following these steps on your desktop computer:

1. Select Backup/Restore from the HPC Explorer Tools menu. The Backup/Restore Properties dialog box shown in Figure 4.6 appears on-screen.

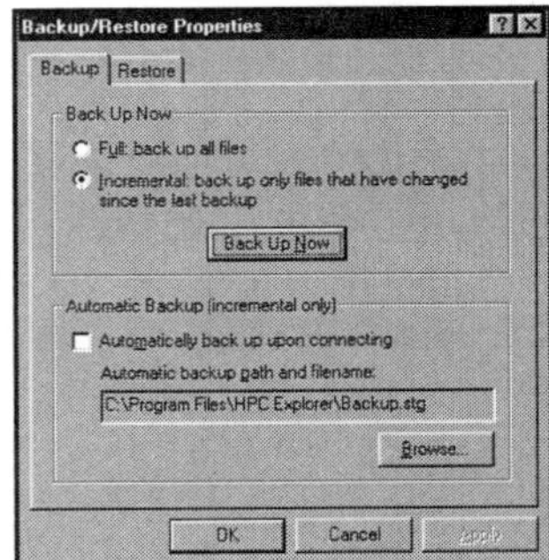

Figure 4.6.
The Backup/Restore Properties dialog box.

2. Choose either incremental or full backup.
3. Click the Back Up Now button.

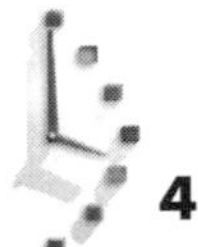

To restore your HPC to the way it was at your last backup, follow these steps on your desktop computer:

1. Select Backup/Restore from the HPC Explorer Tools menu. The Backup/Restore Properties dialog box appears on-screen.
2. Click the Restore tab.
3. Click the Restore Now button, as shown in Figure 4.7.

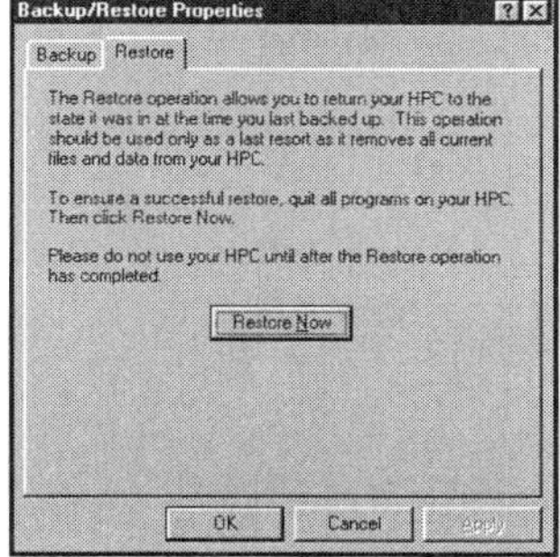

Figure 4.7.
Restoring your data.

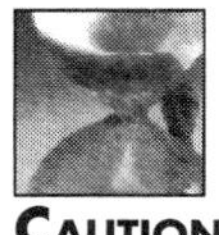

CAUTION

A Restore operation removes all data on your HPC, so only use it with a new HPC or in the event of unrecoverable data loss. Windows CE does not support selective backup or restore—it's either all or nothing.

Troubleshooting

Although synchronization can be one of the most useful aspects of Windows CE, it can also be the most troublesome. This section will help you resolve any potential problems that may arise. In most situations, once you resolve these issues the first time, you will probably not face them again. If you encounter problems not covered in this section, refer to Hour 19, "Having Problems Connecting?"

Problem: The cable supplied with your HPC has a 9-pin serial connector and your desktop computer uses a 25-pin connector.

Solution: Purchase a common 9-pin to 25-pin converter from your local computer store or contact your HPC manufacturer.

Problem: HPC Explorer requires a password while establishing the connection.

Solution: Enter the password you set on your HPC.

Problem: Your computer does not have a CD-ROM drive.

Solution: You will need access to a computer that has a CD-ROM drive so that you can make installation floppy disks for HPC Explorer that you will use later to install Explorer on your desktop PC. On the CD-ROM-equipped computer, follow these instructions for version 1.0 of the Windows CE CD-ROM:

1. Format six 3.5" 1.44M floppy disks. Label the first three disks Exchange Disk 1, Exchange Disk 2, and Exchange Disk 3. Label the next three disks Schedule+ Disk 1, Schedule+ Disk 2, and Schedule+ Disk 3.
2. Open the EXUPDUSA directory on the CD-ROM.
3. Copy all of the files *inside* each of the Disk directories to the corresponding Microsoft Exchange disks.
4. Open the SPLUS70A directory.
5. Copy all of the files *inside* each of the Disk directories to the corresponding Microsoft Schedule + disks.
6. Open the HPC directory.
7. Copy all of the files *inside* each of the Disk directories to the corresponding HPC Explorer disks.

When you have completed this process, you can install each of the Windows CE components by selecting Run from the Start menu, typing **`a:\setup`** for each program's Disk 1, and then clicking the OK button.

Problem: You are having problems establishing the connection between the HPC and your desktop or laptop/notebook computer.

Solution: To resolve connection problems, you must first verify that your serial port is available by using the following criteria:

- The port must be enabled with no conflicts in Windows 95. You can verify these settings from the Windows 95 Control Panel. Also, for power conservation, some notebook computers may have a serial port disabled. To activate the serial port, refer to your notebook computer's user manual.
- Make sure that no other devices are plugged into the desired port.
- Verify that no internal device, such as a modem, is assigned to the port you want to use.

If you have verified that the serial port you want to use is available and you are still having problems connecting, try the following:

- Make sure the cable is securely attached to both your desktop computer and your HPC.
- If you have two serial ports, verify that the cable is attached to the assigned port.
- Verify that your HPC is properly configured by following these instructions:
    1. From the Start menu on the HPC, tap Settings, and then double-tap the Communications icon.
    2. Tap the PC Connection tab.
    3. Verify that the Allow Connection with Desktop Computer check box is checked, and then tap the OK button.
    4. On the desktop computer, double-click the System icon from the Control Panel.
    5. Click the Device Manager tab and double-click Modem from the list of system components.
    6. Double-click the port you are using and click on the Modem tab.
    7. Verify that modem speed is set to 19,200 and click the OK button.

Transferring Files

HPC Explorer displays graphical images of the files and folders on your HPC. This design makes transferring files between your desktop computer and HPC as easy as copying files from your hard drive to a floppy drive. Windows CE continues the Windows 95 legacy by providing a flexible drag-and-drop file transfer feature. With a single click of a mouse, you can transfer a file to/from your HPC.

To transfer a file from your desktop computer to your HPC, follow these steps on your desktop computer:

1. Double-click the HPC Explorer icon to open the program.
2. Open My Computer and locate the file you want to copy.
3. Click the file you want to copy to your HPC.
4. Hold down the mouse button and drag the file to another folder.

To transfer a file from your HPC to your desktop computer, follow these steps on your desktop computer:

1. Double-click the HPC Explorer icon to open it.
2. Open My Computer and go to the directory you want to copy the files to.
3. Click the file you want to copy to your desktop PC.
4. Hold down the mouse button and drag the file to another folder.

Another way to transfer files on your HPC is through a cut and paste procedure. From the Edit menu, use the Cut or Copy command on the files that you want to transfer. Use Paste after you select where you want to copy them to.

When you transfer desktop backgrounds (wallpaper) from your desktop computer to your HPC, Windows CE converts the .bmp files into a format that CE can use. If you are transferring other types of files, you may be asked whether you want to enable file conversions.

If the file type of the file you want to transfer is unsupported, you will still be able to transfer the file although you may have to specify how the file is converted:

1. Select Files Conversion from the Tools menu. The File Conversion Properties dialog box appears on-screen.
2. Click on the HPC to Desktop or Desktop to HPC tab.
3. Select the file type from the list (as shown in Figure 4.8).

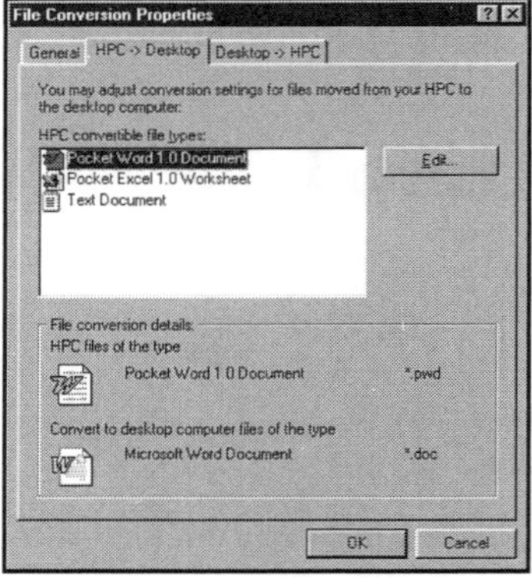

Figure 4.8.
Adjusting conversion settings.

4. Select a conversion file type.

JUST A MINUTE

The desktop and pocket versions of Windows CE applications (like Word and Pocket Word) use different file formats. When transferring Word and Excel documents, Windows CE automatically handles the file conversion. Although the data and much of the formatting is transferred, there is some formatting that may change or be deleted. Hour 1, "Getting Familiar with Windows CE" provided a table that defined many of the compatibility issues.

Printing

Although your HPC does not support printing directly, HPC Explorer does provide a provision to print HPC files while the desktop computer and the HPC are connected. To print from HPC Explorer, follow these steps:

1. Connect your HPC and desktop computer and start HPC Explorer.
2. After the connection is established, select the file that you want to print.
3. Select Print from the File menu.

Summary

In this hour, you learned the fine art of synchronization between your desktop and HPC. You learned how to transfer Pocket Word and Pocket Excel documents to and from your desktop computer. You also learned how to resolve problems that you may have when establishing the connection between the desktop computer and the HPC and how to print, back up, and restore your HPC data.

Q&A

Q What operating systems can I synchronize and transfer Windows CE files with?

A Windows CE currently supports only Microsoft Windows 95, although Windows NT may be supported in the near future. Windows 3.1 and DOS are not supported.

Q Can I convert other desktop PIM (personal information manager) applications with my HPC?

A Yes. With optional software from Datavis and Intellisync, you can synchronize data and transfer files with applications beyond Microsoft Schedule+, Word, and Excel. These optional software packages support applications such as ACT!, WordPerfect, and Lotus 1-2-3.

Q Can I view desktop files from my HPC when connected?

A No.

Q Can I synchronize data with both my home and office PC?

A No, you cannot synchronize data with more than one PC, but you can transfer complete files.

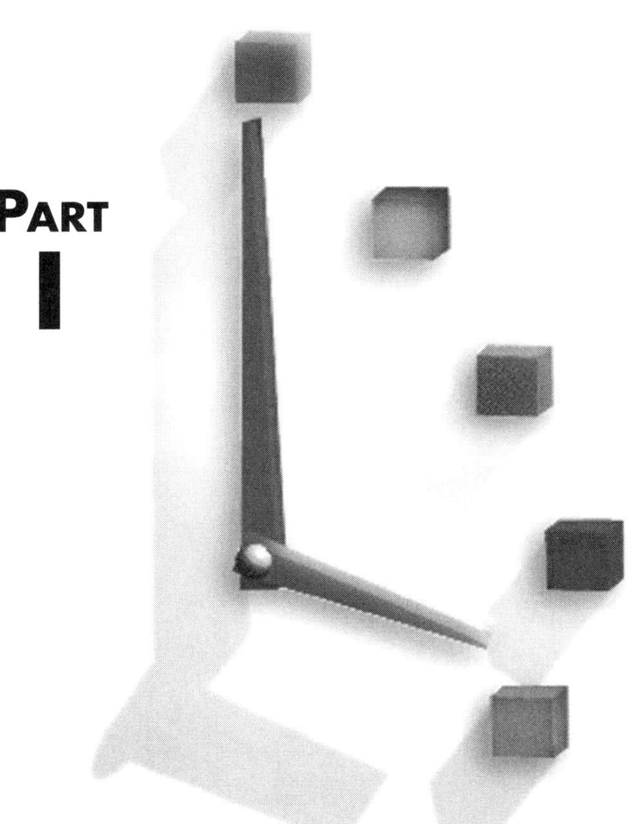

Part I

Hour 5

Call for Help

During this hour, you'll take a short break and check out the Windows CE help system. The following topics will be covered:

- Starting the Windows CE help system
- Navigating the help system
- Exiting the help system

Using the Windows CE Help System

Most Windows CE programs have a ? in the upper-right corner of the screen. Tapping this help button starts the Windows CE help system. Figure 5.1 shows an example of the help system within the Calendar program.

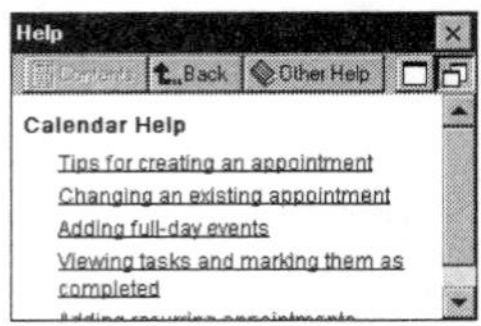

Figure 5.1.
Calendar help.

Within the help system, any text that is underlined has more detailed help associated with it. To select a topic, tap the underlined text. There may be other help topics that are out of view; you can use the scroll bars to reveal the other topics. Tapping the full screen icon in the toolbar (as shown in Figure 5.2) enables you to see more topics on the screen at one time. To return to normal view, tap the double screen icon.

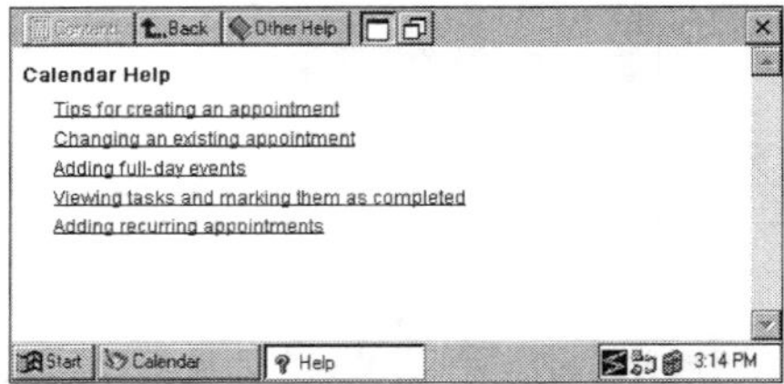

Figure 5.2.
Full-screen help.

Windows CE uses a *context-sensitive* help system, but there may be times when you want help on an unrelated topic. Tap the Other Help icon to see an alphabetized list of all available help topics.

As you go through several layers of help, you can return to the previous section by tapping the Back button in the toolbar. When you are finished with the help system, you can tap the close button to return to where you were before you selected help.

Exploring Help in Windows CE Programs

To give you a better understanding of how the help system works in Windows CE, this section explores the help system in several different Windows CE programs. Pocket Word help, as shown in Figure 5.3, contains information on compatibility issues with Microsoft Word, formatting, using the outline view, and using the keyboard. When you tap the help button in Pocket Excel (as shown in Figure 5.4), you are presented with tips for entering numbers and functions and information concerning compatibility with the desktop version of Excel.

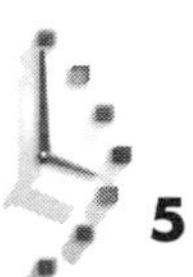

Figure 5.3.
Pocket Word help.

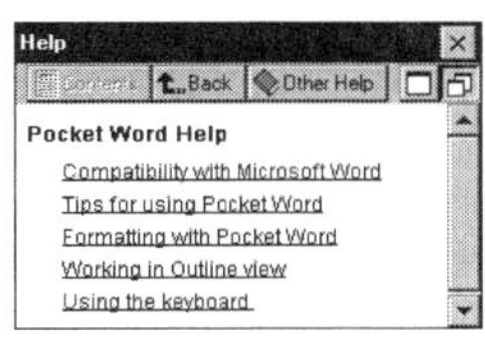

Figure 5.4.
Pocket Excel help.

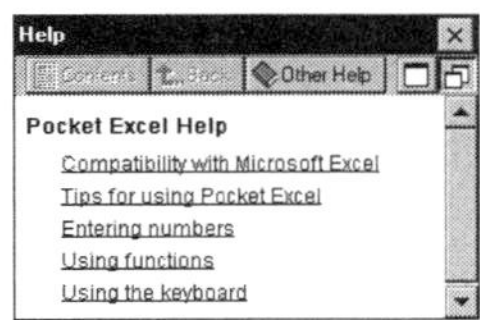

Figure 5.5 shows the help window for Contacts. In addition to basic information, such as using the contact list and looking up contacts, advanced information, such as how to send contact cards between two HPCs via the infrared port, is also available. Help within Calendar and Tasks provides useful information such as instruction on setting up recurring appointments and tasks.

Figure 5.5.
Contacts help.

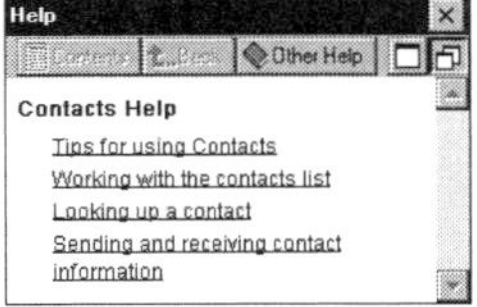

The help screen for Inbox (shown in Figure 5.6) demonstrates how to work with message headers and provides useful information concerning reading, replying to, and sending messages. Other communications programs, such as Pocket Internet Explorer and Terminal, provide guidance in their help systems as well. Even Solitaire, Calculator, and World Clock have help screens that are accessible with a tap of the help button.

Figure 5.6.
Inbox help.

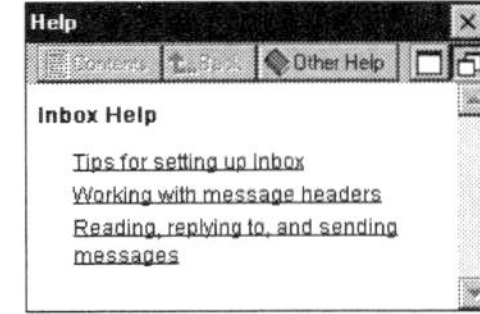

Summary

In this hour, you explored the Windows CE help system. You learned how to navigate and exit help while exploring help sessions in several Windows CE programs.

Q&A

Q I couldn't find the help I needed in the Windows CE help system. Is there any other kind of help available?

A In addition to the help that is built into your HPC and is provided in this book, several other resources are available to you. If you have access to the Internet, you can visit the Microsoft World Wide Web page at `http://www.microsoft.com`. Additionally, Hour 24, "Third-party Products and Services" lists other Web sites with helpful information.

Q Can I access the help system from the keyboard?

A Yes. Press the Windows key and the letter H.

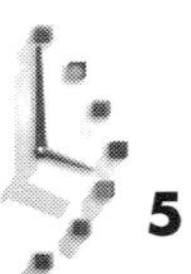

PART II

Getting Organized in the Afternoon

Hour

Part II

Hour 6

Understanding Files and Folders

Think of files as individual items, such as programs or data, and folders as collections of related files. Working with files and folders within Windows CE is very logical, and if you are familiar with Windows 95, you will find it easy to make the transition to Windows CE. You will do most of your work with files and folders from Windows CE Explorer. In this hour, you will examine Windows CE Explorer and learn how to use it efficiently. To access Windows CE Explorer (pictured in Figure 6.1), double-tap the My Handheld PC icon on the HPC desktop or select Explore from the Start menu.

In this hour, you will learn how to do the following:

- View files and folders
- Organize files and folders
- Rename files and folders
- Delete files and folders
- Create shortcuts
- Work with PC memory cards

Figure 6.1.
The Windows CE Explorer.

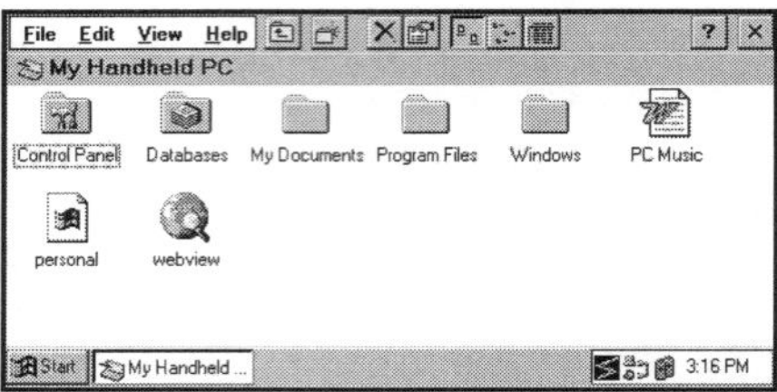

Viewing Files and Folders

Unlike Windows 95, Windows CE allows you to view only one folder at a time. When you open a folder by double-tapping it, you reveal the contents, which may be a list of files and/or additional folders. When you double-tap a folder within a folder, you are "drilling down" to reveal the hierarchy that makes up the file system of Windows CE.

The bar just below the toolbar indicates which folder you are in. As you move within levels of folders, Windows CE changes the information on this bar to display your current location. To see how this works, try a short exercise:

1. If you have not already done so, double-tap the My Handheld PC icon on the desktop.
2. Double-tap the Windows folder, and then double-tap the Programs folder.
3. From the Programs folder, double-tap the Games folder. Your screen should look similar to Figure 6.2.

Figure 6.2.
The title bar displays the file hierarchy.

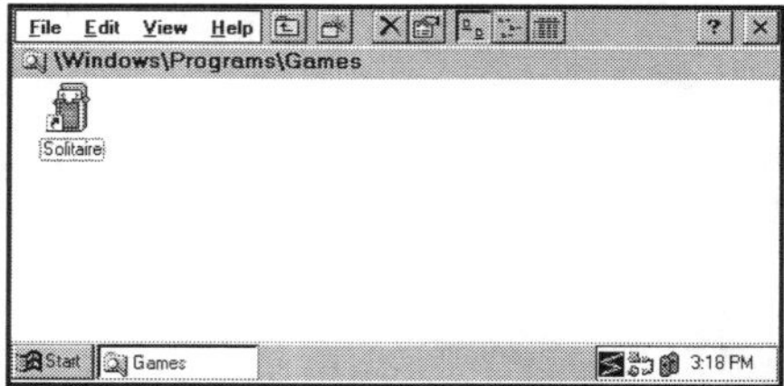

4. Move to a previous folder by tapping the Up Folder icon just to the right of the pull-down menus. Keep tapping the icon until you're back at the Windows CE Explorer screen.

You can view information about a file such as type, file size, and the date it was last changed by tapping the file and then selecting Properties from the File menu. As an alternative, press and hold the Alt key, tap the file you want information from, and then select Properties from the menu that appears. Your screen should look similar to Figure 6.3.

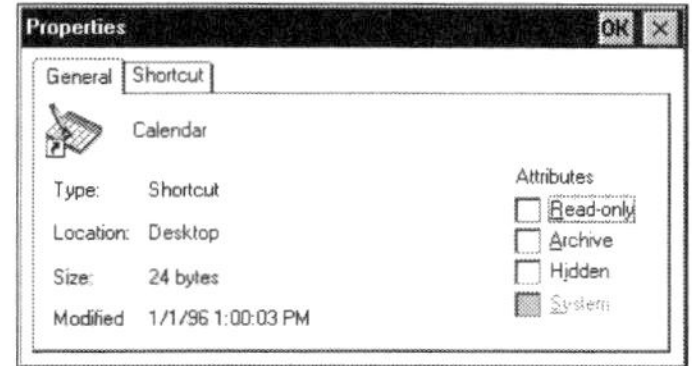

Figure 6.3.
The Properties dialog box reveals information about a file or program.

You can change the look of Windows CE Explorer by tapping one of the view icons on the toolbar or by choosing a view from the View menu. The Windows CE default is to show large icons, as illustrated in Figure 6.4. Figure 6.5 shows the Small Icon view.

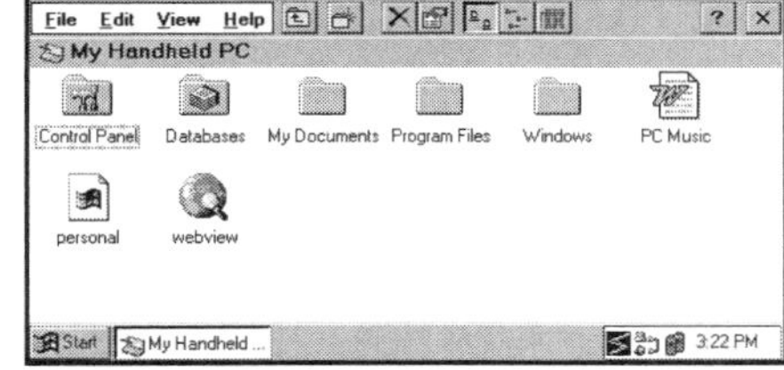

Figure 6.4.
Large Icon view in Explorer.

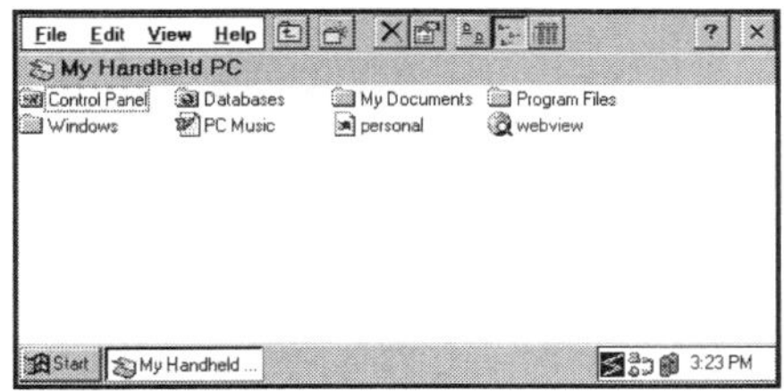

Figure 6.5.
Small Icon view in Explorer.

Figure 6.6 shows Details view. You can change the size of the columns in Details view by tapping and holding the line between the column headers and dragging it to the left or right to set the desired width.

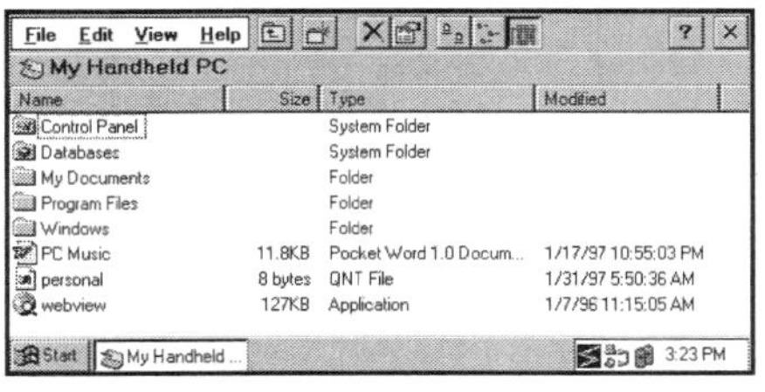

Figure 6.6.
Icons with details in Explorer.

In addition to changing how folders and files are displayed, you can also sort them by several different criteria. To sort within Details view, simply tap the column header of the column you want to sort by. To sort within other views (Large Icon and Small Icon), select one of the following commands:

- From the View menu, select Arrange by Name to sort alphabetically.
- From the View menu, select Arrange by Type to sort by file type.

Organizing Files and Folders

Although the file hierarchy is largely defined, Windows CE provides some flexibility in the structure by enabling you to add files and folders. To create a new folder, follow these steps:

1. Go to the location where you want to add a new folder. You may have to tap Explore from the Start menu and double-tap through several folders until you get to where you want to be.
2. From the File menu, select New Folder.
3. Type the name of the folder, and then press the Enter key.

To move or copy a file or folder, follow these steps:

1. Select the file or folder you want to copy or move by tapping it.
2. From the Edit menu, select Copy (to copy the item) or Cut (to move the item).
3. Go to the location where you want to copy or move the file or folder. You may have to tap Explore from the Start menu and double-tap through several folders until you get to where you want to be.
4. From the Edit menu, select Paste.

You can select more than one file or folder by pressing and holding the Ctrl key as you tap the files or folders you want. If all the files that you want to move or copy are next to each other, tap the first file then hold down the Shift key as you tap the last file. You can select all files within a folder by selecting Select All from the Edit menu.

Renaming Files and Folders

Most files and folders can be renamed. However, be careful not to rename program and system files; they may become inoperable as a result. Windows CE will inform you of this danger if you try to rename a program file or folder.

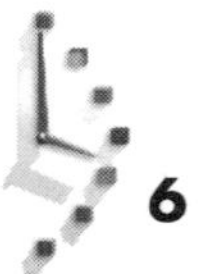

The easiest and quickest way to rename a file is to tap and hold on to the name below the icon of the file or folder you want to change. Enter the new name and press the Enter key. The following is an alternative approach:

1. Tap on the file or folder you want to rename.
2. From the File menu, select Rename.
3. Type the new name, and then press the Enter key.

Deleting Files and Folders

Because the memory on your HPC is very limited, you should delete the files or folders you will not be using again in the future. When you delete a file or folder, it is not permanently removed until you specify that it should be. This feature enables you to retrieve files that you accidentally deleted. Windows CE uses the Recycle Bin to temporarily keep deleted files before they are deleted permanently. The Recycle Bin icon is on your HPC desktop.

Deleting a file is simple. Within Windows CE Explorer, find the file or folder you want to delete and tap the X button in the toolbar. (Note that this is not the close button in the upper-right corner of the screen.) When prompted to confirm that you want to delete the file (as shown in Figure 6.7), tap the Yes button. If you make a mistake, you can undelete the last file deleted by selecting Undo Delete from the Edit menu.

Figure 6.7.
Make sure you want to delete a file.

Removing and Recovering Files from the Recycle Bin

If you want to recover a file other than the last file you deleted, follow these steps:

1. From the desktop, double-tap the Recycle Bin.
2. Tap the file or folder you want to recover.
3. Select Restore from the File menu.

To remove a file from the Recycle Bin, thereby eliminating it forever from your HPC, follow these steps:

1. From the desktop, double-tap the Recycle Bin icon.

2. Tap the file or folder you want to delete permanently.
3. Tap the X button on the toolbar.

If you want to remove all files from the Recycle Bin, select Empty Recycle Bin from the File menu.

Configuring the Recycle Bin

The Recycle Bin, the temporary holding place for deleted files, uses valuable memory until it is emptied. If you want to limit the amount of space that the Recycle Bin uses, you can change the amount of memory used for this feature. You may want to increase the size of the Recycle Bin so that more files can be stored in it before they are permanently deleted.

To change the Recycle Bin settings, follow these steps:

1. From the HPC desktop, double-tap the Recycle Bin icon.
2. Select Properties from the File menu. The Recycle Bin Properties dialog box, shown in Figure 6.8, appears on-screen.
3. Move the slider either by tapping along the line or by tapping the slider and holding and moving along the line.
4. If you want to completely disable the Recycle Bin and permanently remove files when they are deleted, tap the box that reads `Do not move files to the Recycle Bin.`
5. Click the OK button to save your changes.

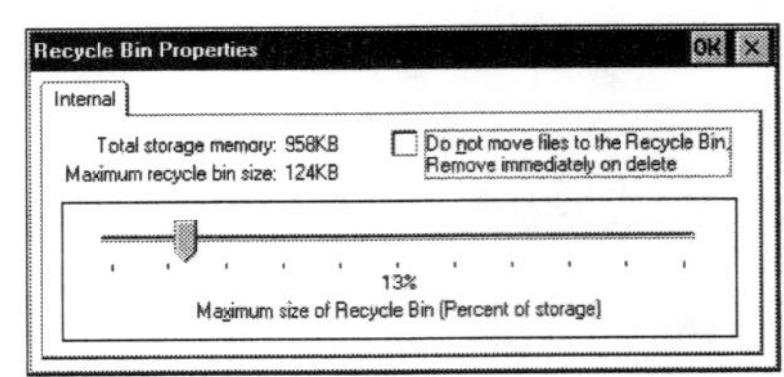

Figure 6.8.
The Recycle Bin Properties dialog box.

When the Recycle Bin is full, you will be prompted to empty it. If you answer Yes, all files will be deleted permanently.

Creating Shortcuts

If there are programs or files that you use often, you may want to create a shortcut to these items. A shortcut is an icon that represents a particular file or program and provides access to that item if you double-tap it.

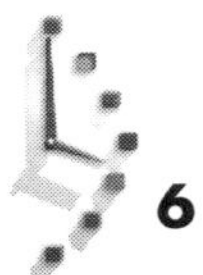

To create a shortcut within a folder, follow these steps:

1. Tap the item you want to create a shortcut for.
2. Select Copy from the Edit menu.
3. Move to where you want to copy the shortcut.
4. Select Paste Shortcut from the Edit menu.

By placing shortcuts on your HPC's desktop, you gain the quickest possible access to the things you use most. To create a shortcut on the desktop, follow these steps:

1. Tap the item you want to create a shortcut for.
2. Select Desktop Shortcut from the File menu.

Windows CE also supports shortcut menus. These menus give you efficient access to a variety of common functions. To access a shortcut menu, press and hold down the Alt key and tap an item. An example is pictured in Figure 6.9.

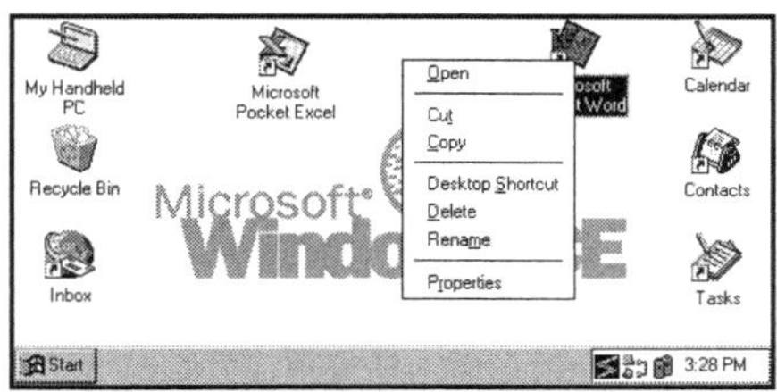

Figure 6.9.
The Windows CE main shortcut menu.

Working with PC Memory Cards

Most HPCs come with an industry-standard PCMCIA slot so you can add things such as a modem and memory cards. Memory cards increase the amount of storage on your HPC. When you install a memory card in your HPC, you are prompted with a message like the one shown in Figure 6.10. Tap the Yes button, and you will notice (see Figure 6.11) a folder named PC Card appearing in the My Handheld PC folder.

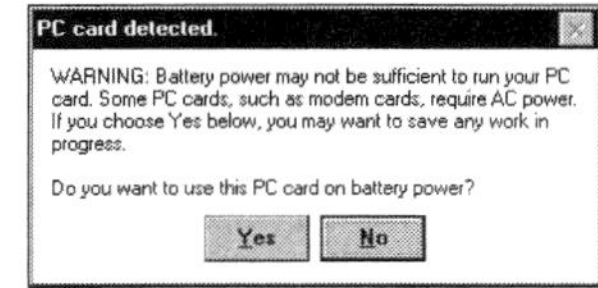

Figure 6.10.
Some PC cards require extra battery power.

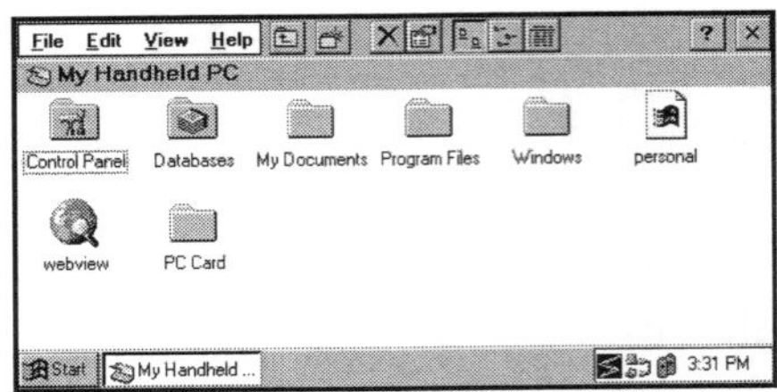

Figure 6.11.
The PC Card folder in Explorer.

To copy or move files to a PC card, follow these steps:

1. Tap the file you want to move or copy and select Cut or Copy from the Edit menu.
2. Double-tap on the PC Card icon and select Paste from the Edit menu.

Summary

In this hour, you learned how to work efficiently with files and folders. You can now copy, move, delete, rename, and view files. You also learned how to use the Recycle Bin and create shortcuts to your programs. Finally, you learned how to copy or move material to memory cards.

Q&A

Q My files and folders have become disorganized. Is there any way to arrange the icons so that they line up?

A Yes. Press the Alt key and then tap the stylus on the screen background.

Q Can hidden files be displayed within Windows CE Explorer?

A Yes. To do this, select Options from the View menu and then select Show All Files.

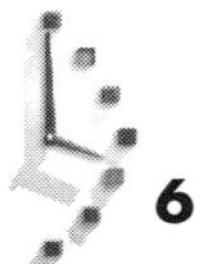

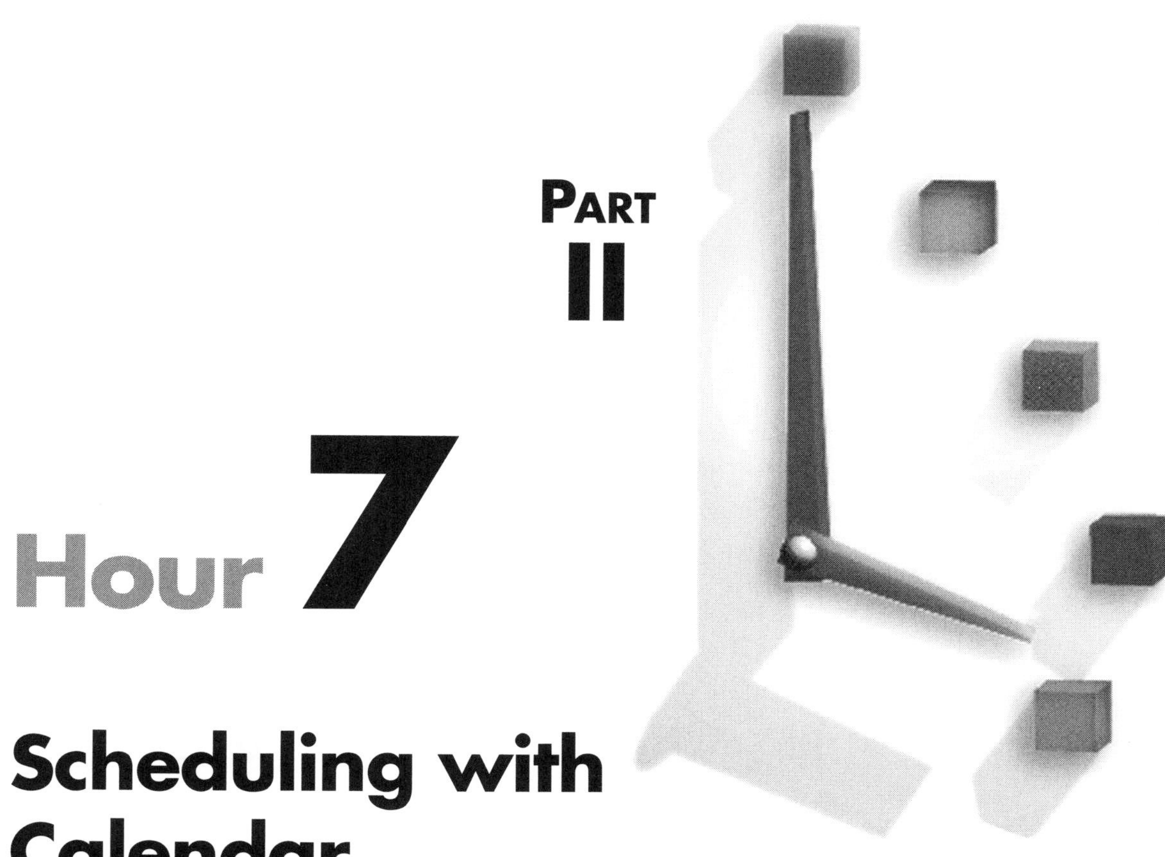

Hour 7

Scheduling with Calendar

In this hour you will explore one of the most frequently used features of Windows CE: Calendar. As part of Windows CE Information Manager, Calendar provides more than simple scheduling functions. With Calendar you add, change, or delete appointments; set up repeating appointments; add full-day events; set a variety of alarms; and view your schedule for a day or a week at a time.

In this hour, you will learn how to do the following:

- Open the Calendar application
- Add a new appointment
- Add a recurring appointment
- Activate and turn off reminders
- Add and modify full-day events
- Move or change the length of appointments
- View your schedule
- Delete appointments and full-day events

Opening the Calendar Application

You can start Calendar by following these steps:

1. Tap the Start button.
2. From the Start menu, tap Programs.
3. Double-tap the Calendar icon.

The layout of the Calendar screen (as shown in Figure 7.1) defaults to the Daily view, with a monthly Calendar at the right and a one-line block for each hour of the currently selected day to the left.

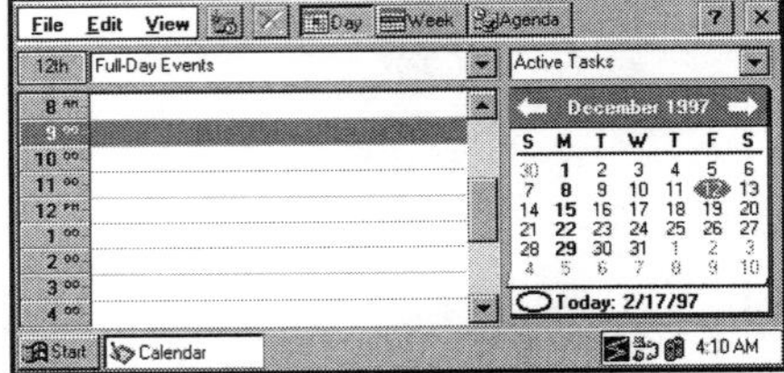

Figure 7.1.
The main Calendar screen.

Adding a New Appointment

You can add an appointment in either Weekly or Daily view. Both use virtually the same procedure:

1. In Daily view, tap the date you want from the monthly calendar. If the month you want is not the current month, tap the right or left arrow next to the month name to move forward or backward until you get to the month you want. In Weekly view, tap the > (greater than) and < (less than) symbols to move to the day you want.
2. Select the time of the appointment by tapping the blank line next to the hour (or the hour closest to) when the appointment starts and tap the New Appointment icon in the toolbar. In Weekly view, tap the box between the corresponding date column and time row.

   If the appointment lasts for several hours, you may want to tap and hold the start time and drag the stylus to the end time, and then tap the New Appointment icon. The Appointment dialog box appears on-screen, as shown in Figure 7.2.
3. Enter a description of the appointment, such as **`Meet with the Big Cheese`**, in the Desc field.
4. Press the Tab key and enter the location of the appointment, such as **`Conference Room`**, in the Location field.

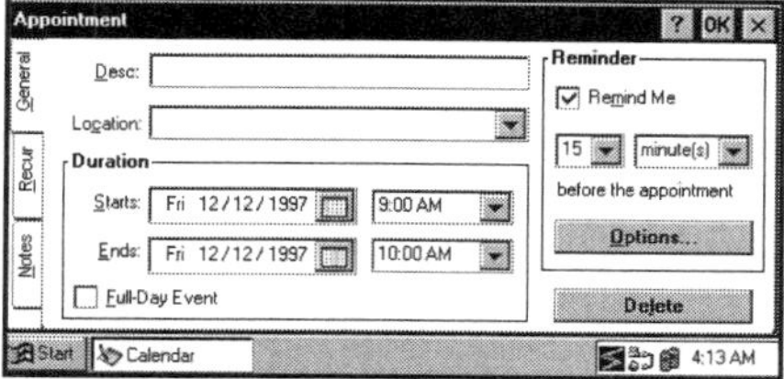

Figure 7.2.
The Appointment dialog box.

5. If you want to change the starting time of the appointment, press the Tab key twice and manually type in the time, or press the down arrow on the keyboard or drop-down list and select the time of the appointment.
6. Tap the OK button to save the appointment.

You can also add an appointment by entering it directly in the Daily view. Simply type a description in one of the time slots. This procedure is an alternative to the preceding steps.

You can add notes to an appointment by tapping the Notes tab in the Appointment dialog box when you are adding or changing an appointment.

Adding a Recurring Appointment

Most appointments are set for a specific time or a specific day. A recurring appointment is useful when an appointment or an event occurs at consistent intervals, such as daily, weekly, monthly, or yearly. An example of a daily recurring appointment is lunch. You might have a weekly staff meeting or a yearly anniversary. To create a recurring appointment, follow these steps:

1. From within Calendar, tap the New Appointment icon in the toolbar. The Appointment dialog box appears on-screen.
2. Enter the description of the appointment in the Desc field.
3. Tap the Recur tab on the left of the screen. Your screen should look similar to Figure 7.3.

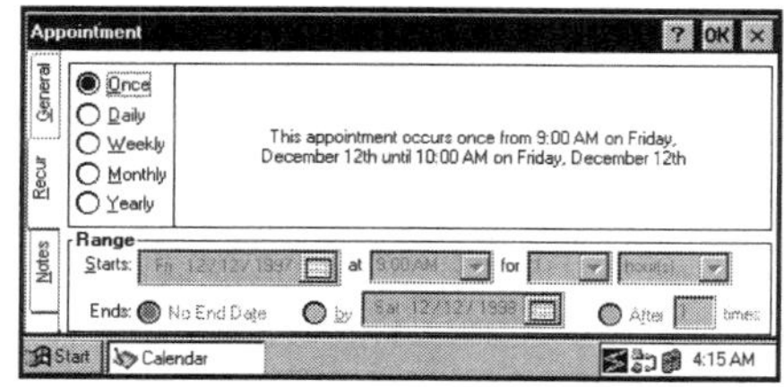

Figure 7.3.
Creating a recurring appointment.

4. Select the interval (Daily, Weekly, Monthly, or Yearly) you want by tapping the appropriate radio button. Figures 7.4, 7.5, and 7.6 show the screens that appear for daily, weekly, and yearly recurring appointments.

Figure 7.4.
Setting up a daily recurring appointment.

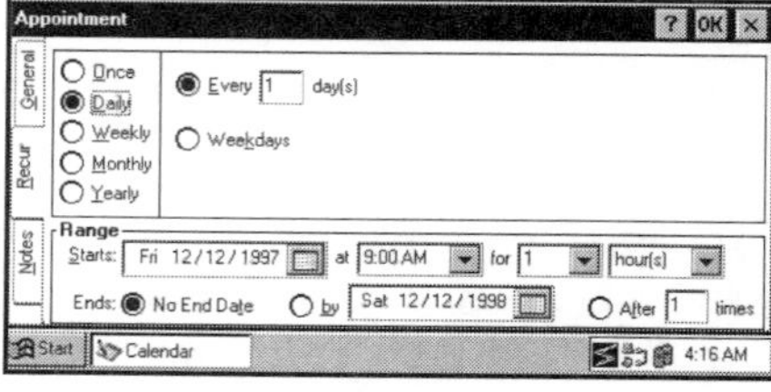

Figure 7.5.
Setting up a weekly recurring appointment.

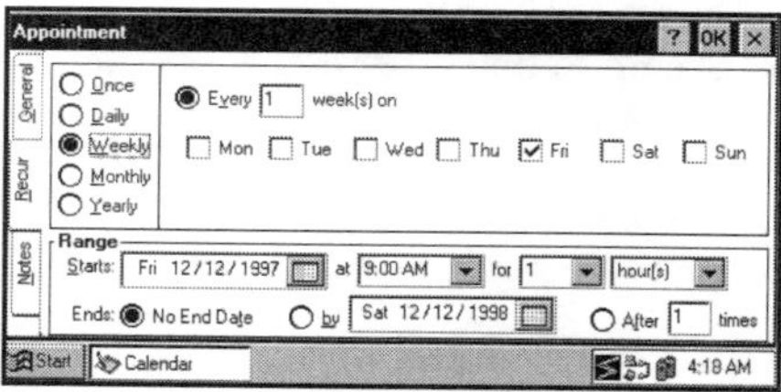

Figure 7.6.
Setting up an annual recurring appointment.

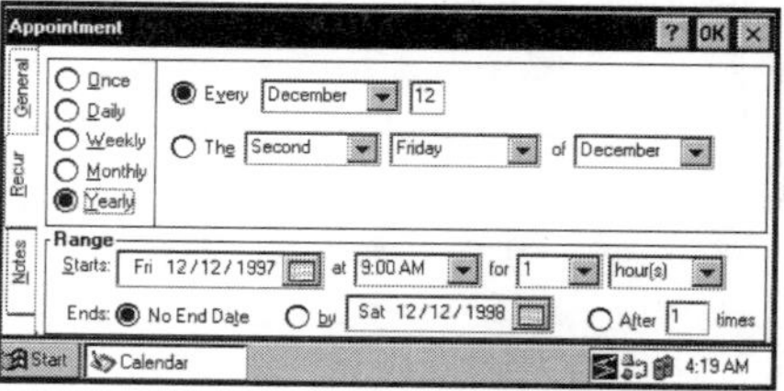

5. Select the frequency of the event by tapping it in the field next to Every. For example, a biweekly meeting would be every two weeks.
6. Select entries from the various check boxes, drop-down lists, and radio buttons that appear for the interval you chose.
7. In the Range box at the bottom of the screen, verify that the Starts date, time, and duration fields are correct by adjusting them from the drop-down lists as necessary. You can use the keyboard for some drop-down lists by typing the first letter of the desired entry, such as F for Friday.
8. If this recurring appointment will go on indefinitely, tap the No End Date radio button. Otherwise, set the End date.
9. Tap the OK button to save the recurring appointment.

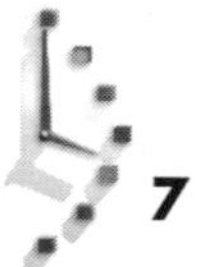

Using Reminders

You can set both Calendar and Tasks (featured in the next hour) applications to notify you of appointments, pending tasks, or events with a dialog box, flashing light (if your HPC supports this feature), or audible alarm. Even if your HPC is turned off, you will be notified with a flashing light. The following sections explain how to set up these reminders and how to turn them off when they occur.

Setting Reminders for an Appointment or Event

From within the Appointment dialog box, follow these instructions to set a reminder:

1. Verify that the Remind Me check box is selected.
2. Select how much time in advance you would like to be notified of the appointment.
3. Tap the Options button. Your screen should look similar to Figure 7.7.

Figure 7.7.
The Notification Options dialog box.

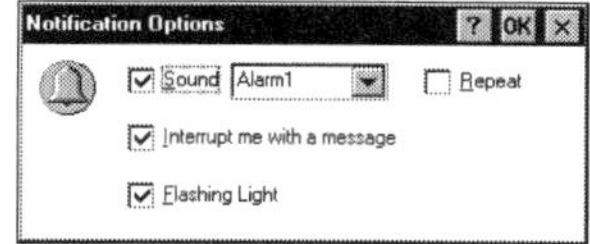

4. From the Notification Options dialog box, select the type of notification you want, a sound message and/or a flashing light (if your HPC is equipped with one), for example. Select the sound you want from the drop-down list.

Time Saver

You can even use your HPC as a traveling alarm clock, as explained in Hour 2, "Getting Started."

Turning Off Reminders

It's 15 minutes before your appointment and your reminder mechanism, either an alarm, light, or dialog box, is activated. What do you do now? Most HPCs have a button on the outside to press in order to turn off the flashing light. If your HPC is not on already, turn it on. No matter which mechanism you chose, the Reminder dialog box displays a message notifying you of an appointment. From the Reminder dialog box, tap the OK button to acknowledge the message and turn off the alarm. If you want another reminder of the

appointment, tap the Snooze button. The Snooze button is set for five minutes and cannot be changed.

Working with Full-Day Events

To add a full-day event to Calendar, follow these steps:

1. Tap the date of the event on the monthly calendar at the right of the main screen. Change the month as necessary by tapping the arrows next to the month name.
2. Tap New Full-Day Event from the drop-down list.
3. Enter the description of the event in the Desc field, and then tap the OK button.

To modify a full-day event, select the event from the Full-Day Events drop-down list and make the desired changes. When finished, tap the OK button to save the changes.

Modifying an Appointment

Modifying an appointment is simply a matter of double-tapping the appointment that you want to change and making the necessary changes. When you are finished making the changes, tap the OK button. The following sections give instructions for specific modifications you may want to make.

Moving an Appointment

To move an appointment to a different time within the same day, tap and hold on the appointment and drag it to the new time. To move an appointment to a different date, follow these steps:

1. Tap the appointment you want to move.
2. Select Cut from the Edit menu.
3. Move to the new date and time.
4. Select Paste from the Edit menu.

Changing the Duration of an Appointment

To change the duration of an appointment, tap the appointment. You will notice two pyramids appear at the top and bottom of the appointment (refer to Figure 7.8). To change the length of the appointment, tap and drag these pyramids to lengthen or shorten the duration of the appointment.

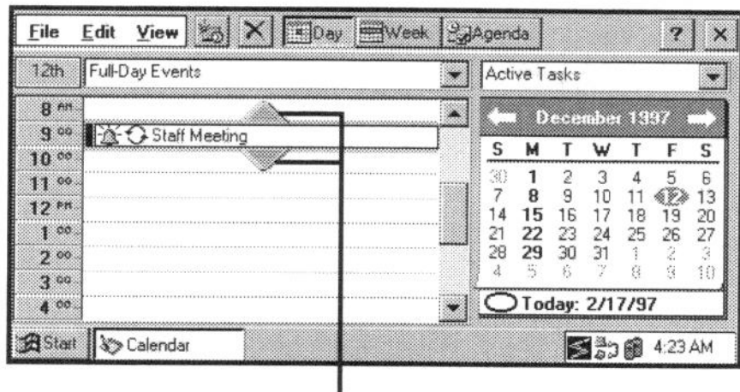

Figure 7.8.
Changing the length of an appointment.

Viewing Your Schedule

You can view your schedule in the default Daily view, Weekly view (refer to Figure 7.9), or the Agenda view (refer to Figure 7.10). To switch between these different views, tap the button on the toolbar that designates the view that you want. Unfortunately, Windows CE does not include a "month-at-a-glance" view. However, the small monthly calendar in the Daily view indicates the days with appointments by displaying the day in bold. The view appearing on the screen when you exit Calendar will become the new default view.

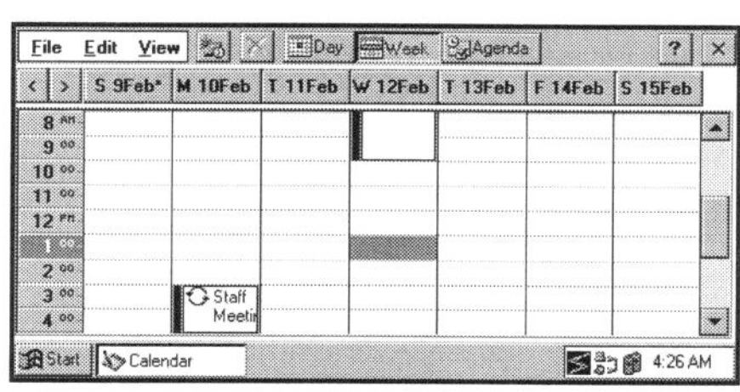

Figure 7.9.
The Calendar's Weekly view.

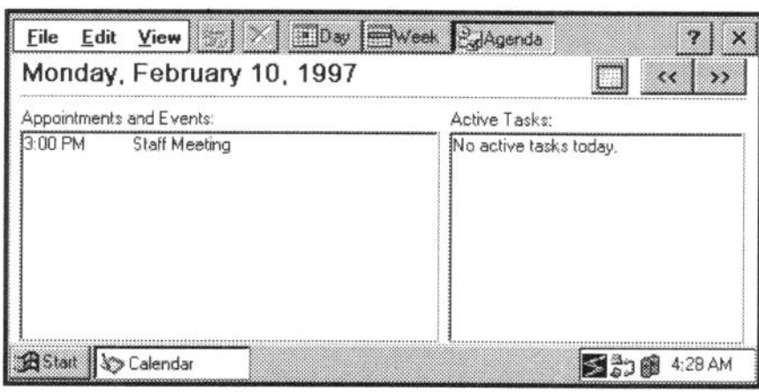

Figure 7.10.
The Calendar's Agenda view.

In the Daily view, tap the date you want to see from the monthly calendar. Weekly view enables you to see your schedule a week at a time. By default, Windows CE displays a week as a five-day work week, although you can change it to a seven-day view by deselecting 5-Day Week View from the View menu.

The Agenda view shows you a summary of all of the appointments, events, and tasks for a particular day. The Tasks section will become clearer when you learn how to create tasks in Hour 9, "The Task at Hand." The Agenda view is read-only; therefore, you can only view, not edit, information.

Deleting an Appointment or Event

There are several ways to delete an appointment:

- Tap the appointment and then tap the X button in the toolbar.
- Select the appointment, and then press the Delete key on your keyboard.
- Select the appointment, and then select Delete Item from the Edit menu.

To delete a full-day event, follow these steps:

1. Select the event from the Full-Day Events drop-down list.
2. Tap the Delete button in the lower-right corner of the screen. (Verify that you are in the General tab.)
3. Tap the OK button in the dialog box that appears.

Unfortunately, Windows CE does not give you the option to delete all appointments prior to a specific date. Therefore, you must manually delete all unnecessary past appointments in order to free up valuable memory storage space.

Summary

In this hour you discovered how to use the Calendar program. You learned how to enter, edit, and delete appointments, create recurring appointments, and view your schedule in a variety of formats.

Q&A

Q Is there any way to improve the speed of Calendar?

A Yes. If you limit the number of recurring appointments that you use, performance will increase.

Q Can I use keyboard shortcuts with Calendar?

A Yes. You can use the arrow keys to move up and down within the Daily view. Use the left and right arrows to change the day. You can also use Shift + an arrow key to select a range of time.

PART
II

Hour 8

Keep in Touch with Contacts

More than just a simple address book, Contacts is a complete contact management program. You can view your contacts together in a list view or one at a time in a detailed card view. However, you must store both personal and business data in a single address book because Windows CE does not support multiple address books. In this hour, you will learn how to do the the following things:

- Open Contacts
- Add a new contact
- Change a contact card
- Create a duplicate contact card
- Use the contact list
- Find contacts
- Delete contacts

Opening Contacts

Follow these steps to open the Contacts application:

1. Tap the Start button to reveal the Start menu.
2. Tap Programs, and then double-tap the Contacts icon.

You can also start Contacts from the Windows CE desktop by double-tapping the Contacts icon.

When you first start Contacts, you see Contacts' list view (refer to Figure 8.1). In this default view, contacts are sorted alphabetically by a person's last name. The list view is a summary view that displays one line for each contact.

Figure 8.1.
The contact list.

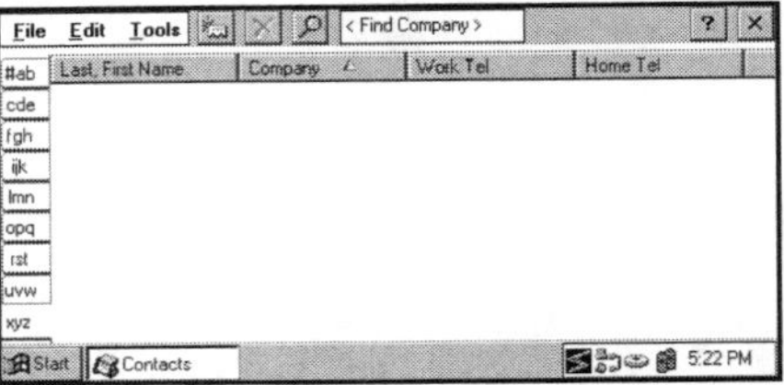

Adding a New Contact

The first thing you will want to do is get your address book handy and enter your contacts. If you prefer to enter contacts first on your desktop PC and then synchronize with your HPC, rather than enter contacts directly in your HPC, you can open Schedule+ on your PC and tap the Contacts tab. To use your HPC to add contacts, follow these steps:

1. Tap the New Card icon in the toolbar.
2. Enter the name of the contact.
3. The first entry screen is the Business tab, which contains mostly work-related information. Tap the Personal Tab to enter information such as home addresses and telephone numbers (refer to Figure 8.2.)
4. Press the Tab key to move from field to field and enter the appropriate information. (You can also move directly to the field you want by tapping on it.)
5. If you want to add notes for your contact, tap the Notes tab and use the free-form text box to enter additional information (refer to Figure 8.3).
6. Tap OK to save the contact.

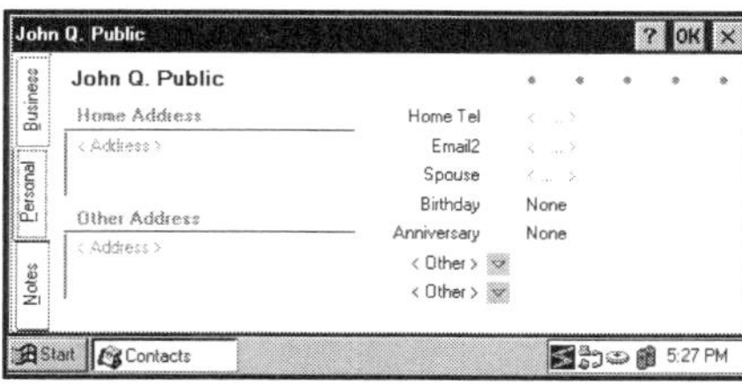

Figure 8.2.
Entering a contact's address.

Figure 8.3.
Adding notes about a contact.

When you add a new contact, a Confirm Address dialog box (shown in Figure 8.4) may appear when you enter the address. Windows CE displays this box when it cannot determine the field (such as City, State, or ZIP) to which a portion of the address belongs. If this box appears, make any necessary changes and tap the OK button. When you are entering an address, you can verify that the information is entered correctly by tapping the Address Tree icon to the right of the address field.

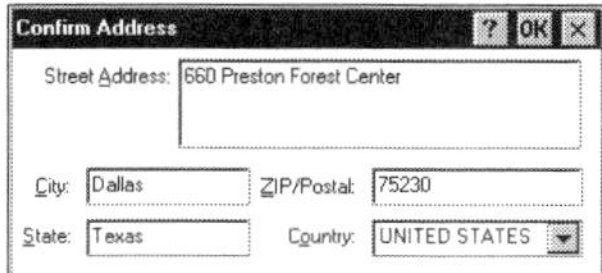

Figure 8.4.
The Confirm Address dialog box.

In the Business tab there are four fields (two fields in the Personal tab) labeled Other that appear on the screen. Because not all available fields are displayed, these Other fields provide you with the option of displaying additional fields (found in Schedule+) you would like to view. To select a field, tap the down arrow to the right of the Other field to display a drop-down list of available fields (refer to Figure 8.5). Tap the field you want, and it will appear in that specific contact card.

When adding a contact, you should be aware of the differences between the fields in Schedule+ and those in Contacts. Contacts contains several fields that are not included in Schedule+. The additional fields are name prefixes, middle names, cellular phone numbers, e-mail addresses, home fax numbers, additional children and spouse names, Web addresses, and other address fields. Although this data will be synchronized, it will not appear in Schedule+.

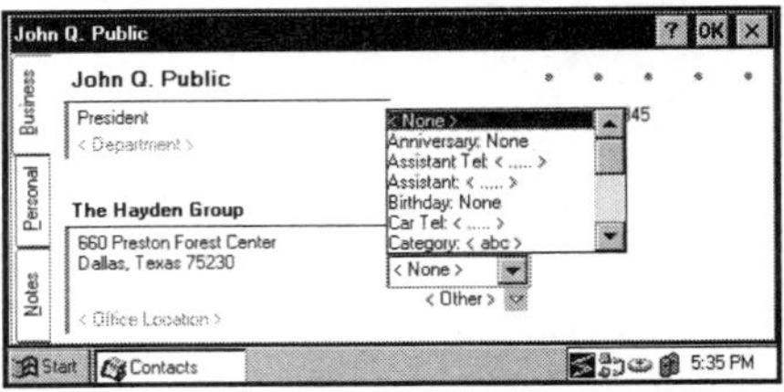

Figure 8.5.
Additional fields for a contact.

Several Schedule+ fields will not be synchronized with your HPC: they are User2, User3, and User4. The User1 field in Schedule+ will be mapped to the Email 1 field on your HPC. The Schedule+ Fax field is mapped to the Work Fax field in Contacts.

Changing a Contact

To change a contact, follow these steps:

1. Double-tap the contact that you want to change from the contact list.
2. Make any changes necessary.
3. Tap the OK button to save the changes.

Creating a Duplicate Contact Card

If you have several contacts from the same company, you can create a duplicate of the first contact and add or change only the information unique to the new contact:

1. Tap the contact that you want to duplicate from the contact list.
2. From the Edit menu, tap Create Copy.
3. Double-tap the new contact and make your changes.

Using the Contact List

To move around the contact list, you can use the up arrow, down arrow, PgDn, and PgUp keys to move up or down a line or screen at a time. Alternatively, you can tap the scroll bars to see additional contacts that are not visible. You can also type the first letter of a contact's last name to move to the first contact whose last name starts with the letter you typed.

Sorting the Contact List

By default, Windows CE sorts contacts alphabetically by last name. You can change this order by tapping the heading column of the field you want Windows CE to sort by. For example, to sort by company name, tap the Company heading (see the results in Figure 8.6). Notice that a small pyramid appears in the heading column of the sorting field.

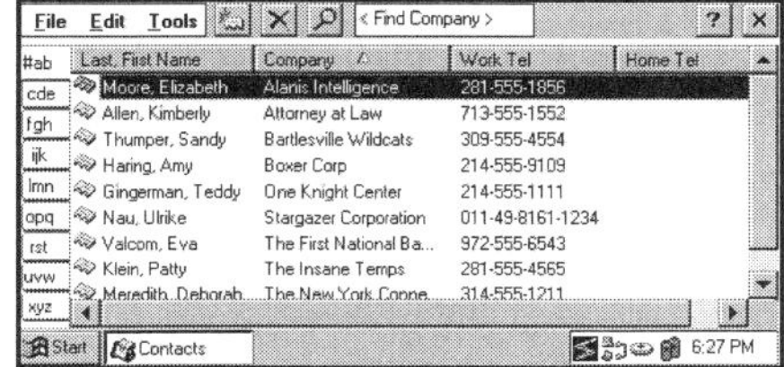

Figure 8.6.
Sorting by company name.

Changing Information Appearing on the Contact List

By default, the fields presented in the Contacts' list view include contact name, company, work phone, and home phone. You can change which columns appear and in what order:

1. Tap the Tools menu and select Options. Your screen should look similar to Figure 8.7.

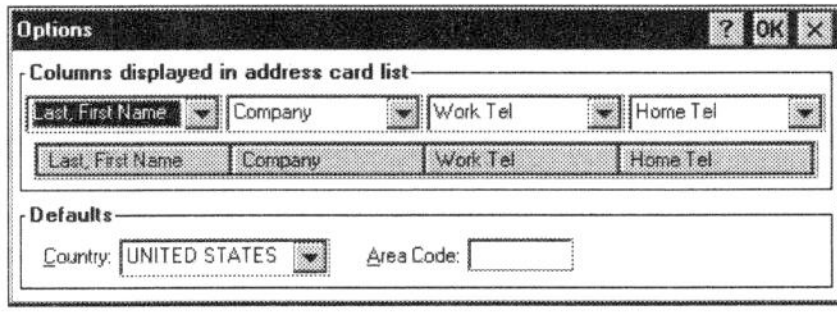

Figure 8.7.
The Options dialog box.

2. Use the drop-down list to select which fields you want to display and in what column.
3. Tap OK when you are finished.

Finding Contacts

If you have a large address book, locating a contact by scrolling can be time-consuming. Also, there may be times when you know a city or phone number for the contact but don't remember the contact's name or the exact spelling. Contacts provides a useful search function that enables you to locate a contact by any word contained within the contact card.

There are a couple of ways to find a contact. The first way limits your searches to the first several characters that the sorted field begins with and only allows you to search on the sorted field. Tap the Quick Find field located in the toolbar next to the magnifying glass. Type the first few letters you want to search for. Notice that highlight bar moves to the first contact that matches what you type and then moves again as you type a more specific match. Suppose your contacts are sorted by last name, and you have two contacts with the last names Allen and Alford. When you type **al**, you are taken directly to Alford, but when you type another **l**, the pointer will move to Allen. Note that searches in Contacts are not case-sensitive.

When you need a more flexible search capability than the Quick Find field provides, follow these steps:

1. Tap the Tools menu, and then select Find. Alternatively, tap the magnifying glass icon in the toolbar.
2. When the Find dialog box appears (as shown in Figure 8.8), type the text you are searching for and press the Enter key or tap the Find Next button.

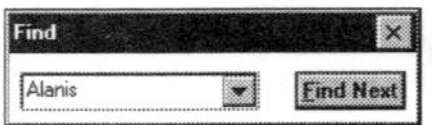

Figure 8.8.
Finding a contact.

3. Tap the X in the upper-right corner of the Find dialog box when you have located the contact you want.

If your text search was successful, you will be taken to the first contact card that matched the criteria. If you want to search for all contacts that contain the information you typed, keep tapping the Find Next button until Contacts has located all matches. If Windows CE cannot find the text you typed within your contacts, a message similar to Figure 8.9 will be displayed.

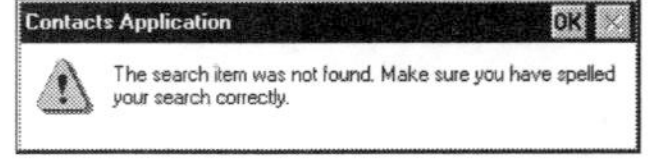

Figure 8.9.
The contact was not found.

Deleting Contacts

There are a couple of ways to delete a contact:

- Select the contact you want to delete and tap the X button in the toolbar.
- Select the contact you want to delete and then press the Delete key on your keyboard. (Note that some HPC keyboards require you to press the Shift or FN key and then the Delete key. Refer to the user's guide that came with your HPC.)

Regardless of which approach you choose, you will see a message warning you that the contact will be permanently deleted. The contact will not be transferred to the Recycle Bin; therefore, it cannot be recovered once it is deleted.

Summary

In this hour, you learned how to use Windows CE's electronic address book, Contacts. You should feel comfortable entering your contacts, moving around the contact list, and searching for and deleting contacts. You also learned how to sort contacts and change the way they are displayed. In Hour 15, "Using Inbox for E-mail," you will learn how to use contact information such as e-mail addresses.

Q&A

Q Can you share contact cards with other HPC users?

A Yes. Windows CE allows you to transfer cards between HPCs via the IR port (see Hour 20, "Using Infrared").

Q What Schedule+ fields are not synchronized?

A The Schedule+ User2, User3, and User4 fields are not synchronized with your HPC.

Part II

Hour 9

The Task at Hand

Tasks is a powerful to-do list that is part of Information Manager. With Tasks you can assign priorities, start dates, and due dates; set alarms; and specify the projects with which the tasks are associated. Once you have completed a task, you can mark it as complete and still maintain a copy for later reference. Additionally, you can view information entered in Tasks from within Calendar.

In this hour, you will learn how to do the following things with Tasks:

- Add tasks to your list
- Change tasks
- Sort tasks
- Mark a task as complete
- Delete a task from the list
- View tasks

Adding Tasks to Your List

Before you begin, start the Tasks program by double-tapping the Tasks icon from the desktop. Alternatively, you can select Programs from the Start menu, and then double-tap the Tasks icon.

To add a new task, follow these steps:

1. Tap the New Task icon on the toolbar. Your screen should look similar to Figure 9.1.

Figure 9.1.
The Task dialog box.

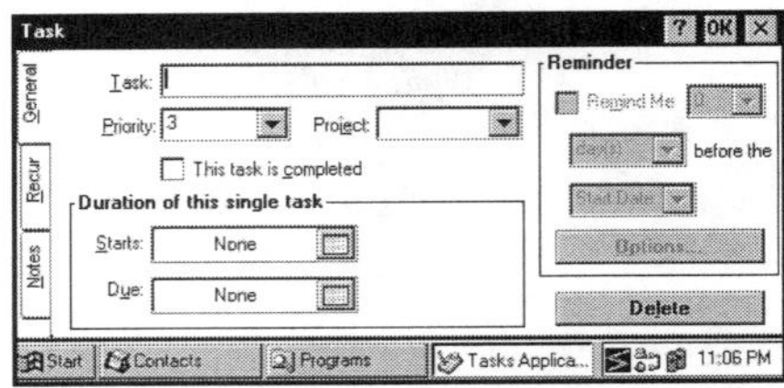

2. Type the name of the task in the Task field.
3. Press the Tab key and select a priority from the Priority drop-down list.
4. Tap the calendar icon next to the Starts field and select the date when the task begins by double-tapping it.
5. Tap the calendar icon next to the Due field and select the date when the task must be finished by double-tapping it. Tap the OK button to add this task to your list.

Adding Recurring Tasks

Just as you can create recurring appointments in Calendar, you can create recurring entries in Tasks. You can set a task to recur on a daily, weekly, monthly, or yearly basis. To create a recurring task, follow these steps:

1. From the Tasks program, tap the New Task icon in the toolbar (if you are not already at the New Tasks screen).
2. Type a description of the task in the Task field.
3. Tap the Recur tab. Your screen should look similar to Figure 9.2.
4. Select the radio button that corresponds to the interval you want: Daily, Weekly, Monthly, or Yearly. The screen changes depending on which interval you select. Figure 9.3 shows the screen for a daily task, Figure 9.4 shows the screen for a weekly task, and Figure 9.5 shows the screen for a monthly task.

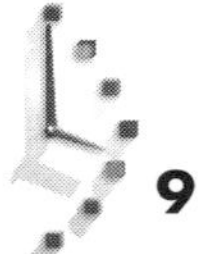

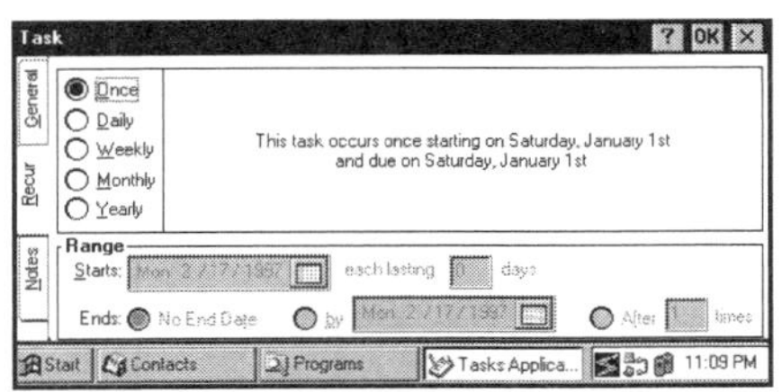

Figure 9.2.
Creating a recurring task.

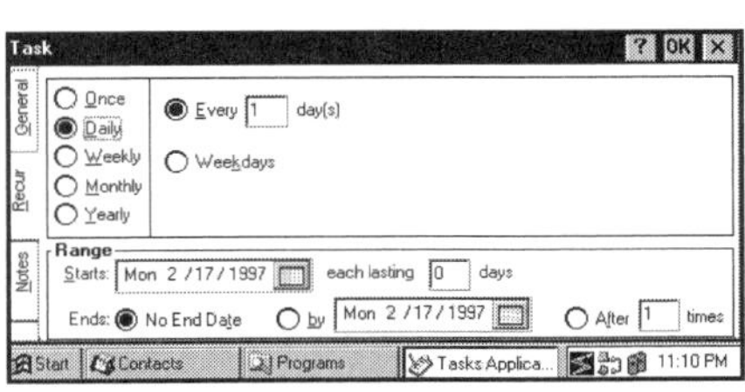

Figure 9.3.
Setting your daily tasks.

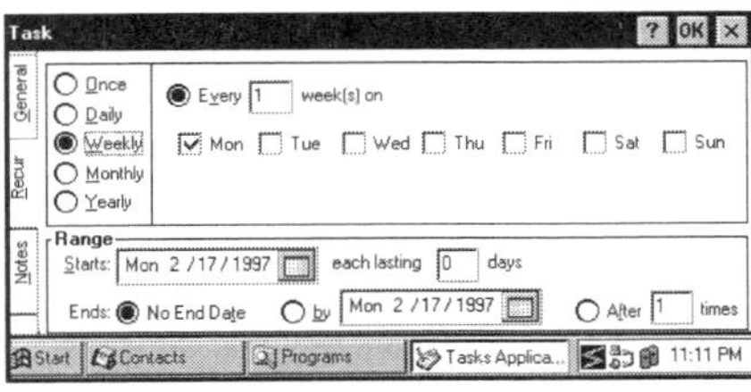

Figure 9.4.
Setting your weekly tasks.

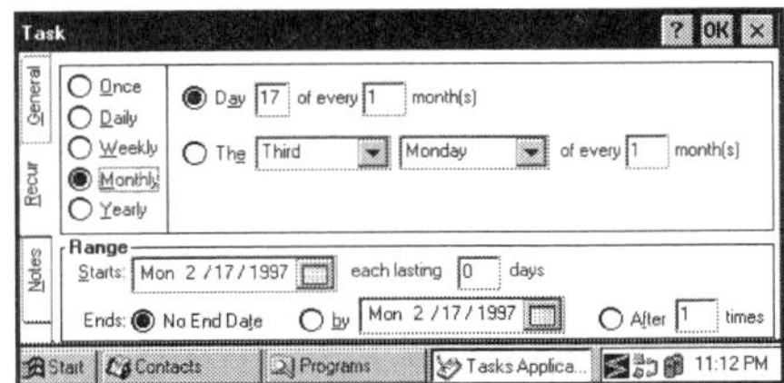

Figure 9.5.
Setting your monthly tasks.

5. Select the options you want from the various check boxes and drop-down lists that are available for the interval you selected. For example, for daily and weekly tasks, select the frequency of the event by entering it in the field next to Every.
6. In the Range box at the bottom of the screen, verify that the Starts date and duration are correct. If they aren't, enter the correct information in the boxes.
7. If this recurring task is indefinite, tap the No End Date radio button; otherwise, set the end date in the box provided. An end date can be a specific date or after the task occurs a certain number of times.
8. Tap the OK button to save the recurring task.

Viewing Tasks

Windows CE provides a couple of ways to view tasks. The following sections provide the details about how you can modify these views to best suit your needs. Figure 9.6 shows a task in Card view. You can also view tasks in a list format that displays all active or completed tasks.

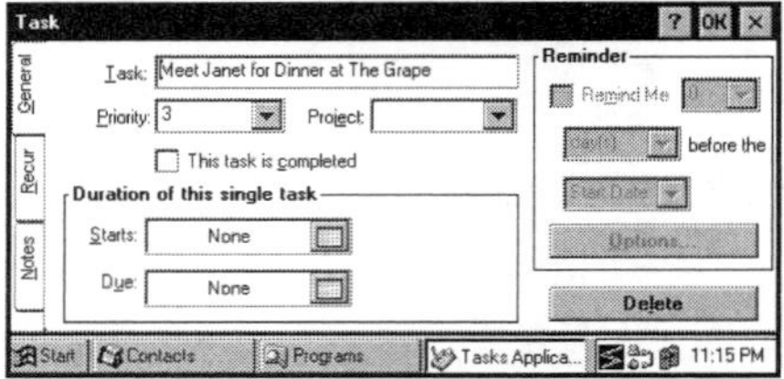

Figure 9.6.
Viewing a task in Card view.

Sorting Tasks

You can sort tasks by any displayed column; just tap the column heading by which you would like to sort. By default, tasks are sorted numerically by priority, then alphabetically. To change the field that tasks are sorted by, tap the desired sort column. You will notice a small pyramid to the right of the heading name that indicates the sort field. If you sort by status, active tasks will be sorted first, followed by completed tasks.

Displaying Only Certain Tasks

Tasks enables you to display only those tasks that meet a certain criterion. For example, you can display only completed tasks or only those that have yet to be completed. Additionally, you can display only tasks that are associated with a particular project.

To display only certain tasks, select the criterion from the drop-down list in the Tasks toolbar, as shown in Figure 9.7. For example, to display only completed tasks, select Completed Tasks from the drop-down list. To view active tasks, select Active Tasks from the list. Once you have created a project, it is added automatically to the drop-down list.

Time Saver

When you enter a new task, one of the optional fields is Project Name. If you want to use Tasks as a project manager or if you want to have an additional field to group your tasks by, enter a project name when adding new tasks.

Figure 9.7.
Viewing specific tasks.

Changing Tasks

After creating a new task, you may want to add notes to it, change its priority or due date, or add a project name to it. To make changes to a task, follow these steps:

1. From the list view, double-tap the task you want to change. This will change your view to Card view.
2. Make the desired changes.
3. Tap the OK button to save changes.

Edit View

Generally you will find that it is easier to make changes in Edit view instead of the default List view. Edit view enables you to see a list of tasks and to change tasks without switching to Card view. To change a task in Edit view, follow these steps:

1. Tap the Edit view icon in the toolbar.
2. Tap the task you want to change.
3. Make the necessary changes directly to the desired field in the Edit panel below the toolbar.
4. Tap the Enter button or press the Enter key to save changes.

Marking a Task as Complete

When you mark a task as complete, that task is no longer displayed in the Agenda view of Calendar, yet Tasks still maintains a record of it. To mark a task as complete, tap the empty box to the left of the task in the default list view. You will notice a check mark appears in the box to indicate the task is complete. If you are in Tasks' Card view, you can tap the This Task Is Completed check box, and then tap the OK button to save the change.

Deleting a Task from the List

To delete a task permanently, follow these steps:

1. Tap the task you want to delete.
2. Tap the X button in the toolbar or press the Del key and tap the OK button to delete the task.

Summary

In this hour you learned how to create to-do lists with the Tasks application. You learned how to view, change, and delete tasks as well as how to set up recurring tasks. Additionally, you learned how to sort a task list and mark tasks as completed.

Q&A

Q When a task is marked as complete, is it deleted?

A No. You have the option to delete a particular task or all completed tasks if you want.

Q Can I create a recurring task?

A Yes. Tap the Recur tab from within a Tasks card and select the frequency with which the task is to be repeated.

PART III

Documents and Spreadsheets at Dinner

Hour

PART
III

Hour 10

Using Pocket Word

It's dinnertime, and Windows CE is serving up a surprisingly powerful word processor: Pocket Word. When the developers at Microsoft designed Pocket Word, they analyzed which features were most frequently used and incorporated most of them into Pocket Word. Although you will not find a spell checker or tables, Pocket Word is still a very capable word processor. Pocket Word offers more than simple note-taking: You can write letters, create reports, or write a memo. In fact, much of this book was written on an HPC during long coast-to-coast flights that lasted longer then a notebook's battery would have.

One of Pocket Word's most useful attributes is its capability to quickly and easily transfer documents to and from Microsoft Word on your desktop PC. Once files are transferred back to your desktop PC, you can check your document for spelling errors and print it. Even if you don't plan on making changes to a document, there are times when just having a Word document available for viewing on your HPC is useful.

In this hour, you will learn how to do the following with Pocket Word:

- Create a new document
- Open a document

- Select and edit text
- Save a document
- Close a document
- Find and replace text
- Change text attributes and justification
- Create bulleted lists

Creating a New Document

When you start Pocket Word by double-tapping the Pocket Word icon, you are automatically put in a new document (refer to Figure 10.1). If you are working on a document and want to create a new document, tap New on the File menu.

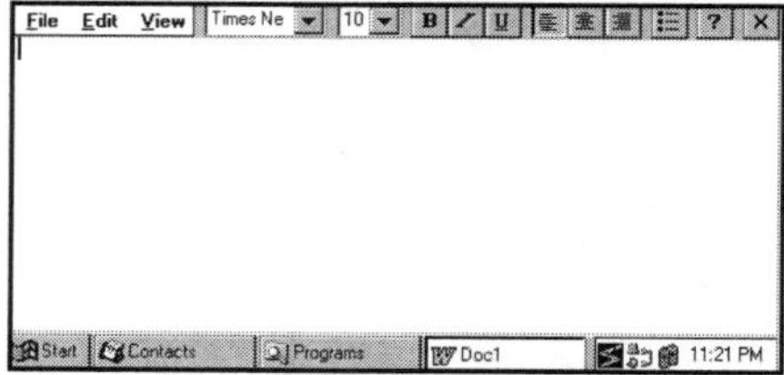

Figure 10.1.
Pocket Word's opening screen.

Pocket Word also provides several templates that you can use to create a document that adheres to a particular format. The My Documents folder includes templates for meeting notes, letters, and memos. If you have created a template or want to use one of the templates provided, follow these steps:

1. From the File menu, select Open.
2. Select the template that you want to use by double-tapping it. Pocket Word displays the template on-screen.
3. Select the template text (surrounded by <> symbols) that you want to change and type in the text you want (refer to Figure 10.2).

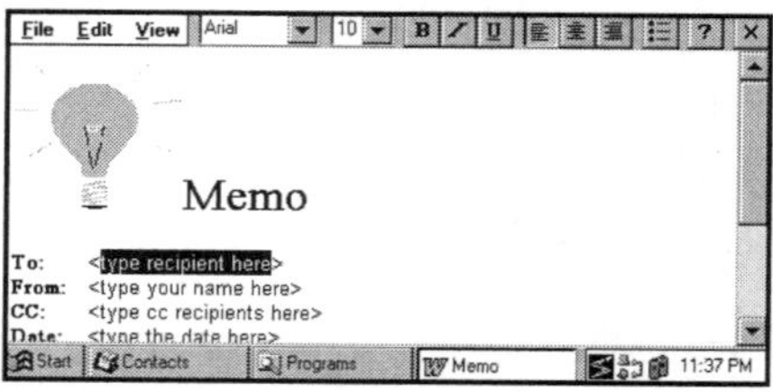

Figure 10.2.
Opening a document template.

4. Save the document when completed by selecting Save from the File menu.

Opening a Document

To open a document within Pocket Word, follow these steps:

1. Tap Open on the File menu. Your screen should look similar to Figure 10.3.

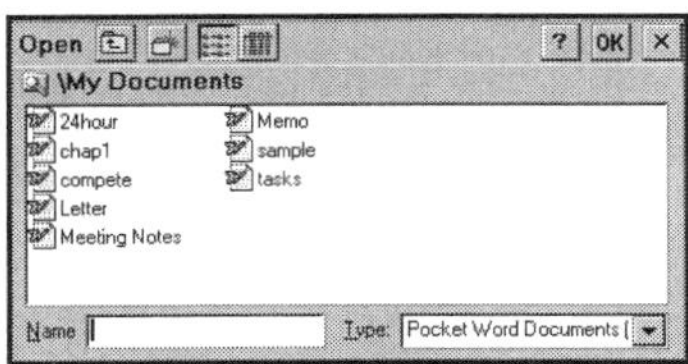

Figure 10.3.
The Open dialog box.

2. From the list of documents, tap the document you want to open and tap the OK button. Alternatively, simply double-tap the one you want to open.

If the document you want to open is one of the last three that you recently worked on, it may appear at the bottom of the File menu. Before selecting Open from the File menu, check to see whether the document you want to open is on the menu. To select one of the documents on the File menu, you can either tap it or type the number to the left of the file name (refer to Figure 10.4).

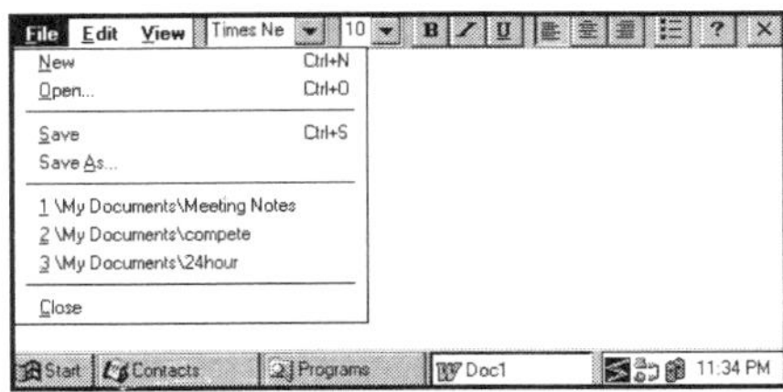

Figure 10.4.
Opening a document from the File menu.

Pocket Word allows you to open more than one document at a time. In fact, you can open as many documents as you want (limited only by available memory). Each document appears in the taskbar for easy access. To reopen a document, tap the desired document from the taskbar.

Selecting and Editing Text

If you want to change fonts and formats or move, delete, or copy text, you will first need to select the text you want to change. There are different instructions depending on how much text you want to select.

To select	*Do this*
A word	Double-tap the word
A paragraph	Triple-tap within the paragraph
The entire document	Tap Select All from the Edit menu
A picture	Tap the picture
A block of text	Tap and drag the entire block

Copying Text

To copy text, follow these steps:

1. Select the text you want to copy.
2. With the text highlighted, select Copy from the Edit menu.
3. Tap the point where you want to insert the selected text.
4. Select Paste from the Edit menu.

Moving Text

To move text within a document, follow these steps:

1. Select the text you want to move.
2. With the text highlighted, select Cut from the Edit menu.
3. Tap the point where you want to insert the selected text.
4. Select Paste from the Edit menu.

Undoing Changes

If you accidentally delete text or make another mistake, you can undo it by selecting Undo from the Edit menu. The Undo feature only works with your most recent command. For example, if you just deleted a paragraph and then you underlined a word, the Undo command will remove the underline because that was your last action. If you have used the Cut command, you can always use the Paste command to recover text. If you deleted text with the Backspace or Delete key, however, Undo will recover only your last key press. If you want to undo an Undo command, select Redo from the Edit menu.

Saving a Document

Pocket Word documents are saved in a unique format with the extension .pwd. This file format is not the same as Microsoft Word, although the conversion to Microsoft Word

format is handled automatically when you use HPC Explorer to transfer documents to and from your HPC.

Pocket Word can also save a document in a .txt file format. This format is a universally compatible file type. However, if you save a file in this format, you will lose all of your formatting, such as centering and boldface, italics, and underlining.

To save a file for the first time, follow these steps:

1. From the File menu, select Save. The Save As dialog box shown in Figure 10.5 appears. If you want to save the file in .txt format, select Plain Text Documents from the Type scroll list. Otherwise, proceed to the next step.
2. Type in the name of your document in the Name text box. Do not type in an extension; the .pwd or .txt extension will be added automatically.

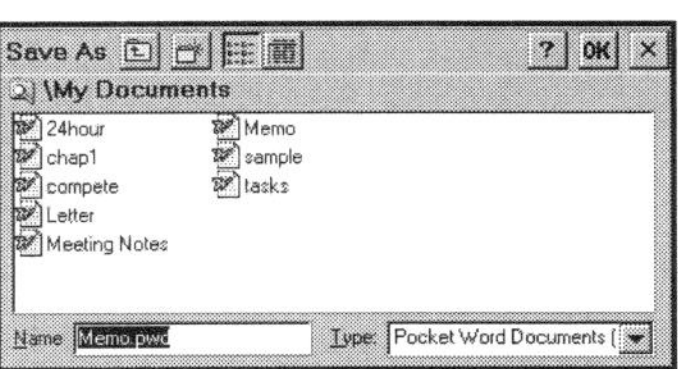

Figure 10.5.
The Save As dialog box.

3. Tap the OK button to save the document.

Murphy's Law says that the batteries on your HPC will die just before you save a long document. Because HPCs do not have a hard disk or floppy drive, all of your data is saved in memory, which requires battery power to prevent data loss. Although a backup battery will save your contents for a period of time after your main batteries have drained, you should save and synchronize frequently.

Closing a Document

When you are finished working with a document, you can close it with one of the following procedures:

- Tap the close button.
- From the File menu, select Close.

If your document has not been saved, a dialog box will appear (shown in Figure 10.6) asking if you want to save changes. If you tap the Yes button, you will be prompted to enter a file name if you have not already entered one. If you tap No, Pocket Word will not save any changes since your last save, and you may lose all of your text. Finally, tapping the Cancel button returns you to the place you were before you attempted to close the file.

Figure 10.6.
The Save Changes dialog box.

You will see this dialog box for each document you have changed. After you handle the last dialog box (or the only one if you opened only one document), Pocket Word will close.

Finding and Replacing Text

Pocket Word enables you to quickly locate a word or several words within a document. In addition, you can replace text throughout a document.

Finding Text

Searches for text begin from the place your cursor is located when you select the Find command and continue to the end of the document and back through from the beginning of the document until they reach the starting point.

To find a word or phrase, follow these steps:

1. Select Find from the Edit menu. The Find dialog box appears on-screen.
2. Type the word(s) you want to locate in the Find What text box (refer to Figure 10.7).

Figure 10.7.
The Find dialog box.

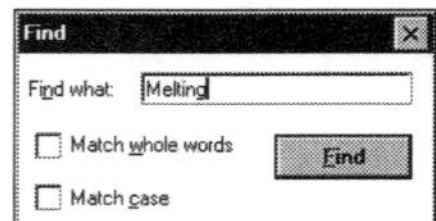

3. From the Find dialog box, tap the Match Case and/or Match Whole Words check boxes if you want to activate these options. If you do not care if the search matches exactly from a capitalization standpoint, leave the Match Case check box blank. If you want to include only whole words in your search, make sure that the Match Whole Words check box is selected. For example, if you type **`start`**, you will not find the word `starting` if the Match Whole Words check box is selected.
4. Tap the Find button to locate the first occurrence of the word(s).
5. Press CTRL+4 repeatedly to move to each subsequent occurrence of the word(s). You can also find the next occurrence by selecting Find Next from the Edit menu.
6. When the document search is complete, a dialog box will display the results of your search.

Replacing Text

To replace a word or phrase, follow these steps:

1. Select Replace from the Edit menu.
2. Type the word(s) you want to replace in the Find What text box (refer to Figure 10.8).

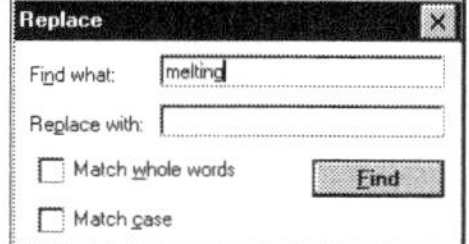

Figure 10.8.
The Replace dialog box.

3. Press the Tab key to move to the Replace With text box and type the word(s) you want to replace the first word you typed.
4. From the Replace dialog box, tap the Match Case and/or Match Whole Words check boxes if you want to activate these options. If you do not care if the word you want to replace matches exactly from a capitalization standpoint, leave the Match Case check box blank. If you want to replace only whole words, make sure that the Match Whole Words check box is selected. For example, if you type **`start`**, you will not alter the word `starting` if the Match Whole Words check box is selected.
5. Tap the Find button to locate the first occurrence of the word(s). When the first word is found, a Find/Replace dialog box will appear (refer to Figure 10.9).

Figure 10.9.
The Find/Replace dialog box.

6. Tap the appropriate button. Tapping the Find button will locate the next match. Tapping the Replace button will replace only that occurrence and move to the next one. Tapping the Replace All button will replace all occurrences of a word within the document.

Changing Text Attributes and Alignment

Without text attributes and justification, documents would look pretty boring. Pocket Word allows you to boldface, underline, and italicize a word or block of text. In addition, you can align text so that it is left-justified, centered, or right-justified. To add a text attribute or align text, select the text you want to change and tap the appropriate toolbar icon.

The toolbar icons offer the following features:

B Tap this icon to make selected text bold.

I Tap this icon to italicize selected text.

U Tap this icon to underline the selected text.

Tap this icon to make the selected text flush with the left side of the screen.

Tap this icon to center the selected text.

Tap this icon to make selected text flush with the right side of the screen.

To remove attributes from text, highlight the text that you want to remove the attributes from. Then deselect the attribute's icon (it should look as though it has been pressed) in the toolbar by tapping it.

Creating Bulleted Lists

When you create a document, a bulleted list can be a useful feature. To create a bulleted list, follow these steps:

1. Move to the point in the document where you want the bulleted list to begin, and then tap the Bulleted List icon on the toolbar.
2. Type in the text for the first bullet.
3. Press the Enter key and enter the text for your second bullet.
4. Continue entering text and pressing Enter until you have completed your list.
5. Press the Enter twice after your last line of bulleted text to turn off the bulleted list feature, or tap the Bulleted List icon on the toolbar again.

Summary

In this hour, you learned how to create documents in Pocket Word. You can now open and save documents, search and replace text, change text attributes, and create bulleted lists. You have also learned how to select text so that you can change formatting and copy or move text. In the next hour, you will learn some of the more advanced features of Pocket Word.

Q&A

Q How can you quickly access a document in the My Documents folder?

A From the Start menu, tap Run. Then type **`pword`** ***`filename`*** (where *`filename`* is the name of the Pocket Word document).

Q Can you transfer Microsoft Word tables to Pocket Word?

A Pocket Word does not support tables, although Microsoft Word tables from your desktop PC will be transferred as columns separated by tabs.

Q Does Pocket Word import pictures?

A Yes. Windows CE can read graphic files with a .bmp extension.

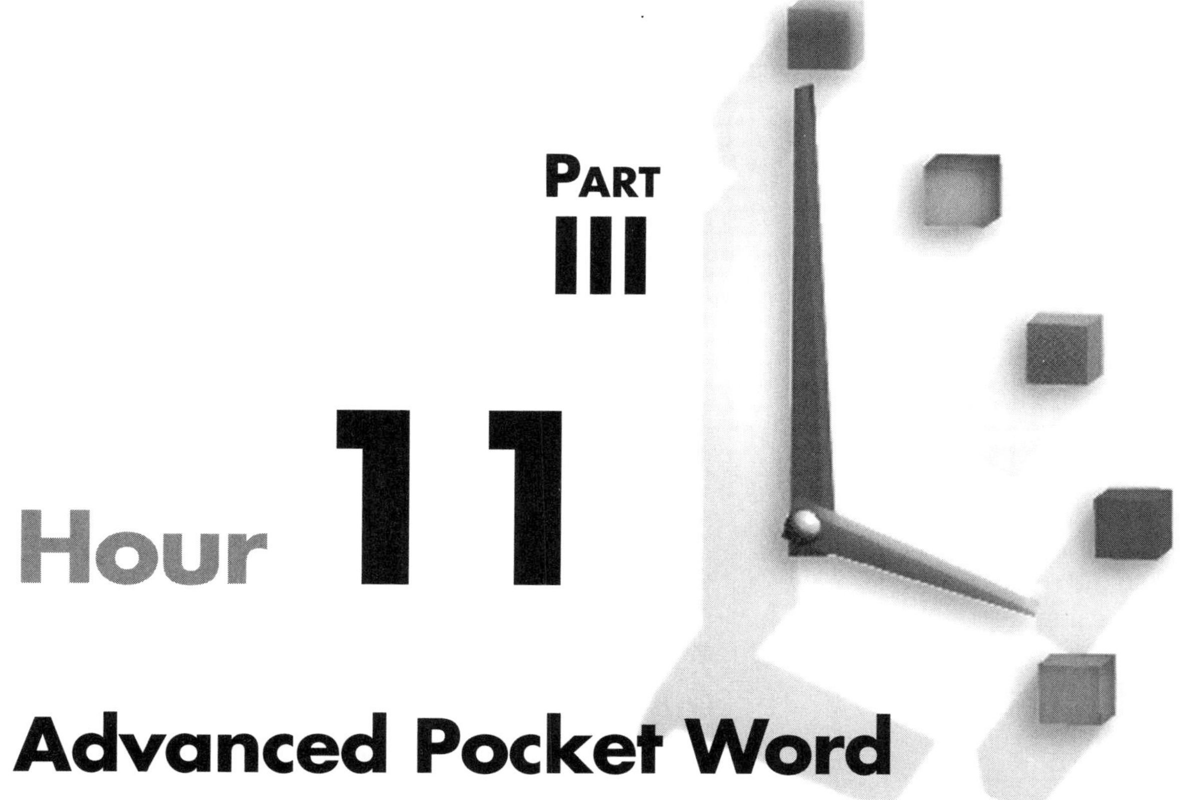

Hour 11

Advanced Pocket Word

In addition to the features you explored during the previous hour, Pocket Word offers even more flexibility with outlining, additional font support, and custom tabs. In this hour, you will learn how to do the following:

- ☐ Work in Outline view
- ☐ Transfer documents to your PC
- ☐ Work with fonts
- ☐ Set tabs

Working in Outline View

The outline feature of Pocket Word is very useful for organizing documents and working with lengthy documents. You also can use the Outline view for taking notes. Pocket Word offers the capability to expand and collapse headings so that you show as much or as little detail as you want. Outlining also enables you to easily move, promote, and demote sections of text.

Switching to Outline View

By default, Pocket Word is in Normal view, which does not display any indentations or symbols (refer to Figure 11.1). To switch to Outline view, select Outline from the View menu. Figure 11.2 shows how the formatting for the document changes when you switch to Outline view.

Figure 11.1.
Normal view in Pocket Word.

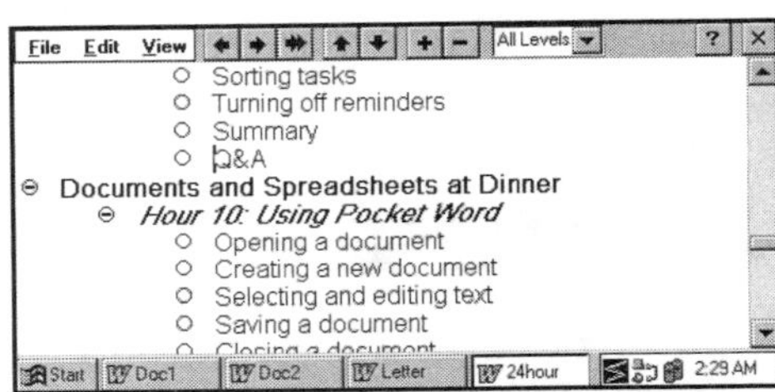

Figure 11.2.
Outline view in Pocket Word.

Using the Toolbar

Most of the outlining features, represented by icons, are accessible from the toolbar:

 Tap this icon to promote a heading by a level.

 Tap this icon to demote a heading by a level.

 Tap this icon to make a block of text part of the previous heading.

 Tap this icon to move the section the cursor is on up a paragraph at a time.

 Tap this icon to move the section the cursor is on down a paragraph at a time.

Tap this icon to display a heading's subheadings and associated text.

Tap this icon to hide a heading's subheadings and associated text.

The toolbar also contains a drop-down list that enables you to determine how many levels of detail you want to display:

1. Tap the drop-down list on the toolbar.
2. From the list, tap the level of detail you want to display.

Using Headings

To create a heading in the Outline view, follow these steps:

1. Switch to Outline view by selecting Outline from the View menu.
2. Tap the left or right arrow in the toolbar to set the level of your heading.
3. Start typing the text for the heading (refer to Figure 11.3).

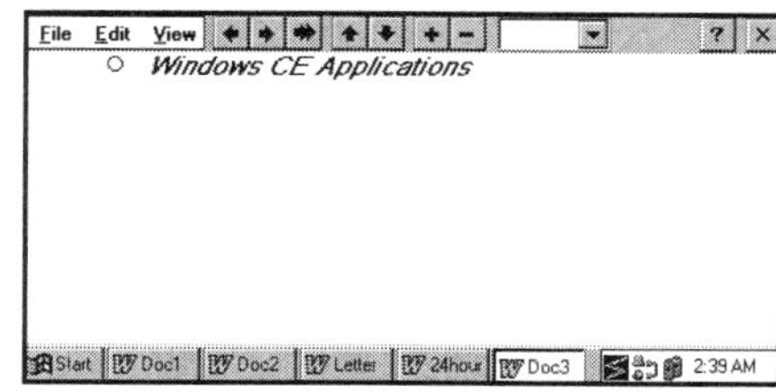

Figure 11.3.
Type the text for the heading.

To apply a heading level to existing text, follow these steps:

1. Switch to Outline view by selecting Outline from the View menu.
2. Tap the text that you want to turn into a heading.
3. Adjust the heading level. Tap the left arrow in the toolbar to increase the heading level. Tap the right arrow in the toolbar to decrease the heading level. Every subsequent tap of the arrow increases or decreases a level at a time.

Expanding and Collapsing Outlines

If you are working with a long document, you may want to collapse sections of text to temporarily hide them from view. Collapsing portions of the text enables you to work with a more manageable document. When you need to work with those hidden sections of text, you can expand the text to reveal it again.

When you are working in Outline view you will notice several symbols that indicate whether text is a heading, with or without body text, expanded, collapsed, or just body text. These symbols are as follows:

- ◘ Body text
- ○ A heading with no subheadings or body text
- ⊕ A heading with subheadings or body text collapsed
- ⊖ A heading with subheadings or body text expanded

To expand all headings and body text, select All Levels from the drop-down list on the toolbar (refer to Figure 11.4).

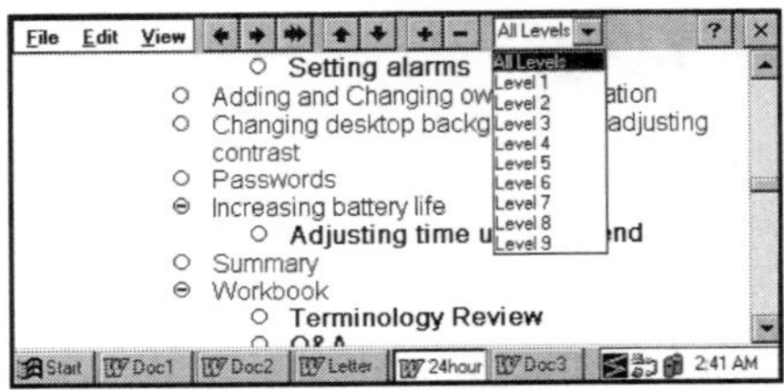

Figure 11.4.
Select All Levels from the scroll list.

To expand a heading or subheading, do one of the following:

- Tap the heading and tap the + symbol in the toolbar.
- Double-tap the circle with the + sign to the left of the heading.

To collapse a heading or subheading, do one of the following:

- Tap the heading and tap the - symbol in the toolbar.
- Double-tap the circle with the - sign to the left of the heading.

To move a heading, tap the heading symbol in the toolbar. Then tap the up arrow in the toolbar to move a heading upward, or tap the down arrow in the toolbar to move a heading downward. Note that if a heading is not collapsed, you will have to collapse it first before moving it. Otherwise the heading text and subheads will not move with the heading.

Transferring Documents to Your PC

One of the most useful features of Pocket Word is the ease with which you can share documents with Microsoft Word on your desktop PC. Using HPC Explorer, you can drag-and-drop files and conversion happens automatically in either direction. When documents are converted, most formatting and attributes are retained. However, some characteristics are affected. For more information about transferring documents between your HPC and desktop PC, refer to Hour 4, "Understanding Synchronization."

Working with Fonts

Windows CE provides a basic set of fonts such as Arial (Helvetica), Times New Roman, and Courier. You may also add the fonts that you use with Windows on your desktop PC. These fonts will be available in Pocket Word and Pocket Excel. TrueType fonts are the primary fonts you will want to use.

Adding Fonts

To add fonts to your HPC, follow these steps:

1. Connect your desktop PC to your HPC.
2. Double-tap the HPC Explorer icon on your desktop PC.
3. Within HPC Explorer, double-tap the My Handheld PC icon, and then double-tap the Windows folder.
4. On your desktop, click the Start menu.
5. Click Settings and then click the Control Panel icon.
6. Double-click the Fonts folder to reveal a list of available fonts (shown in Figure 11.5).

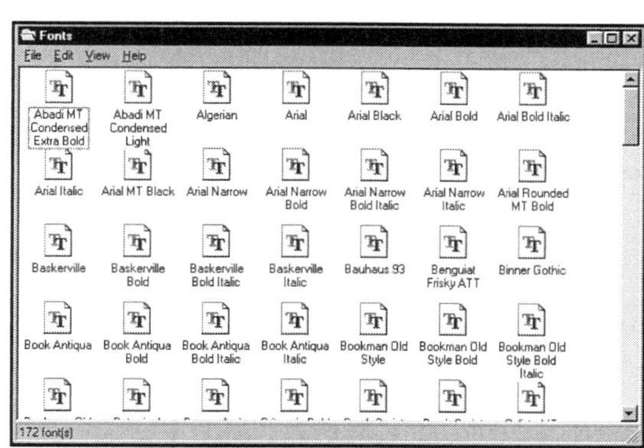

Figure 11.5.
The fonts installed on the system are shown in the Fonts folder.

7. Click and drag the font that you want to convert and drag it to the Windows folder within the Fonts folder of HPC Explorer. The font will be automatically converted. Your screen should look similar to Figure 11.6.

Figure 11.6.
Converting fonts to use on your HPC.

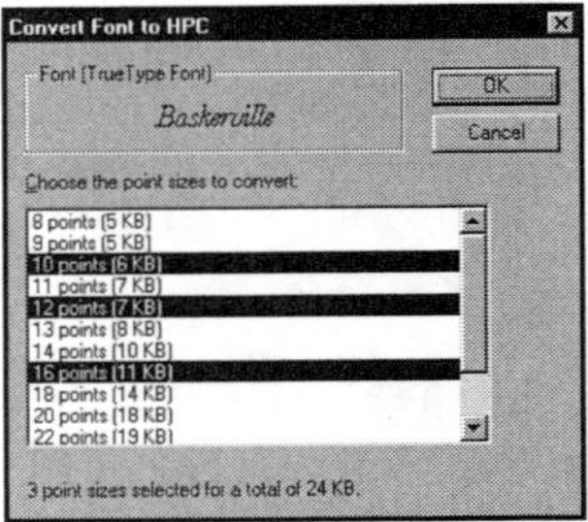

8. Select any other the fonts you want to install, and then click the OK button when you are finished.

Changing the Default Font

To change the default font in a Pocket Word document, follow these steps:

1. From the File menu, tap New to create a new document.
2. Before you begin to type, tap Select All from the Edit menu.
3. Select the font you want to use from the drop-down list on the toolbar.
4. Save this blank document and open it later to default to that font.

Fonts in Converted Files

When you transfer documents from your Windows PC to your HPC, they may contain fonts that are not installed on your HPC. If a font is not installed, Windows CE will convert the text to the closest installed font. When you transfer the document back to your desktop PC, your original font will be restored.

Setting Tabs

Although you cannot change tab settings within Pocket Word (they are set to half-inch intervals), tabs created in Microsoft Word on your desktop PC are preserved. Therefore if your document had one-inch tabs on your desktop PC, they would be set the same way within your HPC document.

Summary

In this hour, you learned some of the more advanced features of Pocket Word. You learned how to effectively work in Outline view and how to expand, collapse, and move headings. Finally, you learned the techniques for adding fonts to your HPC and setting tabs. The next hour explores another productivity application: Pocket Excel.

Q&A

Q What can be done if images disappear in Outline view?

A Select All Levels from the drop-down list in the toolbar.

Q Can character formatting be applied in Outline view?

A Yes. Use keyboard shortcuts such as Ctrl+B for boldface, Ctrl+I for italics, and Ctrl+U for underline. You can also increase the font size with Ctrl+Shift+> or decrease it with Ctrl+Shift+<.

PART

III

Hour 12

Using Pocket Excel

Pocket Excel is a powerful spreadsheet that is compatible with the desktop version of Microsoft Excel. You can use Pocket Excel to do just about anything that requires numbers and calculations. For example, you can use it to track investments, create expense reports, balance your checkbook, or calculate payments on a loan. To access Pocket Excel, double-tap the Pocket Excel icon from the desktop. Figure 12.1 shows the main Pocket Excel screen.

In this hour, you will learn how to do the following things with Pocket Excel:

- Create a new workbook
- Open, save, and close workbooks
- Name and edit cells
- Use worksheets
- Enter data
- Use formulas and functions

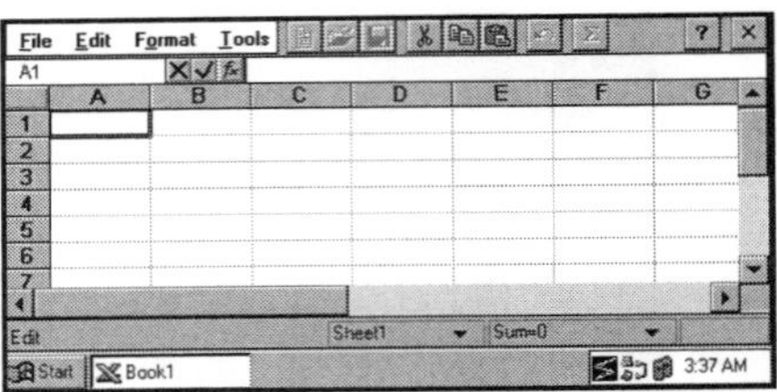

Figure 12.1.
The Pocket Excel opening screen.

Creating a New Workbook

What a document is to Pocket Word, a workbook is to Pocket Excel. To create a new workbook, open Pocket Excel and select New from the File menu. Pocket Excel also includes several sample workbooks, referred to as *templates*, that you can use and modify. To create a new workbook from these templates, follow these steps:

1. Tap Open from the File menu. The Open dialog box (shown in Figure 12.2) appears on-screen.
2. Double-tap one of the templates.

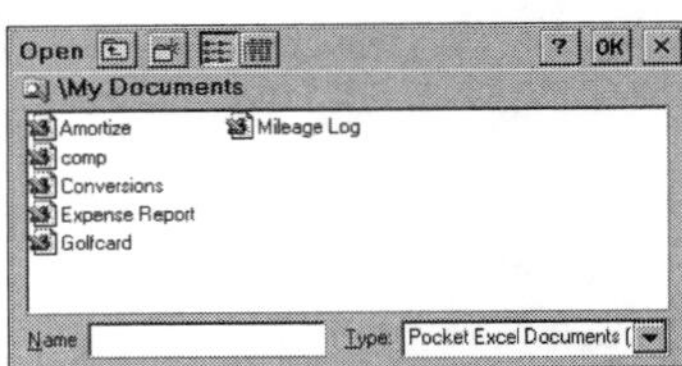

Figure 12.2.
The Open dialog box.

3. Tap Save As from the File menu.
4. Type in the new name for the file, and then press the Enter key.

Opening an Existing Workbook

To open an existing workbook, follow these steps:

1. Select Open from the File menu. The Open dialog box appears on-screen.
2. Locate the workbook you want to open and double-tap it.

Time Saver

The last three workbooks that were opened also appear at the bottom of the File menu so that you can quickly access them by tapping their names.

If you have opened more than one workbook, you can quickly switch from one to the other by tapping the desired workbook's button in the taskbar. You can open as many workbooks as Windows CE's available memory can store.

Using Cells

You have undoubtedly noticed that the workbook grid contains a series of letters along the top and numbers to the left. The intersection of the letters and numbers is called a *cell.* Cells are the individual blocks of numbers or text that build a workbook. Pocket Excel identifies a cell by its coordinates or by its name. For example, when you create a new workbook, your pointer is placed in the upper-left corner in cell A1. This reference, displayed just below File, indicates that your pointer is in column A, row 1. These references will become important when you use functions and formulas.

Selecting and Editing Cells

To use Pocket Excel effectively, you must master selecting and editing. To select a cell, move directly to it and tap. You can select a range of cells by tapping the first cell in the series and dragging the stylus to the last cell of the range. To edit a cell, tap the cell and then tap the edit box just below the toolbar. If the cell that you want to select or edit is not in view, use the horizontal and vertical scroll bars to move around your worksheet.

Naming Cells

A cell reference doesn't tell you anything about the contents of the cell. Therefore, you may find it useful to assign a name to a cell or range of cells. For example, you could name a cell Net_Revenue instead of a cryptic reference such as F29. To name a cell, follow these steps:

1. Select the cell(s) you want to name.
2. Select Define Name from the Tools menu.
3. Type a name of up to 255 characters in the Names in Workbook field.
4. Tap the Add button.

When you assign names, you must adhere to these rules:

- You cannot use spaces in a name. Substitute an underscore character _ for a space.
- The name must begin with a letter and cannot have the same format as a cell reference.

Using Worksheets

Within a single workbook, you can have multiple worksheets. To better understand the relationship between a wookbook and a worksheet, think of a workbook as a novel and worksheets as chapters. Suppose you have a workbook called Budget that covers a five-year period; you might have a separate worksheet for each of the five years.

Adding Worksheets

You can add several worksheets to your workbook to create a more manageable way to view your data. To add a worksheet to a workbook, follow these steps:

1. Select Modify Sheets from the Tools menu.
2. Tap the Insert button.
3. Type the name you want to assign to the worksheet.
4. Tap the OK button.

Switching Between Worksheets

There are two ways to switch between worksheets. The first way is to tap Modify Sheets from the Tools menu and then double-tap the sheet you want to switch to. The second way is to tap on the Sheets shortcut menu just above the taskbar (as seen in Figure 12.3) and then tap the sheet you want to switch to.

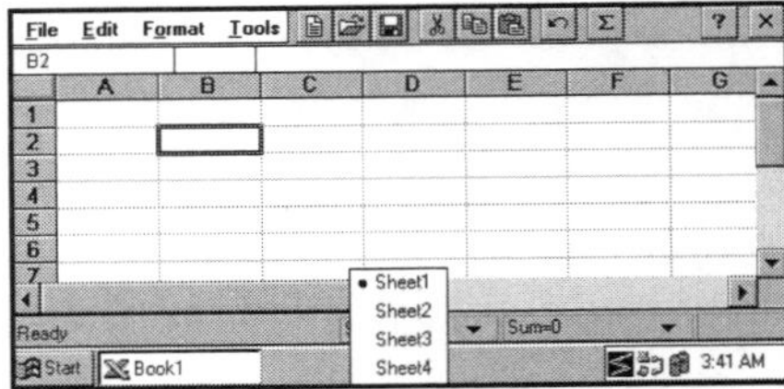

Figure 12.3.
The Sheets shortcut menu.

Renaming Worksheets

To rename a worksheet, follow these steps:

1. Select Modify Sheets from the Tools menu.
2. Tap the sheet you want to rename.
3. Tap the Rename button.

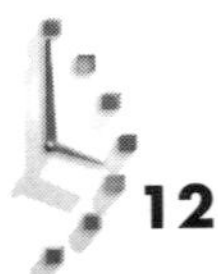

4. Type the new name for the worksheet.
5. Press the Enter key or tap the OK button.

Deleting Worksheets

To delete a worksheet, follow these steps:

1. Select Modify Sheets from the Tools menu.
2. Tap the worksheet that you want to delete.
3. Tap the Delete button.
4. Tap the Yes button to confirm the delete operation.

Changing the Order of Worksheets

To change the order of worksheets, follow these steps:

1. Select Modify Sheets from the Tools menu.
2. Tap the worksheet that you want to move.
3. Tap either the Move Up or the Move Down button until the worksheet is where you want it.

Referring to Cells in Other Worksheets

Because a workbook may contain more than one worksheet, you may want to include formulas or functions that reference a cell from another worksheet. To reference a cell in another worksheet, type the sheet name followed by an exclamation mark and the cell reference (`January!Net_Revenue`, for example). If the sheet name contains a space, surround the name in single quotes.

Entering Data

Data can be entered in several formats, including numbers, currency, text, dates, and times.

Working with Numbers

Pocket Excel defines numbers as 0–9 and as several numeric symbols, such as +, -, /, E, e, (,), $, and %. When you enter numbers, they are right-aligned and can include up to 15 digits. Numbers default to a positive value, but if you place a minus sign in front of a number, it will be negative.

Working with Currency

Numbers entered in a currency format begin with a $ symbol. You can either enter the $ symbol in front of the number you type or format the cell(s) in currency format (explained later in this hour). When you work with currency, there are several ground rules:

- Values are right-aligned.
- You can have up to 15 decimal places, but the default is 2 numbers after the decimal place.
- You can designate negative values by preceding a value with a minus symbol or surrounding a value with parentheses.

Working with Text

Text cells consist of letters, numbers, spaces, and the following symbols:

! @ # $ % ^ & * < > [ ] { } | _~ ' " ; , ? \

You can enter up to 255 characters per cell. For example, *Monthly Sales* is an example of text. Unlike numeric values, which are right-aligned, text is left-aligned within a cell. There will be times when you want to enter a number as text. For example, if you entered an employee number such as 019654, the 0 would be omitted. To format a cell as text, begin the cell entry with an apostrophe.

Working with Dates and Times

When entering dates and times within Pocket Excel, you need to be aware of the following things:

- You can enter the date and time in the same cell by separating the two with a space (8/25/97 9:30, for example).
- You can format the date and time in a variety of ways (Dec-97, 1-Dec-97, and 12/1/97, for example).
- Enter dates with month, day, and year separated with a hyphen or a forward slash. You can identify months either by their numeric equivalent, a three-letter abbreviation, or a full name. The year can range from 1900 to 2078. When entering a year, either type all four numbers or only the last two.
- Enter times with the hour and minute separated with a colon. Keep in mind that time is stored in 24-hour format. You don't need to enter time in military format if you follow the time with AM or PM. Therefore, entering 6:00 PM is the same as entering 18:00.

- Pocket Excel is not case-sensitive.
- If you do not specify a day, the first day of the month is assumed.

Working with Percentages

You can specify a numeric value as a percentage. When entering percentages, you can follow the value with a percent symbol or enter it with a decimal point. For example, to enter 15 percent, you could type either **.15** or **15%**.

Other Formats

Pocket Excel supports a variety of other formats, such as scientific or fraction. You can also customize your own numeric format. To create a custom format, follow these steps:

1. Select Cells from the Format menu.
2. Select the category closest to the custom format you want to create.
3. Change the number of decimal places and/or make any other format changes you want.
4. Tap the OK button to apply that custom format to the selected cell(s).

Using the Fill Command

12

The Fill command is useful for automatically entering data. For example, you may want to enter a series of days in a week or enter the numbers 1 through 50 without having to enter each number individually. When entering days or months, you must spell them entirely or use the three-letter abbreviation. You can also combine text with a series of numbers. For example, Week1, Week2, Week3 could be a series of text supported by Autofill. You can fill a series to the left, right, up, or down.

To automatically enter a series, follow these steps:

1. Type the beginning value in the cell where you want the series to begin.
2. Tap and hold on the first cell and drag to the last cell in the series.
3. Select Fill from the Edit menu.
4. Tap the Series radio button (as shown in Figure 12.4).
5. Select the radio button from the Series Type section that applies to the data you want to fill. Select the Number radio button to fill with numbers, or select Date to fill with days, months, or years. The Autofill series type automatically fills the selected cells with data based on the entry in the first cell.
6. Tap the OK button to execute the Fill command.

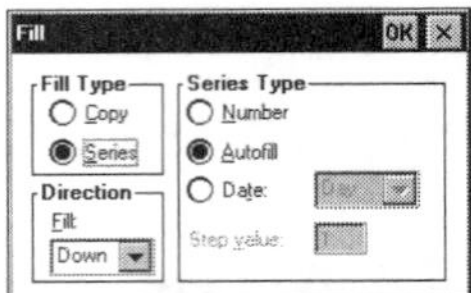

Figure 12.4.
The Fill dialog box.

In addition to being able to increment a series of values automatically, the Fill command can also be used to copy a cell or series of cells to a range of rows or columns:

1. Highlight the cell(s) you want to copy.
2. Select the cell or range of cells you want to fill. (The cell(s) to be copied must be included in the beginning of the range.)
3. Select Fill from the Edit menu.
4. Select Copy from the Fill Type box.
5. Select a direction (right or left, up or down) from the Direction drop-down list.
6. Tap the OK button to execute the Fill command.

Formulas and Functions

A spreadsheet such as Pocket Excel is very useful because, in addition to its capability to work with numbers, it is capable of applying functions and formulas to numeric and text values. Pocket Excel supports about 100 of the most popular functions of Microsoft Excel.

Formulas

A formula allows you to derive numeric results from one or more numbers. In addition to basic addition, subtraction, multiplication, and division, Pocket Excel supports powerful formulas that enable you to analyze your data in more detail. The structure of a formula combines a numeric or text value with an operator. The relationship between cells is defined by the three types of operators supported by Pocket Excel: arithmetic, comparison, and text.

Arithmetic operators include basic addition, subtraction, multiplication, division, percentage, and exponentiation. Comparison operators such as =, <, >, <> (not equal to), <=, and => enable you to compare two cells to derive a TRUE or FALSE result. Finally, text operators enable you to combine two text cells into one.

Formulas always begin with an equal sign. This sign is usually followed by a function and cell or range of cells, which is surrounded by parentheses. Here are a few examples of typical formulas:

```
=SUM(B2:B5)
=(A5+A9)*10
=AVERAGE (A6:F6)
```

Pocket Excel displays the results of the formula in the cell. The formula for the cell is displayed in the formula bar. You can change the formula's values or operators to create a "what-if" scenario.

Functions

The most powerful feature of Pocket Excel is its functions. To see a list of available functions, follow these steps:

1. Select Insert Function from the Tools menu.
2. Tap the up or down arrow of the scroll list to see available functions (as shown in Figure 12.5).

Figure 12.5.
Pocket Excel's functions.

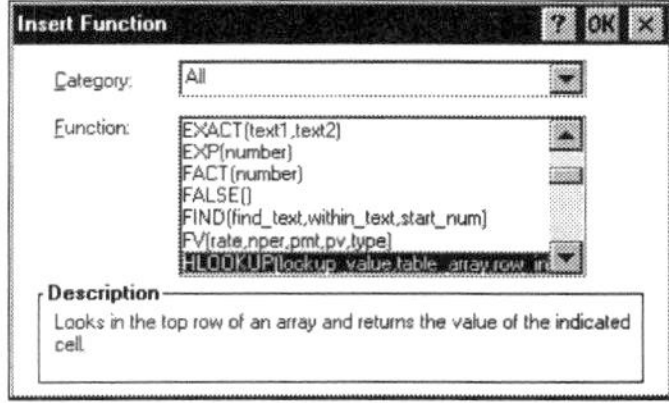

To find out more about a function, tap it to reveal a brief description. For a more detailed description, tap the help button in the upper-right corner of the dialog box. To insert a function in your worksheet, double-tap it.

12

Searching for and Replacing Data

You can search for and replace data within Pocket Excel. To find data, follow these steps:

1. Select Find/Replace from the Edit menu.
2. Type the text you are searching for in the Find What field.
3. Specify where to search (Formulas or Values, for example) in the Look In field.
4. Tap the Find button.

Pocket Excel displays the first match it finds and then stops. If no match is found, the dialog box shown in Figure 12.6 appears. If you want to continue searching for the next match, select Find Next from the Edit menu.

Figure 12.6.
The data was not found in this spreadsheet.

To replace data, follow these steps:

1. Select Find/Replace from the Edit menu.
2. Type the text you want to be replaced in the Find What field.
3. Specify where you want Pocket Excel to search (Formulas or Values, for example) in the Look In field.
4. Tap the Replace button.
5. Type the replacement text in the Replace With field (refer to Figure 12.7).

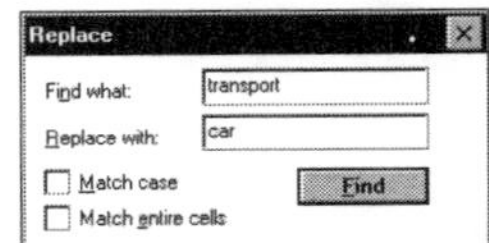

Figure 12.7.
The Replace dialog box.

6. If you want to match case or match entire cells, select those check boxes.
7. Tap the Find button and the Find/Replace dialog box shown in Figure 12.8 will appear.

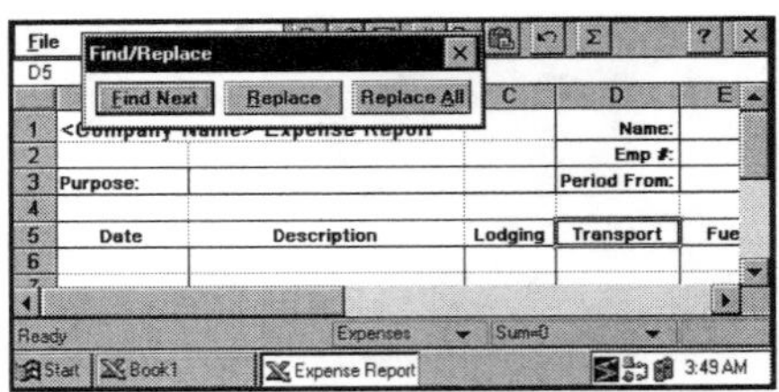

Figure 12.8.
The Find/Replace dialog box.

8. Tap one of the three buttons (Find Next, Replace, or Replace All) or tap the close button to cancel.

Saving a Workbook

It is important to save your work frequently. Pocket Excel saves files in a unique .pxl format, and by default, files are saved in the My Documents folder. To save a workbook, follow these steps:

1. Select Save from the File menu. The Save As dialog box appears on-screen.
2. Type the name you want to assign to the workbook in the Name field (refer to Figure 12.9).

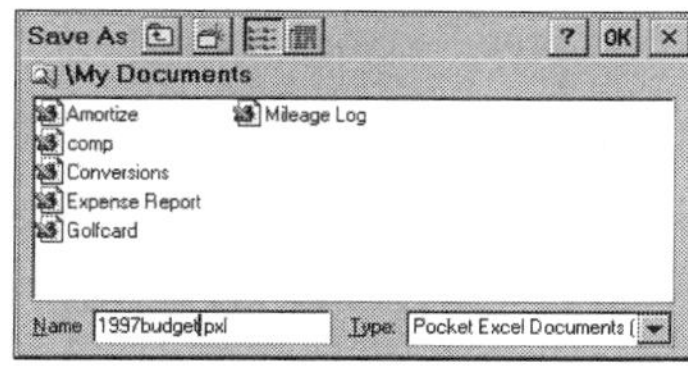

Figure 12.9.
The Save As dialog box.

3. Tap the OK button to save your workbook in the My Documents folder.

Closing a Workbook

When you are finished working with a workbook, you can close it by selecting Close from the File menu or tapping the close button in the upper-right corner of the screen. If you have not saved your workbook, Pocket Excel gives you the opportunity to save it (refer to Figure 12.10).

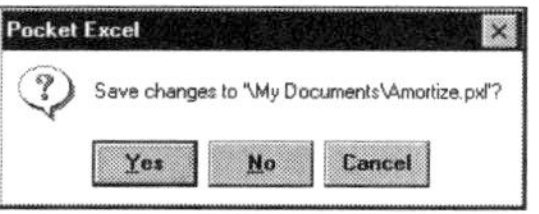

Figure 12.10.
Pocket Excel makes sure that you want to close the spreadsheet.

12

Commonly Used Commands

Table 12.1 lists the most commonly used Pocket Excel commands and the keyboard and stylus sequences required to execute these functions.

Table 12.1. Excel commands.

Command	Stylus	Keyboard
Insert Rows or Columns	Select Insert from Format menu	Alt+O, then I
Delete Rows or Columns	Select Delete from Format menu	Alt+O, then D
Move, Insert, Rename, or Delete Sheet	Select Modify Sheets from Tools menu	Alt+T, then M
Go To	Select Go To from Tools menu	Alt+T, then G

continues

Table 12.1. Excel commands.

Command	Stylus	Keyboard
Insert Functions	Select Insert Function from Tools menu	Alt+T, then I
Hide Columns	Select Column Width from Format menu	Alt+O, then C
Hide Rows	Select Row Height from Format menu	Alt+O, then R

Transferring Excel Files from Your Desktop

By using HPC Explorer, you can easily drag-and-drop workbooks from your desktop PC to your HPC. Although most of the formatting is retained in the conversion process, you should be aware of the following issues:

- Fonts are converted to the closest available font.
- Patterns are removed.
- Borders appear as single lines.
- Unsupported functions are removed (the results of the function are displayed instead of the function).
- Arrays are converted to values.
- Custom numeric formats are converted to closest match.
- Charts, macros, pictures, text boxes, dialog sheets, and drawing objects are removed.
- Pivot table data is converted to values.

Summary

In this hour, you learned about one of the most advanced Windows CE applications: Pocket Excel. You learned how to enter and edit data; add, change, and delete a worksheet; and how to work with functions and formulas. You also learned how to search and replace data, use the Fill command to enter a data series, and access the most commonly used commands. In the next hour, you'll investigate a much simpler program for performing calculations: Calculator.

Q&A

Q How do you quickly open a Pocket Excel workbook?

A From the Start menu, select Run, and then type `pxl` *`file_name`*.

Q How can I load large files more quickly?

A Break up the file into several smaller files, and load only the section that you need.

Q How do you minimize the file size of Microsoft Excel files?

A Remove any blank sheets from the workbook before converting it to Pocket Excel.

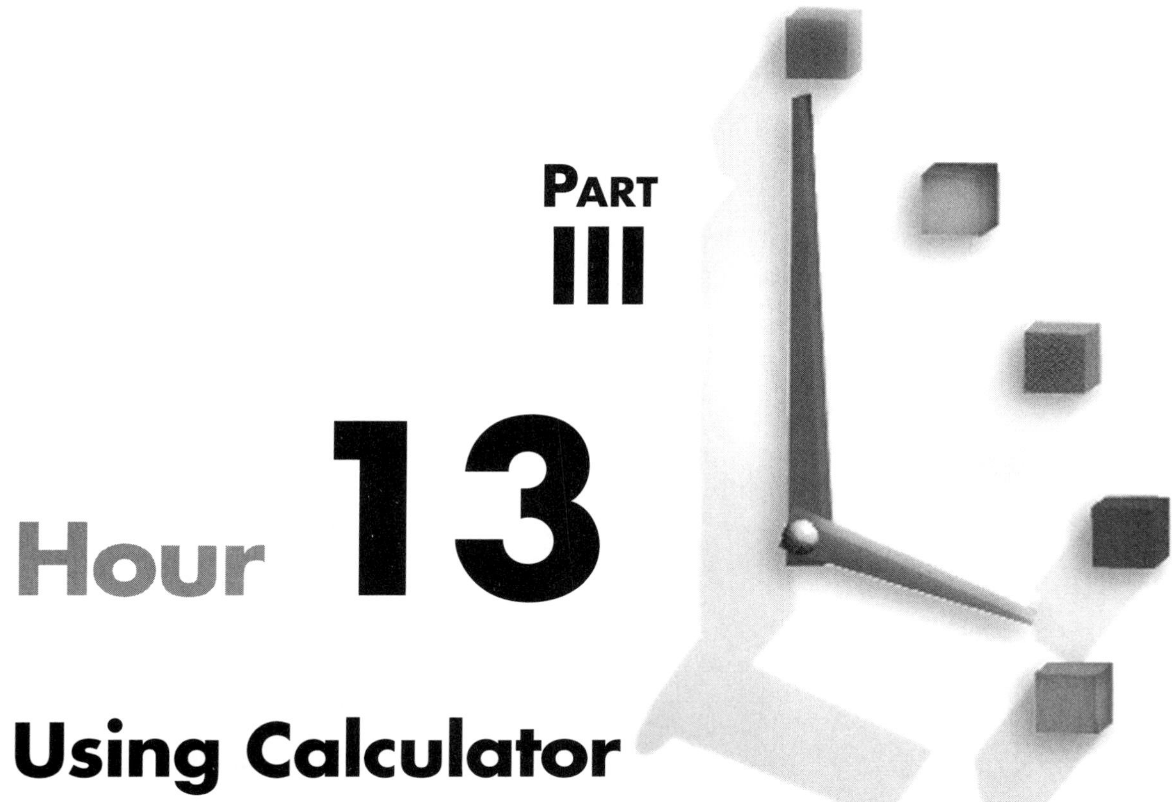

Using Calculator

Calculator is probably the most basic Windows CE program. It can perform simple calculations such as addition, subtraction, multiplication, and division; it also can perform square root calculations and exponentiation. Calculator's features include memory, paper tape simulation, and a Pop-Up view. Noticeably absent from Calculator are conversion and financial calculations. To do those kinds of calculations, you have to use one of the templates included with Pocket Excel or create your own Pocket Excel template.

During this hour, you will learn how to do the following things:

- Open Calculator
- Use Calculator's paper tape feature
- Copy Calculator data to other applications
- Use Calculator's Pop-Up view

Opening Calculator

To open Calculator, follow these steps:

1. Select Programs from the Start menu.
2. Double-tap the Accessories folder.
3. Double-tap the Calculator icon.

Figure 13.1 shows the Calculator interface. Notice that it looks very similar to a desktop calculator.

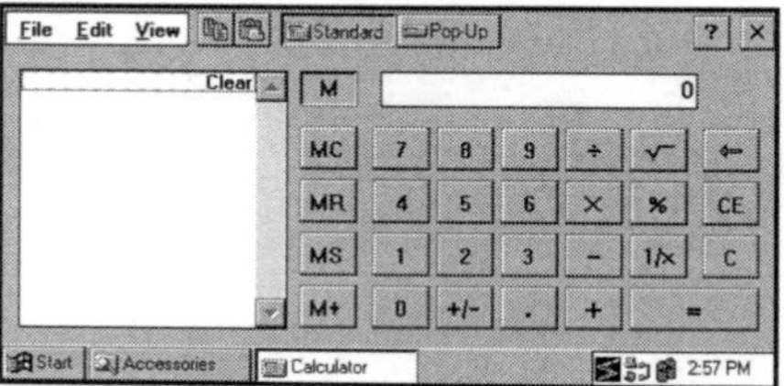

Figure 13.1.
The Calculator program.

To use Calculator, tap on the numbers and functions you want to perform. You also may want to take advantage of Calculator's memory feature. Calculator's memory feature provides four basic functions: add, store, recall, and clear. This feature is useful when you will use a specific number in multiple calculations. For example, when creating an expense report, you may want to store 32 cents in memory for automobile mileage reimbursement.

Try this short exercise:

1. Tap the buttons for the following: **`110 + 246 / 4 =`**.
2. Tap the M+ button to save results, and then tap the C button to clear your tape.
3. Now type **`16 X 3 / 2 =`**.
4. Tap + and then tap MR = to add the results (refer to Figure 13.2).

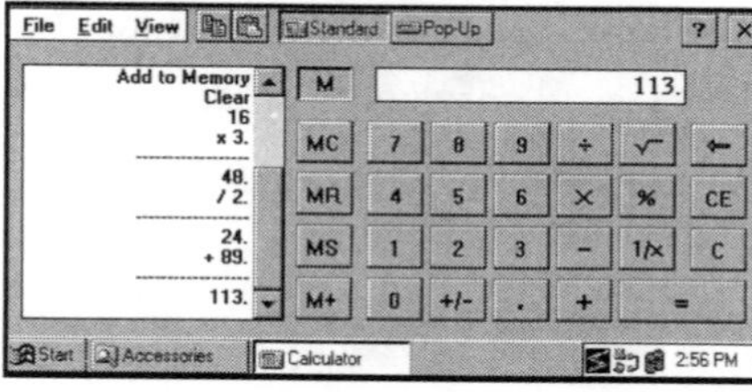

Figure 13.2.
Seeing your results.

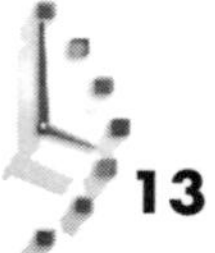

Differences Between Keys and On-screen Buttons

Calculator supports both the keyboard and stylus. Most HPCs do not include a numeric keypad, so you may find that the stylus is more comfortable to use with this program than the keyboard is. If you choose to use the keyboard, be aware that not all keyboard and on-screen buttons operate in the same manner. Table 13.1 illustrates the keyboard and stylus function equivalents.

Table 13.1. Hardware versus software buttons.

Function	Keyboard	Calculator button
Add, subtract, multiply or divide	+, -, *, /	+, -, ×, /
Equal	= or Enter	=
Store display in memory	M	MS
Recall stored memory	R	MR
Add current entry to memory	P	M+
Clear memory	L	MC
Clear entry	C	CE
Clear all	Esc	C
Square root	Q	
Inverse	I	1/x

Using the Paper Tape

Just like a manual adding machine, Calculator displays a paper tape of previous calculations. The paper tape is simulated in a scroll box to the left of the Calculator controls.

You can also use previous paper tape entries in new calculations by double-tapping the tape entry. For example, if you entered a tax rate of 8.25 percent, you could reuse it by double-tapping the entry in the paper tape.

To clear the entire tape display, select Clear Paper Tape from the Edit menu.

Copying Calculator Data

To copy data between Calculator and other programs, follow these steps:

1. From within Calculator, select Copy from the Edit menu.
2. Open the application that you want to copy the data into.
3. Select Paste from the Edit menu of that application.

Using Pop-Up View

Although Calculator is useful as a stand-alone program, you can also use it to perform quick calculations within other Windows CE programs, such as Pocket Word and Pocket Excel. This capability is made possible through the use of Pop-Up view. To use Pop-Up view, follow these steps:

1. Tap the Pop-Up button in the Calculator toolbar.
2. Open the program in which you want to use Pop-Up view.
3. Tap the Calculator button in the taskbar (refer to Figure 13.3).

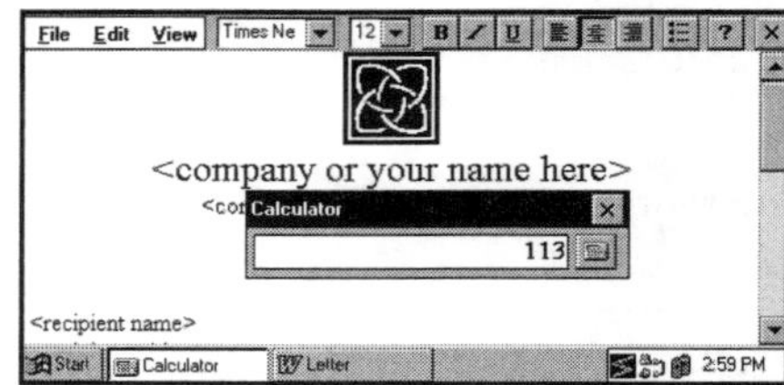

Figure 13.3.
Using Calculator in Pocket Word.

4. Use the keyboard to perform calculations.
5. Press Ctrl+C to copy the Calculator display to the Clipboard.
6. Select Paste from the Edit menu to copy the results into the background program.
7. Tap the close button to close the pop-up window.

When Calculator is in Pop-Up view, you can switch back to Normal view by tapping the Calculator icon.

Summary

During this hour, you learned the basics of Calculator, such as how to enter numbers and perform calculations. You also learned how to use the memory functions as well as how to

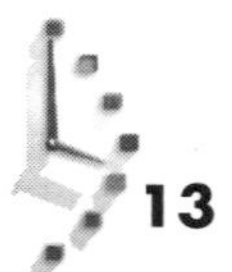

use the paper tape display. Finally, you learned how to copy information from Calculator to other applications by using both standard Copy and Paste commands and Calculator's Pop-Up view.

Q&A

Q How many lines of text can the paper tape store?

A The paper tape can store up to a 100 lines (approximately 13 lines are viewable without scrolling).

Q Does Calculator visually indicate whether a value is in memory?

A Yes. A capital M appears to the left of calculation results windows to indicate that a value is stored in Calculator's memory.

Part III

Hour 14

Take a Break with Solitaire

You know what they say about all work and no play! Now that you've mastered the Windows CE productivity programs, take a break and play a game of Solitaire. Solitaire for Windows CE is similar to the card game Solitaire, with one notable difference: You can't cheat!

In this hour, you'll learn about the following topics:

- How to open Solitaire
- The basic rules and strategy of Solitaire
- How to use Solitaire's controls

Getting Started

To open Solitaire, follow these steps:

1. Select Programs from the Start menu.
2. Double-tap the Games folder.
3. Double-tap the Solitaire icon. Your screen should look like Figure 14.1.

Figure 14.1.
Dealing out Solitaire.

In the upper-left corner, you see a deck of cards. In the upper-right corner are four placeholders where you place the cards, in order, starting with ace, 2, 3 and so on within the same suit. Below these placeholders are seven stacks of cards, the tops of which are turned face up with the cards below them face down.

The goals of Solitaire are as follows:

- Move all of the cards to the four placeholders in the least amount of time.
- Score as many points as possible.
- Have fun!

To achieve these goals, use this strategy at the start of the game:

1. Move the aces from the decks of cards to the placeholders.
2. Reveal face-down cards by stacking the face-up cards on top of each other. Just as in regular Solitaire, you stack cards by decending numerical order and alternating color. For example, if you had a red 10, you could only move it on top of a black Jack, and only a black 9 could be stacked on top of the 10.
3. When there are no cards left to play or place in the placeholder area, use the deck of cards in the upper-right corner of the screen.

To move cards, tap and hold and drag them to the desired location. As you drag a card, make sure that your stylus does not lose contact with the screen until you have reached the desired location. If you try to make an invalid play, the card will be quickly returned to its original location.

To reveal the cards (three at a time) from the main deck in the upper-left corner of the screen, tap on the deck. As each third card is displayed, check to see whether you have any plays with that card.

Using the Controls

A column of five controls along the right of the screen presents several options:

- The Exit button enables you to quit Solitaire with a single tap.
- The Help button provides useful assistance, such as scoring information (refer to Figure 14.2).

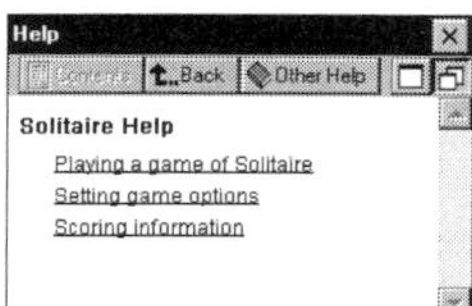

Figure 14.2.
Getting some help.

- The Deal button starts a new game. (There is no way to save a game.)
- The Undo button reverses your previous play.
- The Options button enables you to change elements of the game.

When you tap the Options button, the Options dialog box appears on-screen (refer to Figure 14.3). From this dialog box, you can change the number of cards that are drawn at a time from the main deck, scoring options, card background, and a few other options. To change how many cards are drawn or the scoring system, tap on the radio button for the desired setting. By default, the game is timed and the status is displayed. To change these settings, remove the check mark next to the setting by tapping the appropriate check box. You can choose from six different card backgrounds by tapping the desired pattern and then tapping the OK button.

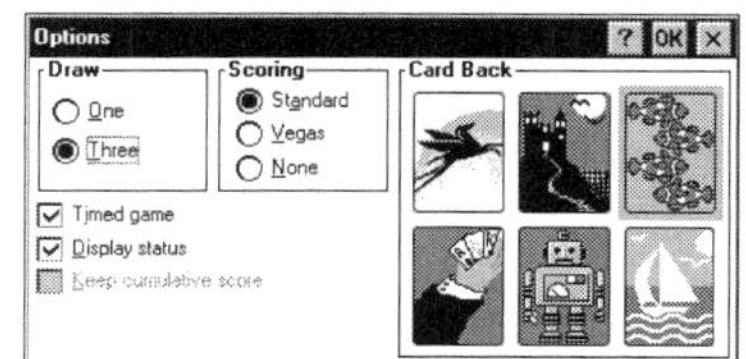

Figure 14.3.
Some playing options.

Summary

You should've had some fun this hour. You learned some of the strategy behind Solitaire and the rules of the game. In addition, you learned how to use the stylus with Solitaire and the function of each of the program buttons.

Q&A

Q What is the difference between the standard and Vegas scoring system?

A The standard scoring system awards points based on time and moves that you make. In Vegas scoring, you ante $52 and are awarded $5 for every card moved to a suit stack.

Q Can you turn off scoring?

A Yes. Select None in the Scoring area in the Options dialog box.

Part IV

Communicating into the Night

Hour

PART IV

Hour 15

Using Inbox for E-mail

Probably the most sophisticated and challenging components of Windows CE are its communications programs. With Windows CE you can browse the Internet, connect to a remote computer, and, as you will learn in this hour, send and receive electronic mail. Inbox is the Windows CE program you use to handle electronic mail. You can also transfer messages between Microsoft Exchange on your desktop computer and Inbox. To use Inbox, you will need a modem (included with some HPCs and optional with others) and an Internet service provider (ISP) with Inbox.

In this hour you will learn how to do the following:

- Set up Inbox
- Get connected
- Use the message list
- Use folders
- Use Microsoft Exchange

Setting Up Inbox

If you already have an ISP account that supports PPP (Point-to-Point protocol), you can set up Inbox. First, you must create a new dial-up connection:

1. From the Start menu, select Programs.
2. Double-tap the Communications folder.
3. Double-tap the Remote Networking folder.
4. Double-tap the Make New Connection icon. The Make New Connection dialog box appears on-screen (refer to Figure 15.1).
5. Type in a name for your connection, such as Compuserve.
6. Tap the Dial-Up Connection radio button if you are using a modem for connection (as seen in Figure 15.1), and then tap the Next button.

Figure 15.1.
Creating a new dial-up connection.

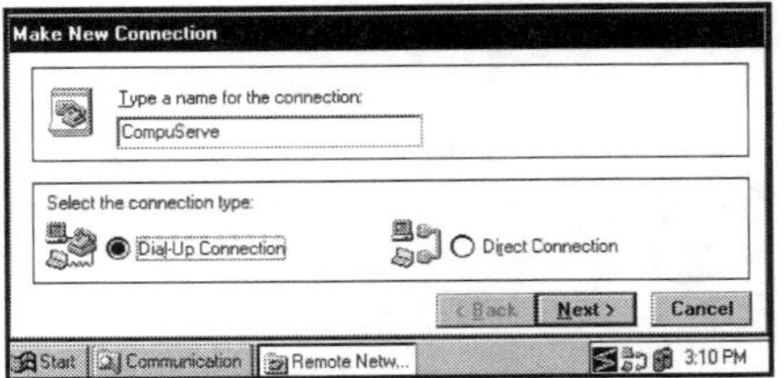

7. Type the telephone number for the connection, and then tap the Finish button.

If the number you are calling is not a local number, make sure that you enter the correct area code and country code and select the Use Country Code And Area Code check box (as shown in Figure 15.2).

Figure 15.2.
Specifying a long-distance call.

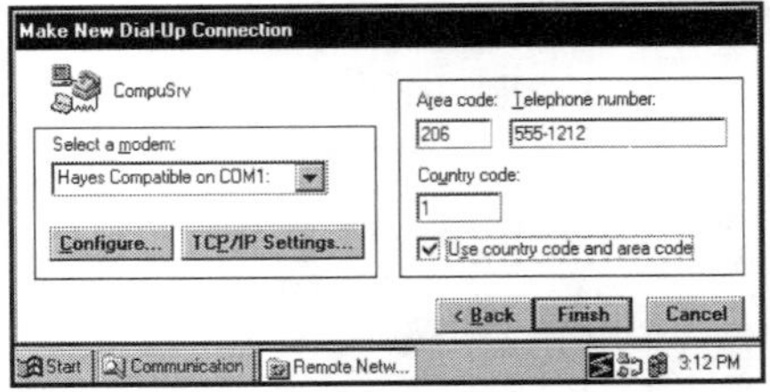

Depending on your ISP, you may need to change the default settings for the dial-up connection you created. To customize the dial-up connection configuration, follow these steps:

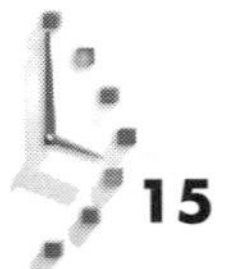

1. From the Remote Networking folder, tap the dial-up connection icon you want to customize so that it is selected.
2. Tap the Edit icon in the toolbar to the right of the X icon.
3. Tap the Configure button.
4. From the Device Properties screen (shown in Figure 15.3), you can change the connection preferences indicated by the speed of your modem and the requirements of your ISP. Some connections may require that you use the terminal window or dial manually. If you are having difficulty with your connection, you may want to experiment with one or both of these check boxes.

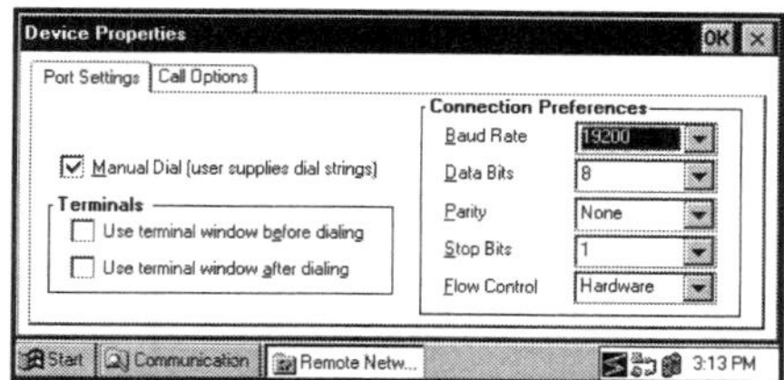

Figure 15.3.
The Port Settings tab of the Device Properties dialog box.

5. The Call Options tab (shown in Figure 15.4) provides several options, such as how long to wait for a connection, credit card tone, or dial tone, as well as a space for additional modem commands that may be necessary for a connection.

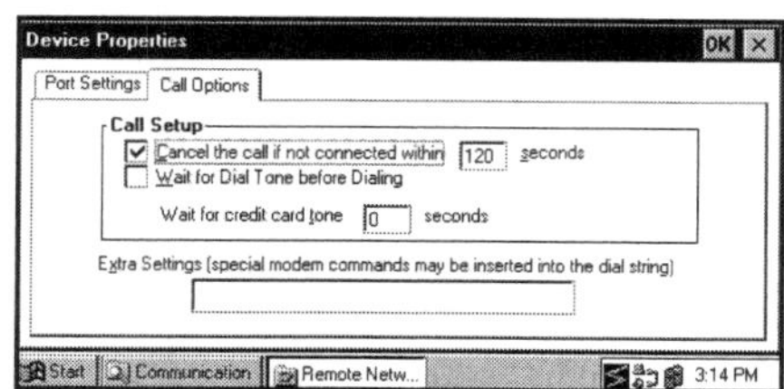

Figure 15.4.
The Call Options tab of the Device Properties dialog box.

6. Tap the OK button when you are finished configuring the connection.

Depending on your ISP, you may also need to configure the TCP/IP settings (contact your Internet Service Provider prior to attempting these steps):

1. From the Remote Networking folder, tap the connection you want to customize so that it is selected.
2. Tap the Edit icon in the toolbar to the right of the X icon.
3. Tap the TCP/IP Settings button.

4. If your ISP requires you to enter DNS (Domain Name System) addresses, deselect the Server-Assigned Name Server Addresses check box and enter the addresses provided by your ISP (refer to Figure 15.5).

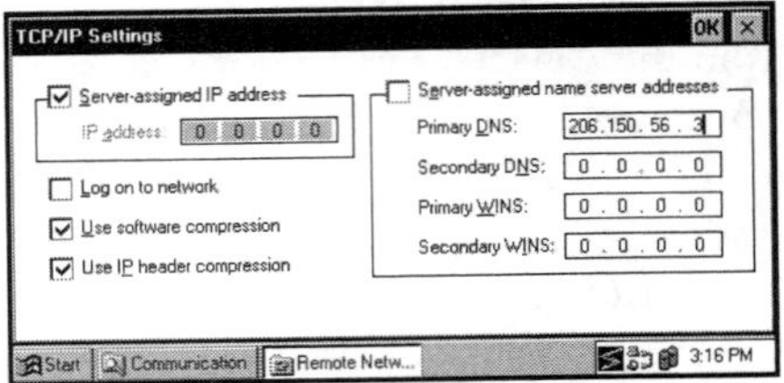

Figure 15.5.
Creating your TCP/IP settings.

5. Tap the OK button to save the changes.

If you are using an external modem, make sure that it is properly connected and turned on. If you are using a PC card modem, make sure that you have answered Yes to the message shown in Figure 15.6. To make sure, remove and reinsert the card to display this message again. Also, because communicating is so battery-intensive, it is highly recommended that you use an AC adapter when communicating.

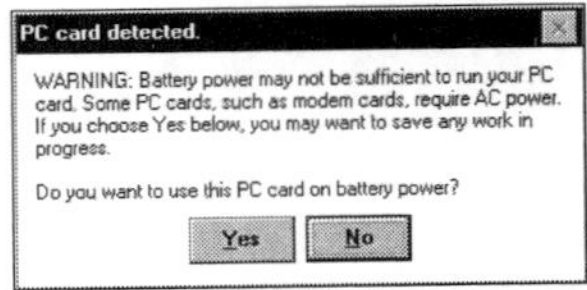

Figure 15.6.
Be cautious. PCMCIA cards use a lot of power.

Also, make sure that you are connected to a standard phone line. If you try to use an office phone line on a PBX system, you may damage your modem. Typically a fax machine uses a standard phone line, so this line may be an option in an office setting.

If you do not have a modem, you can create a direct connection with your desktop PC running Microsoft Exchange. Additionally, you may have access to paging or faxing services if your HPC manufacturer provides those options. Inbox supports the industry-standard POP3 (Post Office Protocol 3) and SMTP (Simple Mail Transport Protocol) for connection via the Internet. Check with your ISP to verify that it conforms to one of these protocols.

Setting Up the Mail Service

Once you have created your connection, you can set up the mail service:

1. Select Programs from the Start menu.
2. Double-tap the Communications folder.

3. Double-tap the Inbox icon.
4. Tap the Options button in the toolbar.
5. From the Options window, tap the Services tab (shown in Figure 15.7).

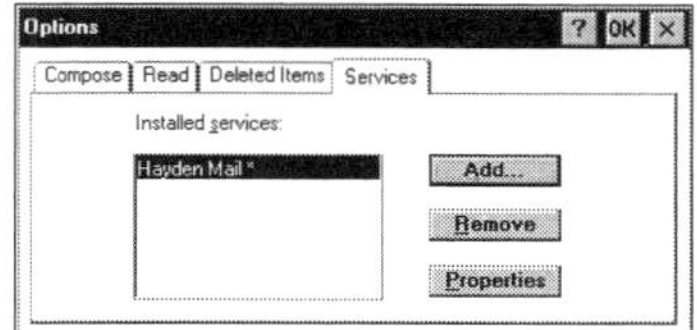

Figure 15.7.
Adding services for your connection.

6. Tap the Add button, and then double-tap Internet Mail Services.
7. Type a name for the service, and then tap the OK button.
8. In the Service Definition dialog box, complete the form (shown in Figure 15.8) with the information provided by your ISP, such as user ID, password, name of the mail host, and return address. From the Connection drop-down list, specify whether this is a dial-up or direct connection. You will have to enter your password each time you connect unless you select the Remember Password check box.

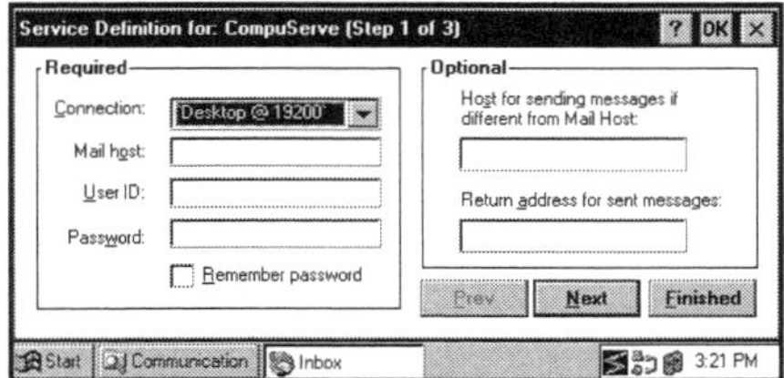

Figure 15.8.
Defining a connection service, in this case, CompuServe.

9. Tap the Next button to view the General Preferences dialog box (shown in Figure 15.9). Specify connections settings such as how often you want the service to check for messages and how you want to be notified of messages. Additionally, you can specify when to disconnect and which e-mail field to use from the Contacts database for the address book. When you have specified the options you want, tap the Next button.

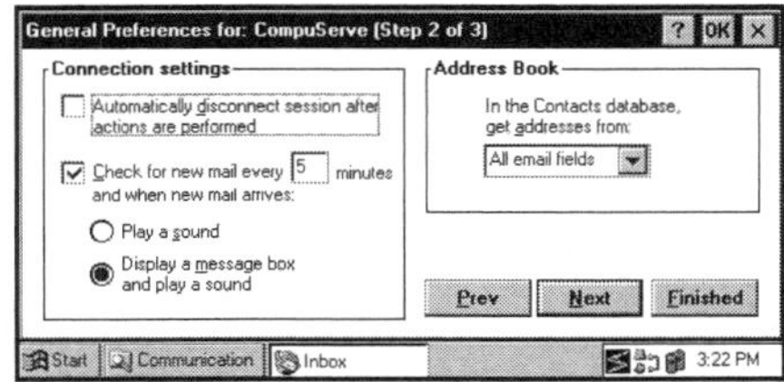

Figure 15.9.
Setting the general preferences for the CompuServe connection.

10. From the Inbox Folder Preferences dialog box (shown in Figure 15.10), you can specify how much of a message is transferred. Depending on the amount of memory in your HPC, you may want to download only message headers or a limited number of lines. When you have completed this screen, tap the Finished button. Then tap the OK button from the Options dialog box.

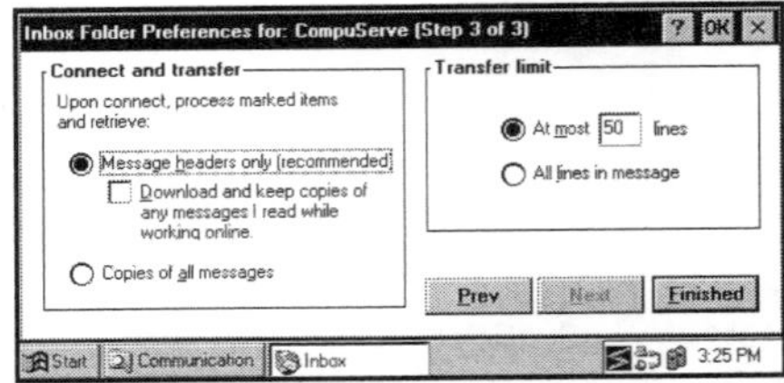

Figure 15.10.
Setting the Inbox folder preferences for the CompuServe connection.

Setting Up Other Services

If you have other services that you want to set up, follow these steps:

1. From within Inbox, tap the Options icon on the toolbar.
2. From the Services tab of the Options dialog box, tap the Add button.
3. Any additional services that are available are listed in the Services dialog box. Select the service that you want, and then tap the OK button.
4. Type the name in the dialog box that appears (refer to Figure 15.11), and then tap the OK button.

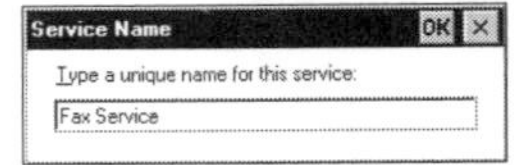

Figure 15.11.
Creating a brand-new connection service.

5. Complete the setup as described in steps 8-10 of the preceding section about creating a mail service.

Getting Connected

Now that you have set up your service, you can connect to it:

1. From Inbox, tap the name of the service you want to connect to from the Service menu.
2. Tap the toolbar icon that shows a hand holding the HPC.

3. Enter the service password if necessary (refer to Figure 15.12); then tap the OK button.

Figure 15.12.
Setting the service's password.

4. Complete the information in the next screen, such as user ID and password. Some ISPs require you to enter a domain name, which is typically a word followed by a `.com`, such as `compuserve.com`. When you have completed the information on this screen, tap the Connect button.

In a perfect world, the following tasks are performed:

1. A dialog box appears on-screen to indicate that a connection is being attempted.
2. The connection is established, and you hear a tone and see a message.
3. Any messages in the Outbox are sent.
4. Waiting messages are transferred or copied to your Inbox.
5. Message headers are displayed.
6. You are automatically disconnected if you selected this option.

The reality is that most users will have some problems connecting the first time. Here are some tips and tricks to getting connected quickly:

- If you are using an external modem, make sure that it is turned on.
- If you are using a PC card modem, make sure that your HPC recognizes it (remove and reinsert it if necessary). Make sure the card-lock switch is in the locked position.
- Confirm that you have entered all of your ISP information correctly. A single incorrect number or letter in your user ID, password, or DNS address fields could prevent you from connecting.
- Deselect Use Software Compression and/or Use IP Header Compression within the TCP/IP settings and try the connection again.
- Verify that you are using a valid phone line and phone number and that the number is not continually busy. Some phone lines may require you to place a 9 before the number to get a valid phone line.
- Confirm that if you are calling from work or home you have specified the location appropriately in your dialing settings.
- If you are dialing a number that is long distance, verify that the Use Country Code and Area Code check box is selected within the settings.

Using the Message List

The message list is command central for Inbox. The message list displays information about messages you receive, such as who the message is from, subject, date and time, size of the message, and a graphical icon indicating whether the message is stored on your HPC and if it has been read. To the left of the message window are several folders, including Inbox, Outbox, Sent Items, and Deleted Items (refer to Figure 15.13).

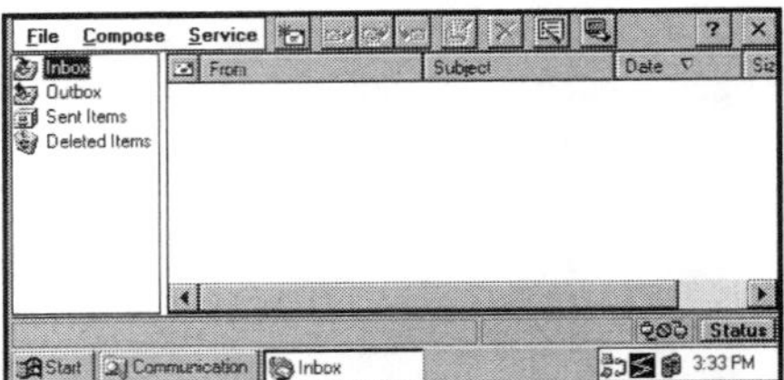

Figure 15.13.
The main Inbox window.

The message list displays both the amount of memory that the message uses on your HPC and the size of the message. Very large files may indicate that there is an attachment that the first version of Windows CE does not allow you to view. Although you cannot view the attachment, it is still downloaded into your HPC.

Working Online or Offline

There are a number of factors to consider when deciding whether to work online or offline. First and foremost, if you are running your HPC off of battery power, your online time will be very limited (approximately 5-30 minutes), depending on the power drain of your modem. If possible, use an AC adapter when working online to avoid this problem.

Working online provides the most flexibility and is very similar to using commercial online services, such as CompuServe and America Online, or a company e-mail system. You can immediately send, read, reply, move, and delete messages, although it may be necessary to select Refresh from the Service menu to update your screen. Another advantage of working online is that much less memory is required because you do not have to retrieve messages to read them.

Working offline is akin to a batch accounting system where you initiate a number of tasks but they are not executed until later. If your ISP charges by the hour, working offline can be much less expensive than working online. Any actions that are initiated offline will be executed the next time you are connected.

Creating and Sending Messages

To create a new message, follow these steps:

1. From Inbox, tap the New Message icon in the toolbar.
2. Type the Internet address of the person you want to send the message to, and then press the Tab key.
3. Type your message (refer to Figure 15.14).

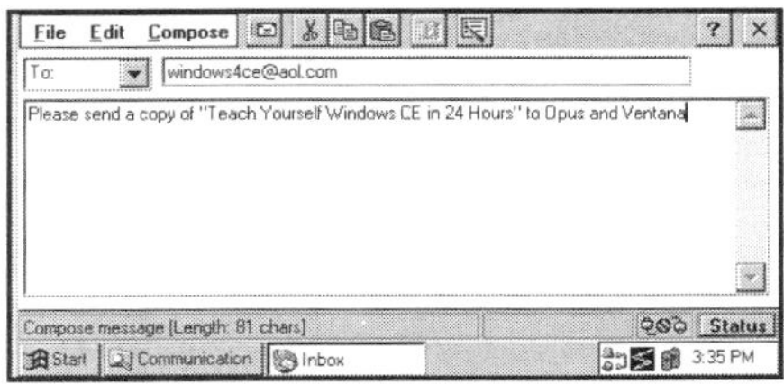

Figure 15.14.
A typical e-mail message.

4. If you want to enter a subject or Cc: someone else, tap the To scroll list (refer to Figure 15.15) and select the appropriate item from the list.

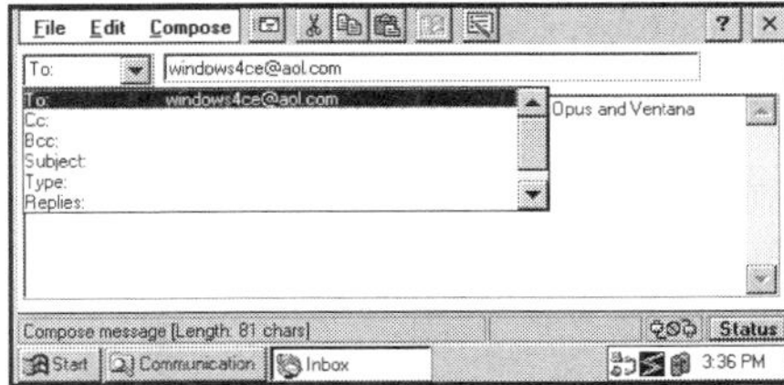

Figure 15.15.
Selecting message recipients.

5. Tap the Send icon in the toolbar to send the message. If you are offline, the message will be sent the next time you log on.

Getting Messages

Message headers and/or text are retrieved automatically when the connection is established. The settings you specified in the Inbox Folder Preferences options during setup determine what is transferred. Once you have received the messages and/or headers, you can double-tap each header to retrieve the text while online or during the next online session if you are offline.

If you limited the number of lines transferred in your settings, you can override that setting for a particular message by selecting the header and selecting Retrieve Full Text Copy from the Services menu. To copy many messages within the line transfer parameters, select the headers you want, and then select Retrieve a Copy from the Service menu.

Reading Messages

To read a message, double-tap the message header. If you are online and you have retrieved the message, the message will be displayed. If you are offline, you will not be able to view the message until the next time you are online, unless you have already retrieved the message. If you are online, you can use the Up and Down buttons while viewing messages to view the next or previous message.

Replying to and Forwarding Messages

While reading a message, you have several options, including replying to, forwarding, and deleting messages. You can reply to the sender or all recipients of a message. To reply to sender, tap the Reply to Sender icon in the toolbar. To reply to all recipients, tap the associated icon in the toolbar. When you tap these icons, a reply window appears.

Several reply options are available. To change these options, follow these steps:

1. Select Options from the Compose menu.
2. Select the check boxes for the options you want (refer to Figure 15.16).
3. Tap the OK button to save changes.

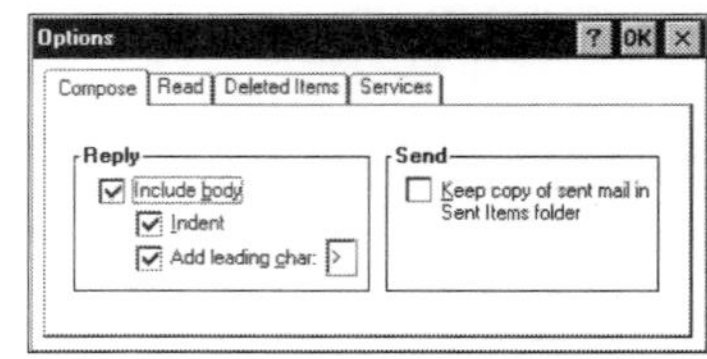

Figure 15.16.
Setting the Reply options.

You can also have a message forwarded to another recipient by tapping the Forward icon in the toolbar.

Moving Messages

Inbox also provides the capability to move and delete messages. Use these features with caution because the messages are permanently deleted from the server. If you move or delete messages with attachments, they will be lost because Inbox cannot read attachments.

To move a message from the server to your HPC, follow these steps:

1. From the Inbox message list, tap the message header that you want to move.
2. Select Move To from the File menu, and then select the folder that you want the message moved to.

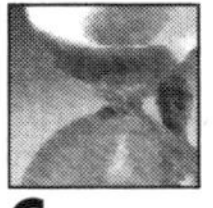

CAUTION

> If you have specified a limited number of lines to be downloaded in your options settings, part of the message may be deleted and unrecoverable if you try to move it.

Deleting Messages

To delete a message, follow these steps:

1. Tap the message header that you want to delete.
2. Tap the X button in the toolbar.

If you are working offline, the message will not be deleted until the next time you are connected. Therefore, you have the option of dragging the message from the Deleted Items folder back to the Inbox before you connect again, if you change your mind.

Using Folders

To make working with messages more organized, Inbox uses folders to arrange messages. By default, four folders are already created: Inbox, Outbox, Sent Items, and Deleted Items. These folders are permanent; you cannot delete or rename them. The Inbox folder is for received messages, and the Outbox folder is for messages that have been created but not yet sent. If you have selected the option of having a copy of all sent messages saved, they are stored in the Sent Items folder. Finally, the Deleted Items folder is a temporary holding place for messages that have been marked for deletion.

You can create other folders to supplement the built-in folders:

1. Select New Folder from the File menu.
2. Type the name of the folder (refer to Figure 15.17).

Figure 15.17.
Creating a new Inbox folder.

3. Tap the OK button.

Once you have created a folder, you can rename or delete it. To rename a folder, double-tap it, type the new name, and press the Enter key. To delete a folder, follow these steps:

1. Select the folder that you want to delete.
2. Tap the X button in the toolbar.
3. When the Delete Folder dialog box appears (shown in Figure 15.18), tap the Yes button to delete the folder and its contents.

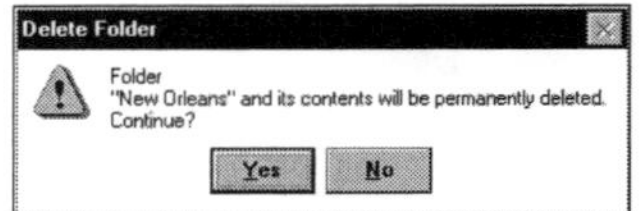

Figure 15.18.
Be sure you want to delete the folder.

Transfer Microsoft Exchange Messages

Although Inbox can work as a stand-alone application, you can also use it to share messages between your HPC and desktop PC. The CD-ROM included with your HPC contains a version of Microsoft Exchange for your desktop computer. You can transfer messages from the Microsoft Exchange Inbox to and from the Inbox on your HPC:

1. Connect your desktop PC to your HPC with the cable that came with your HPC.
2. Within Microsoft Exchange, select any messages you want to transfer to the HPC, and then select HPC Inbox Transfer.
3. In the HPC Inbox Transfer dialog box, select whether you want to transfer messages to or from your HPC.
4. Click the OK button.
5. If you're copying messages from the HPC to Microsoft Exchange, choose the Microsoft Exchange folder from the dialog box that opens.

Summary

You are probably ready for a break after this hour. You learned how to set up your e-mail service and connect to a remote computer. You can now receive, send, reply, forward, move, copy, and delete messages either online or offline. In addition, you learned how to create and modify folders and transfer messages between Inbox and Microsoft Exchange on your desktop computer.

Q&A

Q Does Inbox support file attachments?

A Version 1 of Windows CE does not support file attachments.

Q Can you remove all messages from the Inbox?

A Yes. Select Clear All from the Services menu.

Q Can I use a phone line with call waiting to connect?

A Yes. Select the Disable Call Waiting by Dialing check box within Dialing Properties.

PART IV

Hour 16

Surfing the Net

A word that was once reserved for describing a sport for dudes from California has now taken on a whole new meaning. Surfing in the late 1990s describes what about 17 million people do over the Internet. Whether you use the Internet to find out the up-to-the-minute weather forecast, read a newspaper before it has even made it to the newsstands, or make travel reservations, the Net is a wealth of information at your fingertips. With your modem-equipped HPC and Pocket Internet Explorer, you can now surf the Net from virtually anywhere.

Pocket Internet Explorer (IE) opens up a world of communications options available over the Internet. For example, you can see graphics as well as text. The requirements for Pocket IE are the same as those listed for Inbox in Hour 15, "Using Inbox for E-mail."

In this hour, you will learn how to do the following things:

- Set up Pocket IE
- Connect to the Internet
- Cruise the Internet
- Fine-tune Pocket IE

Setting Up Pocket Internet Explorer

Although most Windows CE programs are built into your HPC, Pocket Internet Explorer is on the CD-ROM that came with your HPC. To install pocket Internet Explorer on your HPC, select it when you install HPC Explorer on your desktop computer. Refer to Hour 4, "Understanding Synchronization," for more details about using HPC Explorer. If you have already installed HPC Explorer, you can quickly install Pocket IE:

1. Connect your HPC and desktop computer with the cable that was included with your HPC.
2. Select Programs from the Start menu.
3. Click the HPC Explorer folder and select Setup Microsoft Pocket Internet Explorer. You should see the screen shown in Figure 16.1.
4. Click the Next button, and then answer the on-screen questions.

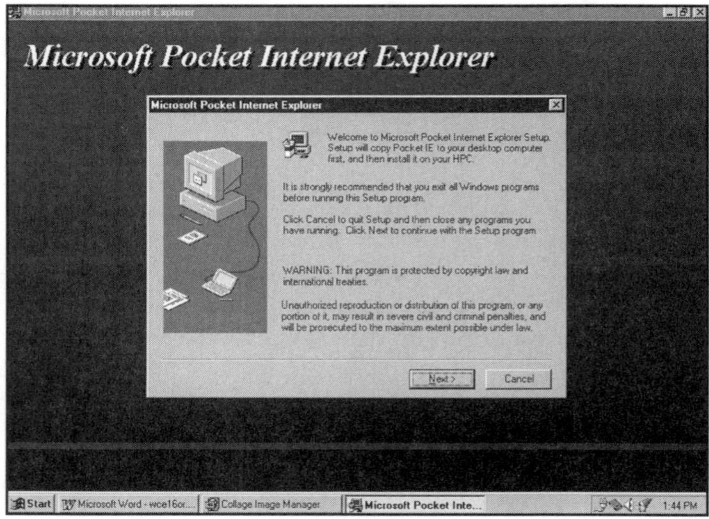

Figure 16.1.
Setting up Pocket Internet Explorer.

Microsoft includes free updates to Pocket Internet Explorer on its Web site located at `www.microsoft.com`. Once you are on the Microsoft home page, you will be able to access the Windows CE Web page.

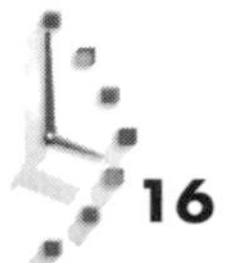

Connecting to the Net

If have not done so already, set up your dial-up connection as explained in the previous hour. You have two options for getting connected:

- Double-tap the dial-up connection icon you created, and then tap the Connect button.
- Set up the AutoDial feature within Pocket Internet Explorer.

16

To set up AutoDial, follow these steps:

1. Double tap the Pocket IE icon.
2. Select Options from the View menu.
3. Tap the Auto Dial tab (shown in Figure 16.2).

Figure 16.2.
Configuring AutoDial.

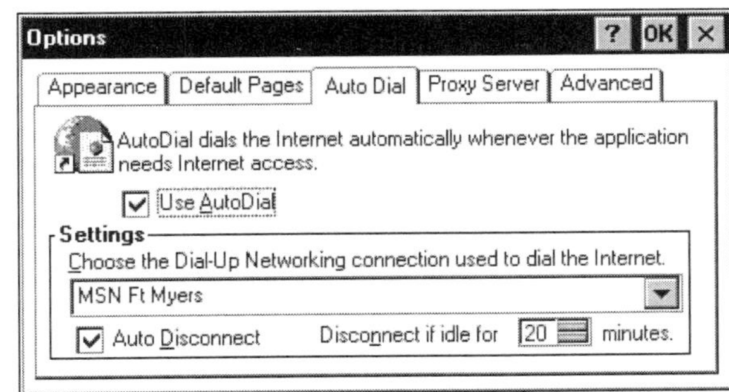

4. Tap the Use AutoDial check box to select it. The Settings area of the tab becomes available.
5. In the Settings area, select the dial-up connection that you want to use.
6. Tap the OK button.

If you have problems connecting, refer to Hour 19, "Having Problems Connecting?"

Cruising the Internet

Now that you are connected, the real fun begins. If you have not done so already, double-tap the Pocket IE icon. Your screen should look similar to Figure 16.3.

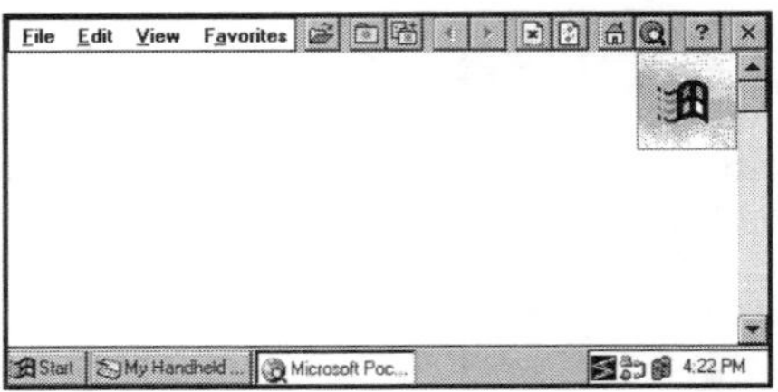

Figure 16.3.
Pocket Explorer's main screen.

Try to access a few Web sites. Start by accessing the Windows CE Web site:

1. Select Open from the File menu or tap the Open icon from the toolbar. The Open Internet Address dialog box appears.
2. Type **`www.microsoft.com/windowsce`**, and then press the Enter key. Note that although the address (also called an URL) for a Web site is prefaced with `http://`, Pocket IE does not require you to type this part. The Windows logo shown in Figure 16.3 will appear while the page is being loaded.

If you have used Pocket IE previously, you can access a list of sites you have visited from the Address drop-down list (refer to Figure 16.4). While you are online, Pocket IE keeps track of the sites you have visited during the current session. You can return to a previous screen by tapping the back arrow button on the toolbar until you reach the desired screen. Conversely, to move forward, tap the forward arrow button.

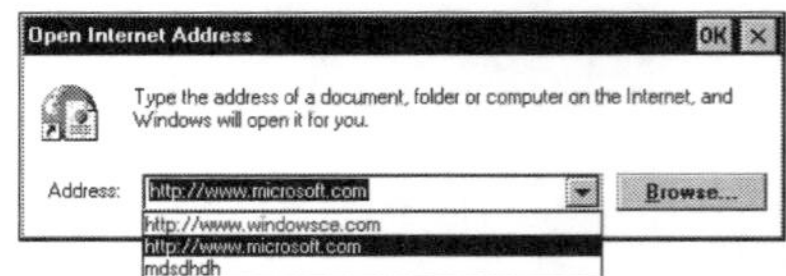

Figure 16.4.
Recording where you've surfed.

If there are sites that you visit regularly, you can add them to your Favorites folder so that you can easily access them in the future:

1. Tap the Open Address icon on the toolbar.
2. Type the address of the site that you want to add, and then press the Enter key.
3. When the site is loaded, select Add to Favorites from the Favorites menu. Alternatively, you can tap the Favorites icon on the toolbar.
4. Tap the OK button to add the site.

To access your Favorites folder, follow these steps:

1. Select Open Favorites Folder from the Favorites menu. The Open Favorites dialog box appears.
2. Select the site you want to access by tapping it twice.

In addition to setting up your Favorites folder, you can also create a desktop shortcut icon for even faster access. A desktop shortcut will load Pocket IE, make the connection, and jump to a specific page, all with just a double-tap. To create a desktop shortcut, load the page you want to create the shortcut for and select Desktop Shortcut from the File menu. To delete a shortcut from your desktop, drag it to the Recycle Bin.

Like Pocket Word and Excel, Pocket IE enables you to access previous pages from the taskbar. For each new page that you access, follow these instructions:

1. Select New Window from the File menu.
2. Select Open from the File menu.
3. Type the address for the page you want to access or choose it from the drop-down list.

Each page that you open in this way will appear in the taskbar and can be accessed by tapping it on the taskbar.

Fine-tuning Pocket IE

To enhance the usability of Pocket IE, you can customize it to your particular preferences. The following sections detail some of the options you can set to make Pocket IE work best for you.

Changing the Default Home Page

Each time you start Pocket IE, you are taken to the start page, sometimes referred to as your home page, defined in your options settings. On most HPCs, the default page is `file:/windows/default.htm`, which is a file on your HPC. You can change this page to your most commonly accessed Web page:

1. Access the page that you want to set as your start page.
2. Select Options from the View menu.
3. Tap the Default Pages tab.
4. Tap the Use Current Page check box.
5. Tap the OK button.

Each time you start Pocket IE, you will be taken automatically to this site. While you are online accessing other sites, you can return to the start page by tapping the Home icon in the toolbar.

Setting Up a Search Page

Because of the magnitude of sites in the Internet, the question is seldom "Is it there?" but rather "Can I find it?" The Internet provides several search sites that will search throughout the entire Internet for sites that contain the keyword that you enter. Two of the most common sites are `www.yahoo.com` and `www.excite.com`. You can quickly access a search site from within Pocket IE by setting up your default search page:

1. Access the search page that you want (for example, `www.yahoo.com`).
2. Select Options from the View menu.
3. Tap the Default Pages tab.
4. Tap the Start Page drop-down list and select Search Page.
5. Tap the Use Current Page check box.
6. Tap the OK button.

Changing Web Page Appearances

The Appearance tab in the Options dialog box enables you to specify such options as whether to play sounds and display graphics. Because your HPC's display is much smaller than a typical desktop display, Pocket IE defaults to forcing an Internet page to fit within the current window so that it is easy to navigate. This default setting may result in some images being too small to read. You can change this setting by following these steps:

1. Select Options from the View menu.
2. Select the Appearance tab.
3. Tap the Make Page Fit Window check box to deselect it (refer to Figure 16.5).

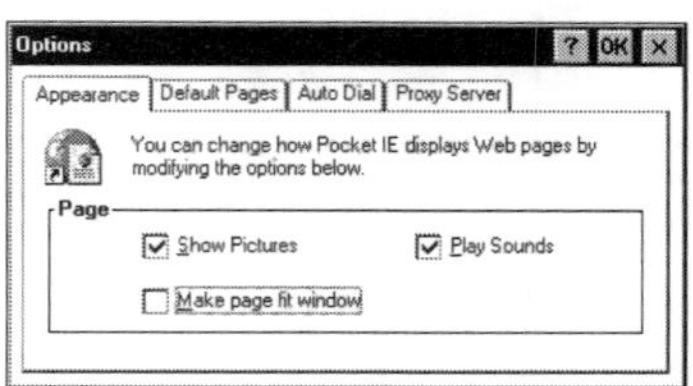

Figure 16.5.
Seeing the whole page.

4. Tap the OK button.

After changing this setting, you will have to use scroll bars in order to be able to see the entire page.

Summary

In this hour, you learned how to conquer the Internet. You installed Pocket IE, configured the AutoDial feature, and cruised to various Web sites. You now can create a desktop shortcut and add your most commonly accessed sites to your Favorites folder. Finally, you learned how change your default home and search pages.

Q&A

Q Can I access the Web from a corporate intranet?

A Yes. Before you can access a corporate intranet, you must first configure a proxy server. Before you do so, you will need to get the proxy service address from your company's intranet administrator. The proxy server must comply with the CERN proxy server standard. Servers using SOCKS security or ANS proxy servers are not supported.

To configure a proxy server, follow these steps:

1. Select Options from the View menu.
2. Tap the Proxy Server tab.
3. Tap the Use Proxy Server check box.
4. Enter the information supplied by your intranet administrator.
5. Tap the OK button.

PART IV

Hour 17

Remote Computing

In addition to enabling you to access the Internet and check e-mail, Windows CE also enables you to connect to a remote computer, such as a remote access server on a company network. To do this, you can use the Terminal program described in the next hour, "Using Terminal," or you can use a third-party program such as Symantec's PC Anywhere for Windows CE. When you deal with remote computing, you need to be aware of several things and configure many options. In this hour, you'll learn about the following topics:

- Modifying dial-up connections
- Manual dialing
- Dialing strings
- Configuring settings for a different city

Modifying Dial-up Connections

In Hour 15, "Using Inbox for E-mail," you learned how to set up a dial-up connection. If your service provider changes IP addresses or other settings, you will have to modify the dial-up connection. You may also have to modify the dial-up connection if you change phone lines or services. The following sections explain how to change both general connection settings and TCP/IP settings.

Changing General Connection Settings

To change the dial-up connection settings, follow these steps:

1. From the Remote Networking folder, tap the dial-up connection icon you want to modify.
2. From the toolbar, tap the Modify Settings icon.
3. Tap the Configure button (shown in Figure 17.1).

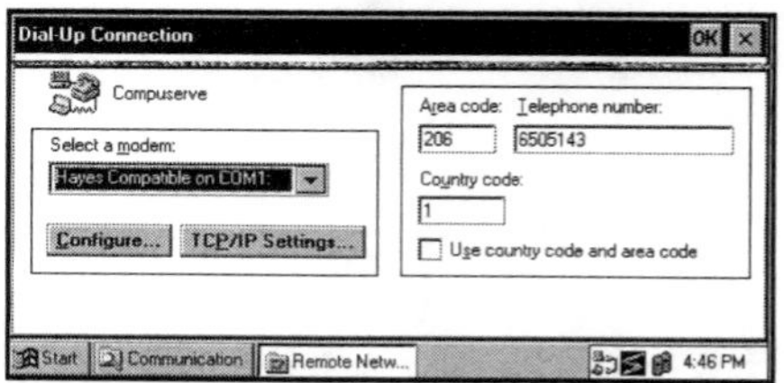

Figure 17.1.
The Dial-Up Connection dialog box.

4. From the Device Properties dialog box (shown in Figure 17.2), make any necessary changes and then tap the OK button until you return to the highlighted dial-up connection icon.

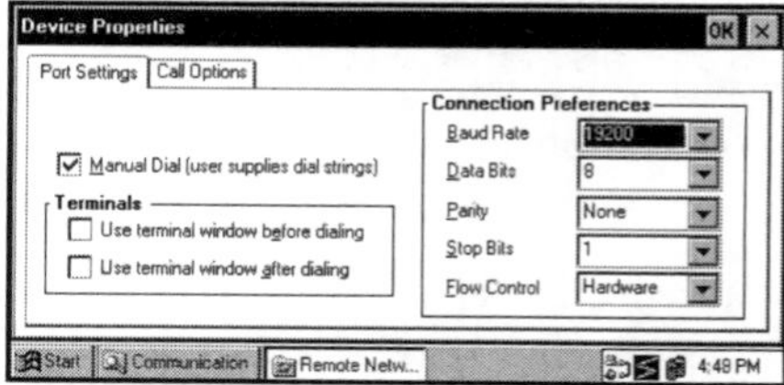

Figure 17.2.
The Device Properties dialog box.

Changing TCP/IP Settings

To change TCP/IP settings, follow these steps:

1. From the Remote Networking folder, tap the dial-up connection icon you want to modify.
2. From the toolbar, tap the Modify Settings icon.

3. Tap the TCP/IP Settings button. A dialog box appears on-screen to enable you to change the IP addresses as necessary as well as settings such as software and header compression.
4. Make any necessary changes and then tap the OK button until you return to the highlighted dial-up connection icon.

Manual Dialing

In certain situations, if you are in another country or your modem is not one of the Windows CE–supported modems, you may need to use manual dialing in order to make a connection. To set up manual dialing, follow these steps:

17

1. From the Remote Networking folder, tap the dial-up connection icon you want to modify.
2. From the toolbar, tap the Modify Settings icon.
3. Tap the Configure button.
4. In the Device Properties dialog box select the Manual Dial check box (refer to Figure 17.2).
5. In the window that appears, enter the command identified in the modem's user manual for your modem to make the connection. The most common command is `ATDT5558643` where `5558643` is the telephone number you want to connect to. Then press Enter.

Entering Modem Commands

In addition to the commands necessary for manual dialing, you can enter any other modem commands that are required to make a connection. To add these commands, follow these steps:

1. From the Remote Networking folder, tap the dial-up connection icon that you want to modify.
2. From the toolbar, tap the Modify Settings icon.
3. Tap the Configure button.
4. Tap the Call Options tab.
5. Enter the commands in the Extra Settings box (refer to Figure 17.3).

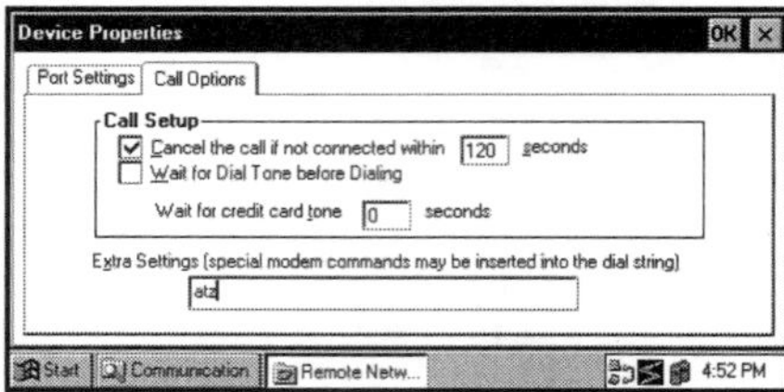

Figure 17.3.
Setting call options.

Using Dialing Strings

Because dialing with a modem is not always as simple as entering the telephone number, Windows CE provides a number of dialing options, referred to as dial strings. One of the most common strings is the one that disables call waiting. You can configure Windows CE to enter this string automatically:

1. From the Remote Networking folder, double-tap one of the dial-up connection icons.
2. Tap the Dial Properties button. The Communications Properties dialog box opens.
3. From the Dialing tab, tap the Disable Call Waiting by Dialing check box (refer to Figure 17.4).

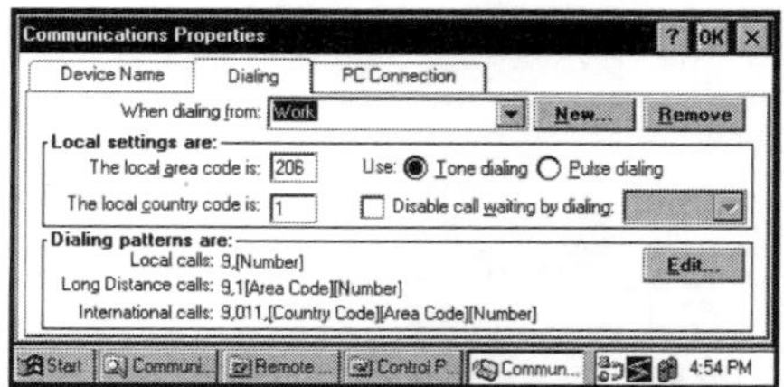

Figure 17.4.
Setting advanced dialing properties.

4. From the scroll list to the right of the Disable Call Waiting check box, tap the down arrow and select the command required by your phone company (refer to Figure 17.5).

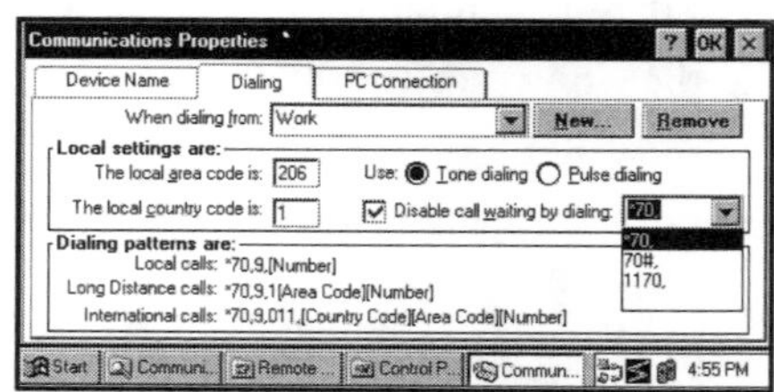

Figure 17.5.
Specifying the disable call waiting command.

5. Tap the OK button.

You can also specify a dialing string as part of the telephone number in a remote networking entry. Dialing strings are most often used when making a connection from a hotel room. A 9 is usually required to get an outside line and precedes the telephone number. You may also want to have your calling card number automatically entered.

Here are a couple of examples of dialing strings that you may need:

9,5558643	Dials a 9, pauses for 2 seconds, then dials the number
8,07135551234,1234567891	Dials an 8, pauses for 2 seconds, dials zero, dials the number, and then enters the calling card number

Telephone numbers may also be preceded with symbols such as T for tone dialing, P for pulse dialing, and W to wait for a dial tone.

Configuring Settings for a Different City

When traveling, you may need to change the dialing patterns or local settings for the city that you are in. To change these settings, follow these steps:

1. Double-tap the dial-up connection icon that you are going to use.
2. Tap the Dialing Properties icon.
3. Select Work or Home from the When Dialing From field or tap the New button to create a configuration for another location.
4. Make any changes necessary to the local settings.
5. Tap the Edit button in the Dialing Patterns window.
6. Make the necessary changes in the Edit Dialing Patterns dialog box (shown in Figure 17.6).
7. Tap the OK button until you return to the selected dial-up connection icon.

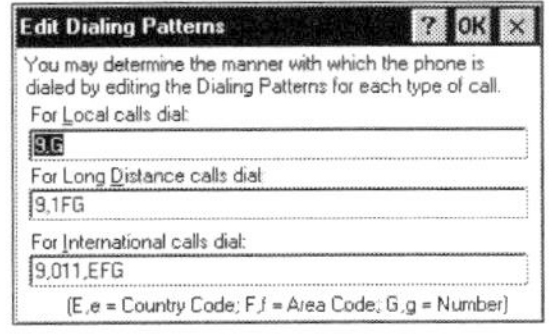

Figure 17.6.
The Edit Dialing Patterns dialog box.

Summary

In this hour you learned how to change your dial-up connection settings. You also learned how to enter dialing strings and patterns as well as set up manual dialing. In the next hour you will be able to get online with a bulletin board or an online service.

Q&A

Q Does Windows CE have the capability to run Windows 95 programs remotely?

A No. But Symantec's pcAnywhere CE program offers this capability.

Q Does Windows CE support dialing in to my Novell NetWare Connect server?

A No. Windows CE only supports dialing into servers that support TCP/IP and PPP.

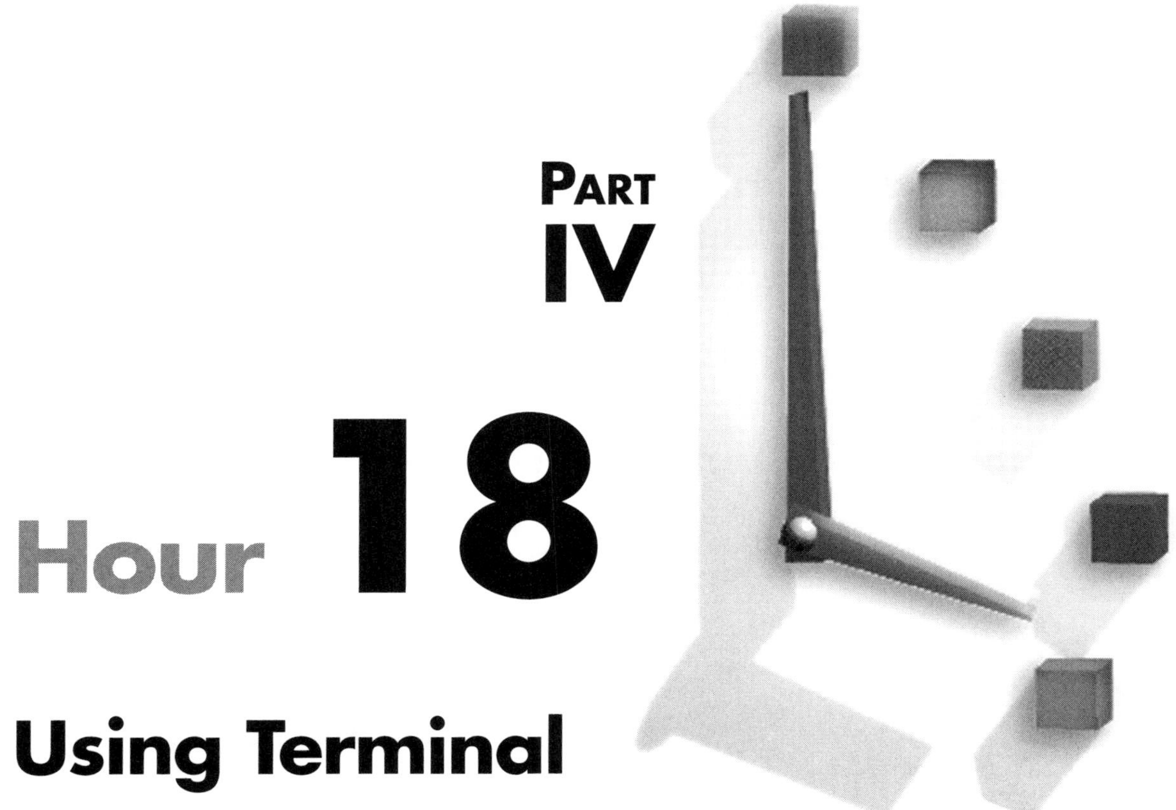

Hour 18

Using Terminal

Inbox enables you to get your e-mail, and Pocket Internet Explorer gives you Web access, but you may need to access an electronic bulletin board system (BBS) or an e-mail system such as MCI Mail that is not supported by Inbox. Windows CE's Terminal program provides VT-100 and TTY terminal emulation so that you can connect to virtually any remote computer.

In this hour, you will learn about the following topics:

- Starting Terminal
- Creating a Terminal dial-up connection
- Connecting with Terminal
- Advanced configuration
- Changing character size

Starting Terminal

Starting Terminal, like starting all programs in Windows CE, is pretty straightforward:

1. Select Programs from the Start menu.
2. Double-tap the Communications folder.
3. Double-tap the Terminal icon.

Creating a Terminal Dial-up Connection

In Hour 15, "Using Inbox for E-mail," you learned how to create a dial-up connection icon. Creating a dial-up connection for Terminal is similar to what you learned in Hour 15, with some key differences. To create a new dial-up connection for Terminal, follow these steps:

1. From the Terminal folder, double-tap the Make a New Connection icon.
2. Type in the Session Name (as shown in Figure 18.1).

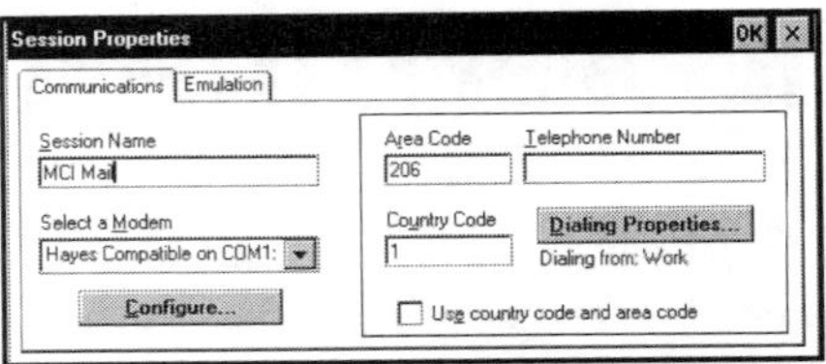

Figure 18.1.
The Session Properties dialog.

3. Choose your modem from the Select a Modem scroll list.
4. Type in the area code and telephone number.
5. Tap the OK button.

Connecting with Terminal

Before you can connect, you must have a modem that is supported and recognized by your HPC connected to a standard analog phone line. Digital phone lines, such as those used by many offices, are not supported. Therefore, you may need to connect to a fax line if no other analog lines are available.

To connect to an online service or BBS, follow these steps:

1. Double-tap the dial-up connection icon created in the previous section (in the Terminal folder). If your settings are correct and the number is not busy, a dialog

box will appear, and the connection will be made. Once you are connected, the Terminal window opens.

2. When you are finished with your online session, select Close from the File menu to disconnect.

Advanced Configuration

If you have problems connecting or want to fine-tune your settings, you can modify your dial-up connection icon:

1. From the Terminal folder, tap the dial-up connection icon that you want to modify.
2. Tap the Modify Connection icon in the toolbar.
3. Tap the Emulation tab (as seen in Figure 18.2).

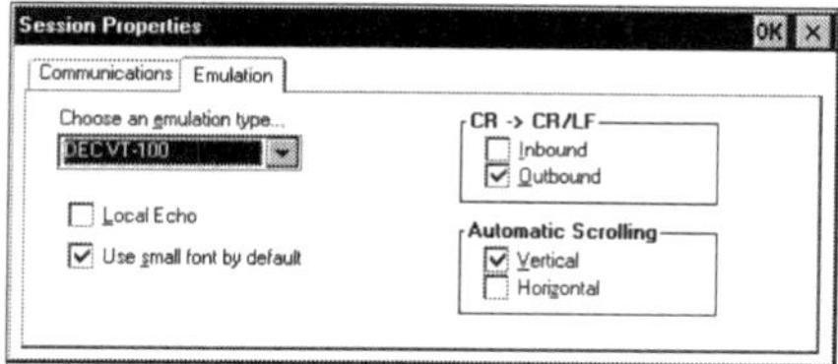

Figure 18.2.
Setting the Terminal emulation.

4. From the Choose an Emulation Type scroll list, select DEC VT-100 or TTY.
5. Select and deselect the other options depending on the BBS you are using. For example, if you are seeing double characters or a blank screen, you may have to change the local echo setting. If every line is separated by a space or your entire display is on one line, you may have to change the CR settings.
6. Tap the Communications tab, and then tap the Configure button.
7. From the Port Settings tab of the Device Properties dialog box (shown in Figure 18.3), you can change connection preferences such as the baud rate of your modem and other communications options specified by your online service provider.

Figure 18.3.
Setting the device properties.

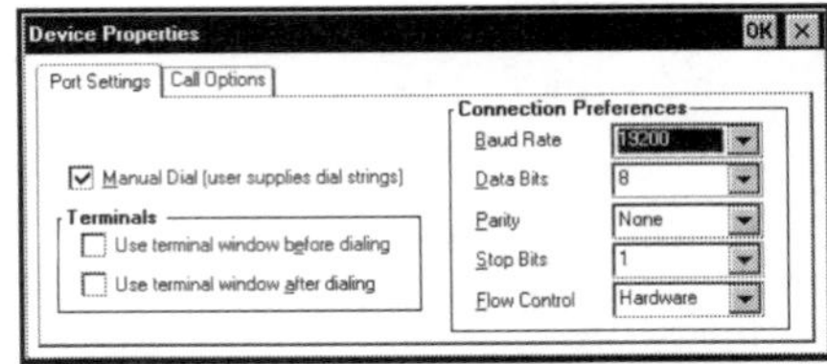

8. Tap the Call Options tab (shown in Figure 18.4) to change options such as how long to wait for a connection, credit card tone, or dial tone and enter additional modem commands that may be necessary for a connection.

Figure 18.4.
Setting the call options.

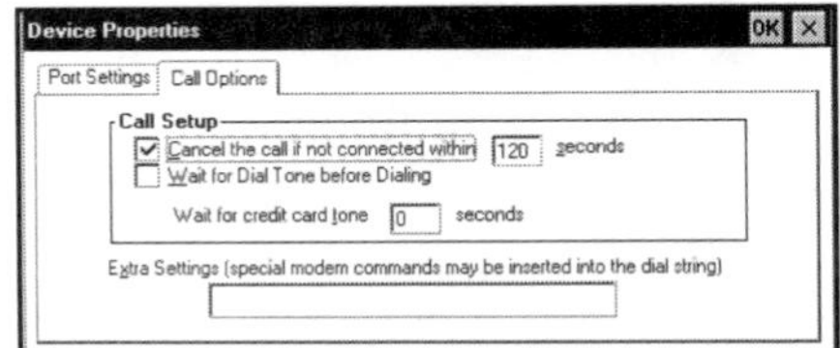

9. Tap the OK button.
10. Tap the Dialing Properties button.
11. Select Work or Home from the When Dialing From field or tap the New button to create a configuration for another location.
12. Make any changes necessary to the local settings. For example, if you have call waiting on the phone line you are using, tap the Disable Call Waiting check box.
13. Tap the Edit button in the Dialing Patterns window and make the necessary changes in the Edit Dialing Patterns dialog (shown in Figure 18.5).

Figure 18.5.
You can create different dialing scenarios for Terminal.

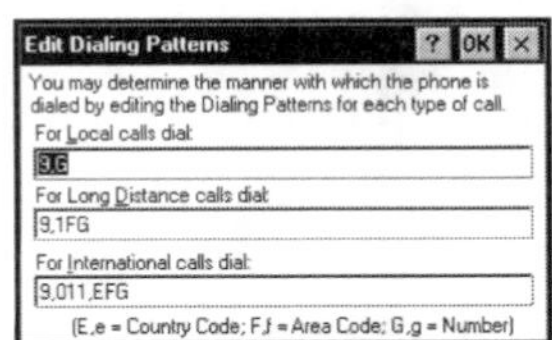

14. Tap the OK button twice when finished.

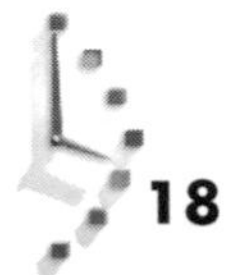

Changing Character Size

Because the screen size of your HPC is much smaller than what the service you are connecting to is expecting, characters may appear very small. Terminal provides a simple solution for this problem. To increase the character size, tap the large A icon in the toolbar. To revert to the small size, tap the small A icon.

Summary

In this hour you learned how to customize, connect, and enhance connection to an online service or bulletin board system using Terminal. In the next hour, "Having Problems Connecting?," you will learn how to resolve any connection problems you may have with Terminal, Inbox, Pocket IE, or any other communications program.

Q&A

Q Does Terminal support file transfer?

A No. The first version of Windows CE Terminal does not support file transfer.

Q Can I connect to a bulletin board system that uses ANSI terminal emulation?

A No. Terminal only supports TTY and VT-100.

Part IV

Hour 19

Having Problems Connecting?

For the most part, Windows CE is very easy to use. Going online with your HPC and communication programs such as Pocket IE, Inbox, and Terminal can be the exception to this rule. Most of the problems that you will encounter are connection problems that are related to configuration. In this hour, you will learn how to check for and deal with the following common problems:

- Your modem is not compatible with or recognized by your HPC
- Your IP addresses are entered incorrectly for Internet access
- Software and IP header compression settings are incorrect
- Windows CE thinks the local number you are dialing is long distance
- Serial port conflicts occur on your desktop computer when you use HPC Explorer
- The PC Connection settings on your HPC are set incorrectly
- The telephone line you're using is not analog
- Your Internet service provider (ISP) does not support PPP protocol
- Your baud rate is set too high for a reliable connection
- You have call waiting

Your Modem Is Not Compatible with or Recognized by Your HPC

Because HPCs are battery-operated and online communications require more power than any other component, you cannot effectively use every modem with your HPC. Some HPCs have built-in modems that require less power than a typical PC card modem.

As a general rule, you cannot use PC card modems with speeds over 14.4Kbps effectively while running your HPC on batteries. Battery life may be reduced to five minutes online with a 28.8Kbps modem. Even low-power (3 volt) 14.4Kbps modems can limit battery life to 30 minutes or less of online time. For this reason, it is highly recommended that you connect your HPC to a manufacturer-approved AC adapter when you are using online communications.

The following modems have been tested by Microsoft and have beed confirmed to work with Windows CE:

- Compaq Speedpaq 288 Telephony Modem and 288 Fax Modem
- EXP ThinFax 1414LXM and DataFax 1414
- Hayes Optima 14.4 and 28.8 + FAX for PCMCIA
- Megahertz PC Card Modem (XJ1144 and XJ2288)
- Microcom TravelCard 28.8P and Fast 28P
- Motorola Montana 33.6 and SecurID V.34
- Practical Peripherals ProClass PC144T2 and PC288T2
- SanDisk 144000bps Fax/Modem
- Simple Technologies 28.8 Communicator
- U.S. Robotics Sportster 14.4, 28.8 V.34 PC Card FaxModem, SP1336 and XJ/CC1336
- Xircom CreditCard Modem 28.8 and 33.6

Another common problem relating to PC card modems is that the HPC will not recognize the modem unless it is locked in and receiving power. When you first install a PC card modem, you will see a message asking you if you want to run the card off battery power. Answer Yes to the question unless you are using an AC adapter for connection.

When using your HPC internationally, be aware of modems using only two pins. International phone systems often reverse the pins, and these modems aren't able to compensate. A null modem adapter may correct this problem.

You can also use an external modem with your HPC. You will need a null modem cable and a 9-pin to 25-pin adapter in addition to the cable that came with your HPC. Follow these steps when connecting with an external modem:

1. Configure your dial-up connection to be a generic modem on COM1. (Modem types are not supported for external modems.)
2. Turn on your modem.
3. Proceed with your connection as you would for any other connection.

Your IP Addresses Are Entered Incorrectly for Internet Access

Although some ISPs assign IP addresses automatically, most will require that you enter the address into your settings. At a minimum, you will need the primary and secondary DNS numbers and may also need WINS numbers. To change or modify these settings, follow these steps:

1. From the Remote Networking folder, tap the dial-up connection icon that you want to modify.
2. Tap the Modify Connection icon in the toolbar.
3. Tap the TCP/IP Settings button.
4. Deselect the Server-Assigned Name Server Addresses check box by tapping it.
5. Enter the primary and secondary DNS numbers provided by your ISP (refer to Figure 19.1).

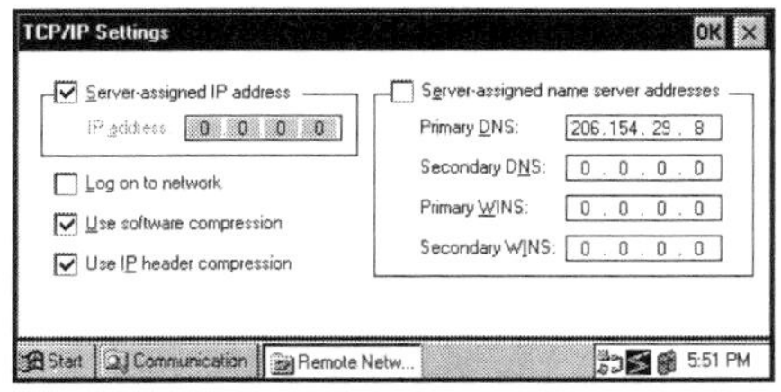

Figure 19.1.
Setting your TCP/IP options.

6. Tap the OK button twice.

JUST A MINUTE

From time to time, your ISP may change its DNS numbers. If you are having problems making a connection that worked previously, contact your ISP for updated DNS numbers.

Software and IP Header Compression Settings Are Incorrect

The settings that will commonly prevent you from connecting are software and IP header compression. To change these settings, follow these steps:

1. From the Remote Networking folder, tap the dial-up connection icon that you want to modify.
2. Tap the Modify Connection icon in the toolbar.
3. Tap the TCP/IP Settings button.
4. Deselect the Software and/or IP Header Compression check boxes by tapping them.
5. Tap the OK button twice.

Windows CE Thinks the Local Number You Are Dialing Is Long Distance

When the telephone number of your connection is a local number, make sure that you have not selected the Use Country Code and Area Code check box. Also make sure that your dialing properties indicate your correct local area code.

To check the Use Country Code setting, follow these steps:

1. From the Remote Networking folder, tap the dial-up connection icon that you want to verify.
2. Tap the Properties icon in the toolbar. Verify that the Use Country Code and Area Code check box has not been selected.

Serial Port Conflicts Exist on Your Desktop Computer When You Use HPC Explorer

The most common problems with the connection between your HPC and your desktop computer are serial port conflicts. If after you install HPC Explorer a connection is not created, you probably have a serial port conflict on your desktop computer. You can check to see whether you have an obvious conflict by following these steps:

1. From the Start menu on your desktop computer, click Settings, and then click the Control Panel.

19

2. From Control Panel, double-click the System icon.
3. Click the Device Manager tab.
4. Double-click Ports (COM & LPT) to display available ports and any conflicts (refer to Figure 19.2). Conflicts are identified with a small yellow yield sign with an exclamation mark in the middle.

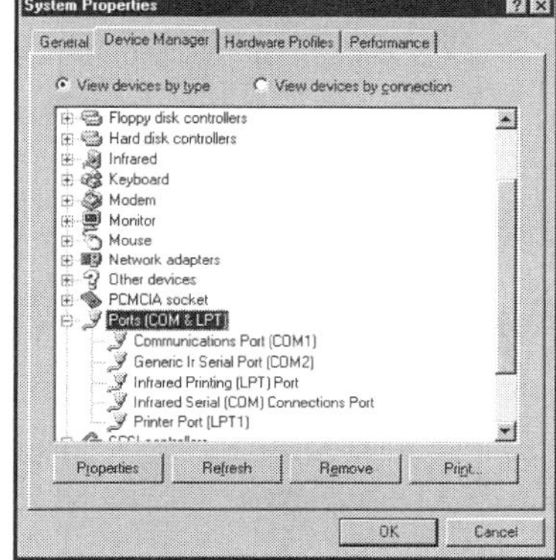

Figure 19.2.
Checking for port conflicts on your desktop computer.

If you have a serial port conflict, you will have to reconfigure your computer's hardware to resolve the conflict. Consult your computer's documentation or the manufacturer's technical support line for more information on reconfiguring your particular hardware.

If the serial port that you want to use is available and no conflicts are identified, you may have a problem on the HPC end. In some rare circumstances, you may have to double-tap the PC Link icon in the Communications folder to initiate the connection.

The PC Connection Settings on Your HPC Are Set Incorrectly

To verify your connection settings on your HPC, follow these steps:

1. Select Settings from the Start menu.
2. Double-tap the Communications icon.
3. Tap the PC Connection tab.
4. Verify that the Connect Using setting indicates Desktop @ 19200.
5. Tap the OK button.

The Telephone Line Is Not Analog

Communications on your HPC require a standard analog phone line like the kind usually used in your home. Most offices use a digital PBX line that is incompatible with your HPC and could damage your modem. Before connecting to an office phone line, verify that it is not a digital line. If you are unable to verify the phone type, you can purchase an inexpensive phone line polarity and voltage tester from Radio Shack or a product from IBM called a Modem Saver. This kind of product can also be very useful when connecting to a phone line in a foreign country.

Your Internet Service Provider (ISP) Does Not Support PPP Protocol

Most ISPs support Point-to-Point (PPP) protocol, which is required for connection. America Online and CompuServe are examples of common online service providers that support PPP. Check with your ISP to verify that it supports PPP.

Your Baud Rate Is Set Too High for a Reliable Connection

Although your modem may be able to communicate at the speed specified in your settings, you may not be able to maintain a reliable connection at maximum speed. If you are having connection problems, try lowering the connection speed:

1. From the Remote Networking folder, tap the dial-up connection icon you want to modify.
2. Tap the Properties icon on the toolbar.
3. Tap the Configure button.
4. Choose a lower baud rate in the Baud Rate scroll box.
5. Tap the OK button twice.

You Have Call Waiting but Have Not Disabled It in Your Settings

If you have the call waiting service on your phone line, you may be interrupted in the middle of a connection if you receive an incoming call. To prevent this situation from occurring, disable call waiting when you are connected by following these steps:

1. From the Remote Networking folder, double-tap the dial-up connection icon you want to modify.
2. Tap the Dial Properties icon.
3. Tap the Disable Call Waiting by Dialing check box.
4. From the scroll list, select the code used by your telephone company to disable call waiting (in most cases *70, is the setting).
5. Tap the OK button.

Other Connection Problems

Although the problems and solutions this hour has already addressed will resolve most of your connection problems, you should be aware of some other issues that can cause problems.

If your modem is not on the list of supported modems, you may have to experiment with several selections until you find the one that is correct. If you are still unsuccessful connecting, select the Generic modem setting and add your own modem commands (as specified in your modem's user manual). To add these commands, follow these steps:

1. Tap the dial-up connection icon that you want to modify.
2. Tap the Modify Connection icon in the toolbar.
3. Tap the Configure button.
4. Tap the Call Options tab (shown in Figure 19.3).

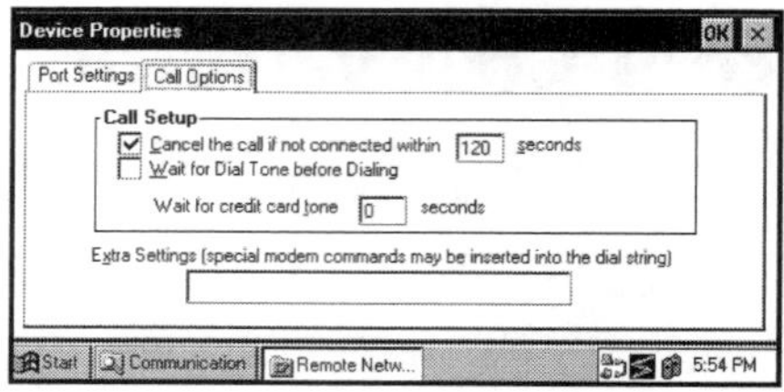

Figure 19.3.
Adding extra commands for your modem.

5. Enter the modem commands in the Extra Settings box near the bottom of the screen.
6. Tap the OK button twice to save your settings.

Another common connection problem is that you have entered your user ID, password, and domain incorrectly. Double-tap your dial-up connection icon to view your settings. Make sure that you have entered your User ID and password correctly and tap the Save Password check box. The Domain field is used when dialing in to a company intranet. Check with your network administrator for the correct domain name.

Summary

In this hour, you learned how to resolve problems you may have when connecting to online services and connecting to your desktop computer. You learned the 10 most common connection problems and the steps necessary to correct these problems. You should now be on your way to surfing the Net, getting e-mail, and synchronizing with your desktop.

Q&A

Q Does HPC Explorer Setup begin automatically after you insert the CD?

A Yes. On most systems, it will run automatically. If this does not happen, select Run from the Start menu and type `D:setup`. Then press the Enter key.

Q Does Windows CE support two desktop partnerships? For example, can your HPC synchronize with both your home and work desktop PCs?

A No. Version 1.0 does not support more than one partnership.

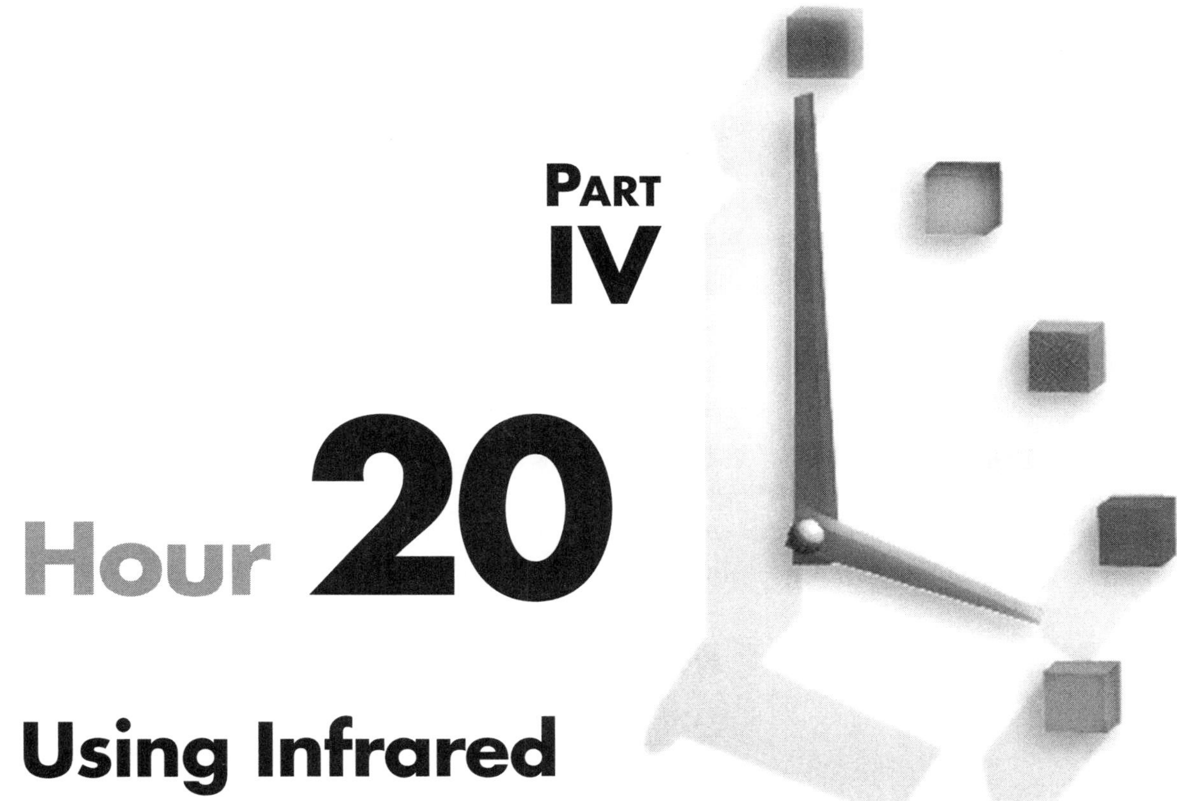

Hour 20

Using Infrared

A unique feature common to all HPCs is an infrared port (IR) for transferring data to other HPCs. With IR you can transfer files such as a document or spreadsheet to a colleague or transfer a contact card to a business associate. Although the first version of Windows CE does not support the use of IR transfer between HPCs and IR-equipped notebook and desktop computers, several third-party software developers have indicated that they plan to support this feature.

In this hour, you will learn how to do the following:

- Transfer information
- Send and receive files
- Troubleshoot IR transfers

Transferring Information

One set of data that many users will want to transfer back and forth will be contact information. By following these instructions, you will be able to easily shift this information back and forth via the HPC's IR port:

1. Double-tap the Contacts icon on your HPC's desktop.
2. Select the contact that you want to transfer. You can select multiple contacts by holding down the Ctrl key while tapping each contact you want to select.
3. Align the HPCs so that the IR ports are facing each other and are no more than three feet apart.
4. From the File menu, select Send on the sending end.
5. From within Contacts on the receiving end, tap Receive from the File menu.

Sending and Receiving Files

To send and receive files between two HPCs, follow these steps:

1. Select the file that you want to send.
2. Align the HPCs so that the IR ports are facing each other and are no more than three feet apart.
3. Select Send from the File menu.
4. On the receiving end, select Receive from the File menu.

Troubleshooting IR Transfers

If you are encountering problems using infrared communications, check for the following situations:

- Make sure that the two units are aligned within three feet of each other and that nothing is blocking the line of sight between the two.
- Indoor lighting, such as fluorescent lights in an office, may cause interference with the IR port. Try turning off the lights or moving the units away from the lights.
- You cannot transfer more than one file at a time. Therefore, to transfer an entire folder's contents, you must transfer one file at a time.

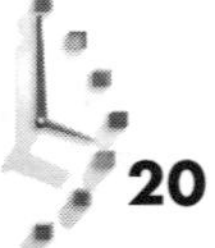

Summary

In this hour, you learned how to use the wireless infrared feature to transfer files and data. You learned how to easily share contact cards from one HPC to another and how to troubleshoot any problems that you encounter.

Q&A

Q Can I use the infrared port to transfer files to my notebook computer?

A No. The current version of Windows CE does not support file transfer or synchronization with the infrared port found on most notebook computers. Several third-party software developers have promised to deliver this technology to the Windows CE platform. Contact Microsoft at `www.microsoft.com` for information on available software to support this feature.

Q Can I use the infrared port to print to an IR-equipped printer?

A Some HPCs, such as the Hewlett Packard, support wireless printing, although Windows CE version 1.0 does not directly support this feature. In addition, printing support is available from some third-party developers.

Part IV

Hour 21

Sending and Receiving Faxes

Although many HPCs do not have fax software built in, all HPCs support faxing when you use a PC card fax modem. Bsquare Development offers a free trial version of their bFAX software for Windows CE. You can download bFAX Lite from the World Wide Web at `http://www.bsquare.com/development` to your desktop PC and then install it on your HPC. A more powerful version of this software is included with the Casio Cassiopeia HPC. bFAX Lite does not support the reception of faxes, the Contacts database, or files other than text.

In this hour, you will use bFAX Lite to do the following things:

- Configure a fax modem
- Send faxes
- Troubleshoot fax problems

Configuring a Fax Modem

Most PC card modems supported by Windows CE also have faxing capabilities. Install and configure your modem as you would for any other communications. Refer to Hour 15, "Using Inbox for E-mail," for information on creating a dial-up connection icon.

To use bFAX Lite, your HPC and modem must meet the following requirements:

- HPC Explorer must be installed on your desktop computer.
- Your modem must be a standard class 2.0 PC card fax modem.

If you are using a 2M memory HPC, you may have to increase the memory available for running programs. Refer to Hour 22, "Fine-tuning and Troubleshooting," for information on how to adjust the memory size.

Installing bFAX Lite

To install bFAX Lite on your desktop computer, follow these steps:

1. Download bFAX Lite from the Internet at `http://www.bsquare.com/development` to your desktop computer.
2. After you have decompressed the files, double-click the Setup icon.
3. Click the Install button.
4. Connect the HPC to your desktop computer and follow the installation instructions on the screen.

If after the installation is complete you see a message indicating the trial version has expired, contact Bsquare Development at 888-820-4500 for an update or change the date of your HPC to January 1, 1997.

Starting bFAX Lite

To start bFAX Lite on your HPC, follow these steps:

1. Double-tap the Bsquare Fax Lite icon on your desktop.
2. In the message box that appears (refer to Figure 21.1), tap the I Agree button and bFAX Lite will open.

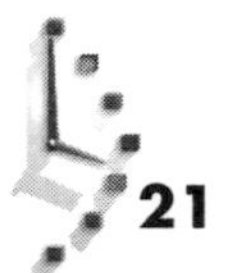

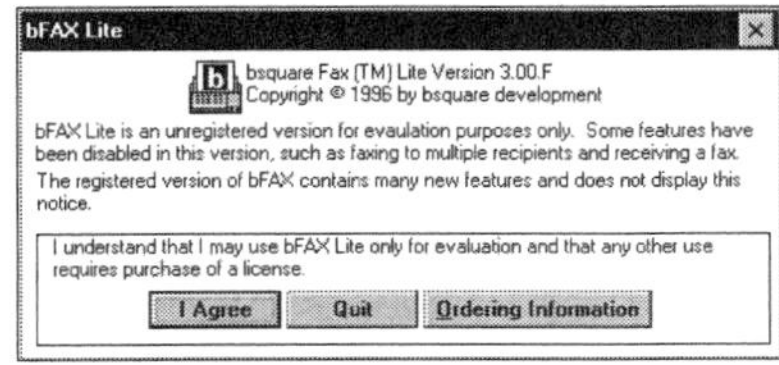

Figure 21.1.
You must first agree to use bFAX only for your own evaluation.

JUST A MINUTE

Because a full version of bFAX is included with the Cassiopeia HPC, you will not see a message that the trial version has expired if you have that HPC.

Sending Faxes

The basic steps for sending a fax are as follows:

1. Create a new fax.
2. Add recipients.
3. Add files.
4. Send the fax.

To create a new fax in bFAX Lite, follow these steps:

1. Select New Fax from the Fax menu.
2. Type a name for the fax that you want to create, and then press the Enter key.
3. Select Add Recipient from the Fax menu.
4. Type the name of the person that you want to send the fax to and that person's telephone number (see Figure 21.2), and then tap the OK button. The recipient will appear in the upper right pane of the bFAX window (shown in Figure 21.3)

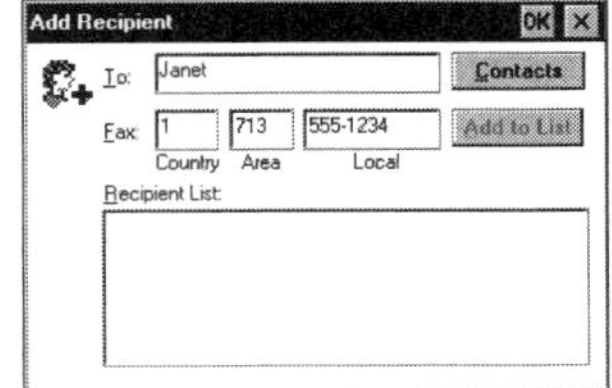

Figure 21.2.
Adding a fax recipient.

21

Figure 21.3.
Listing the fax recipient.

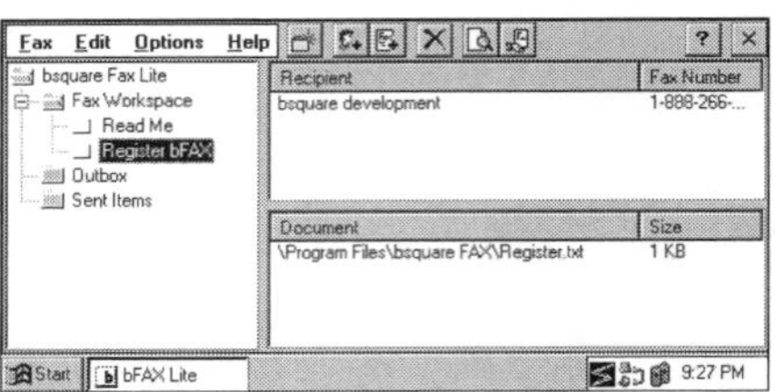

5. Select Add Document from the Fax menu and double-tap the document that you want to fax. The Lite version of bFAX only supports text files with a .txt extension. Refer to the section "Faxing a Pocket Word Document with bFAX Lite" for instructions on how to convert Pocket Word documents to text files. The professional version supports graphics files and Pocket Word documents.
6. Verify that your modem is installed and plugged into the phone line.
7. From the Fax menu, select Send Fax.

Changing Fax Options

To conserve space, documents are deleted after they are faxed successfully. You can change this option:

1. Select Preferences from the Options menu.
2. Tap the Options tab (shown in Figure 21.4).

Figure 21.4.
Configuring bFAX.

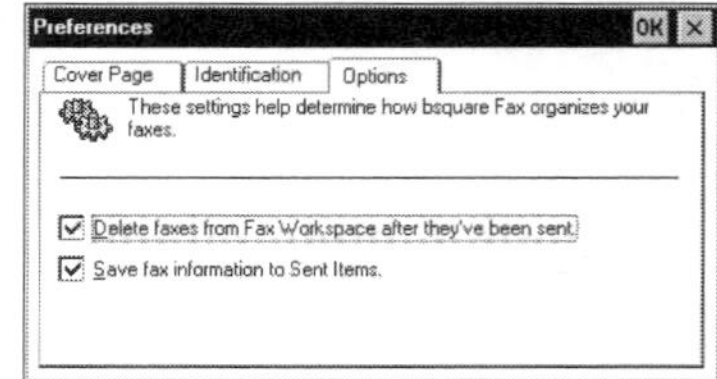

3. Deselect the Delete Faxes from Fax Workspace check box.
4. Tap the OK button.

Faxing a Pocket Word Document with bFAX Lite

If you want to fax a Pocket Word document using bFAX Lite, you first have to save it as a text file:

1. Open Pocket Word and the document that you want to fax.
2. Select Save As from the File menu.

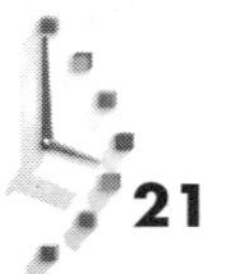

3. Type the name of the document followed by the extension **`.txt`**.
4. Select Plain Text Document from the Type scroll list (shown in Figure 21.5).

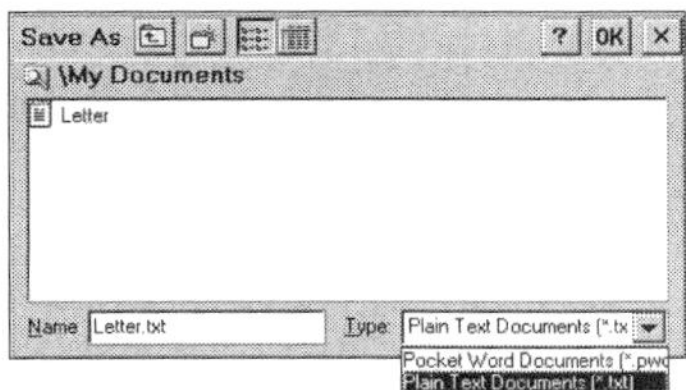

Figure 21.5.
Choosing the file type for the fax document.

5. Tap the OK button.

Troubleshooting

If you see the error message `Your modem reported a general error`, you could have one of several problems:

- The phone number dialed is incorrect. This could be a result of a long-distance number being dialed as a local number. Check the Fax Progress dialog box to verify the number that is being dialed.
- The modem could have encountered a voice mail system or operator message that generated this error message. Verify that you have entered the correct fax number.
- The fax number you entered may contain characters not supported by your fax modem. Verify that you have entered the correct fax number.

If you see the error message `Your modem could not be found`, the modem is probably not locked into place or is not receiving battery power. Remove and reinsert the modem, lock it in place, and answer Yes to the battery power question.

Summary

In this hour, you learned how to use your HPC as a portable fax machine. You learned how to install the bFAX Lite software on your HPC, convert Pocket Word documents, enter the contact information, select the documents to fax, and send the fax. You also learned the limitations of bFAX Lite and how to resolve any problems encountered.

Q&A

Q Can a document be modified after it is added to the outgoing fax list?

A Yes. Double-tap the document to open it for editing.

Q Can a recipient be modified after it is added to the outgoing fax list?

A No, not in bFAX Lite.

Q How do you uninstall bFAX Lite?

A Select Control Panel from the Start menu and select Remove Programs. Select bFAX and tap the Remove button.

PART V

Burning the Midnight Oil

Hour

Part V

Hour 22

Fine-tuning and Troubleshooting

To get the most out of your HPC, you may have to fine-tune some of the settings. For example, you may need to adjust the memory allocation. This hour covers details about the following topics:

- Memory
- Screen problems
- Passwords
- Synchronizing
- Volume and sound
- Battery power
- Removing programs

Memory

Most desktop and notebook computers store programs and data on a hard drive and use memory to run programs. Your HPC uses memory to store programs and data as well as to run programs. Windows CE enables you to split this memory allocation in any manner you choose. If you have a lot of data that you want to store on your HPC, you may want to increase the storage memory. On the other hand, if you are running programs that require a lot of memory, such as Pocket IE, or want to run several programs at the same time, you may want to increase program memory.

To change memory allocation, follow these steps:

1. Select Settings from the Start menu.
2. Double-tap the System icon.
3. Tap the Memory tab (shown in Figure 22.1).

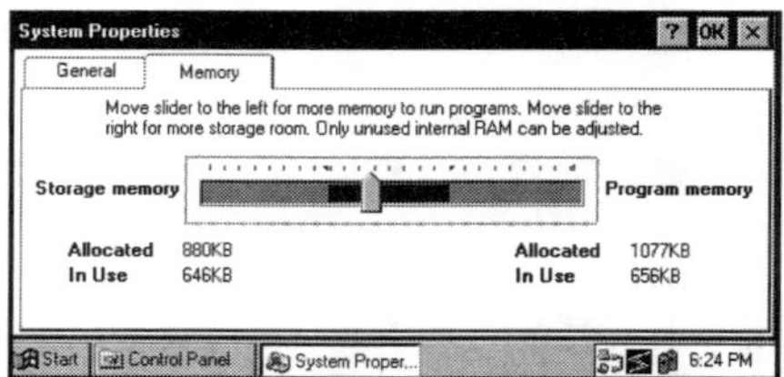

Figure 22.1.
The Memory properties of the HPC.

4. Move the slider by tapping and holding while moving the slider in the desired direction.
5. Tap the OK button to save changes.

If you notice that your HPC is operating more slowly than normal, you may want to try restarting your HPC. Make sure that you close all applications before doing so. Increasing the amount of program memory can also make your HPC run faster.

To display the total memory that is available on your HPC, follow these steps:

1. Select Settings from the Start menu.
2. Double-tap the System icon.

Screen Problems

One of the most common problems reported on Windows CE technical support lines is that the HPC is not working or that the screen is blank. In most circumstances, this problem is easily solved:

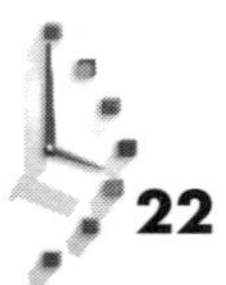

- Change the contrast setting. If your HPC has an external control, it may have been inadvertently changed to make the screen appear to be off.
- Change batteries and verify that battery lock is set correctly.
- Push the reset button.

If your HPC has been exposed to extreme temperatures or prolonged direct sunlight, the LCD screen may become darker. Remove the display from these conditions, and the display will return to normal after a short period of time.

Many HPCs may be difficult to read under poor lighting conditions. Some HPCs, such as those from Compaq, Casio, and Philips, contain backlit screens for easier viewing. You may also want to adjust your light so that it shines directly on the screen.

Passwords

Don't forget your password! If you forget your password, you must completely reset your HPC, resulting in a complete loss of data. If you have not synchronized with your desktop computer recently, this reset operation can be catastrophic. Refer to your HPC's user's guide for instructions on how to perform a complete reset. Even if you have a reset button, you may have to remove all batteries, including the backup battery, to perform a complete reset.

Synchronizing

If you are having problems synchronizing data between your HPC and desktop computer, check for these common causes:

- You have not installed Microsoft Schedule+ 7.0a onto your desktop computer.
- You selected Guest when you connected to your desktop computer and HPC. You cannot synchronize in Guest mode. To correct this problem, you may have to create a new partnership.
- You have a configuration or cable problem.

Windows CE enables you to specify how often to synchronize and whether or not to synchronize automatically upon connecting. You can speed up synchronization by following these rules:

- Delete appointments and tasks that have been completed and that you no longer need for reference.
- Do not create large notes. In addition to slowing data transfer, notes take up a lot of space on your HPC.

- ☐ Limit the number of items that you synchronize by selecting Synchronization Manager from the Tools menu of HPC Explorer. From there, select Options from the Database tab. For each database, choose the number of weeks of information to synchronize.

Volume and Sound

Your HPC contains a speaker that can play sounds, alarms, and .wav files. You can modify most of the settings related to sound and volume from the Control Panel:

1. Select Settings from the Start menu.
2. Double-tap the Volume & Sounds icon.
3. To adjust volume, tap and hold the slider and move it in the desired direction (refer to Figure 22.2).

Figure 22.2.
Crank up that HPC.

4. Select the desired check boxes to enable and disable sounds.
5. Tap the Sound tab (shown in Figure 22.3).

Figure 22.3.
Assign sounds to system events.

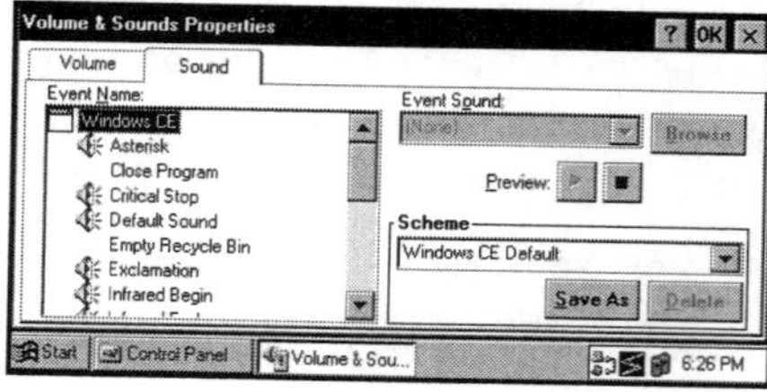

6. If you want to change the sound that goes with a certain event, select the event from the Event Name list, and then tap the Browse button to select the .wav file you want to use for that event.
7. Tap the OK button when you are finished modifying sounds.

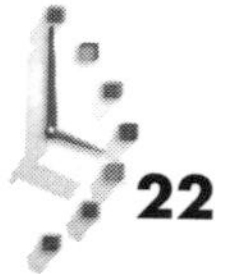

Verify that any sound files that are transferred from your desktop computer to your HPC are 8-bit, 11-KHz, mono .wav files.

Battery Power

To check battery life, double-tap the battery icon in your taskbar to load the Power Properties dialog box (shown in Figure 22.4). Depending on your HPC, the percentage of main battery power left may be displayed. Your HPC turns off automatically after three minutes of inactivity. You can change this setting from the Power Off tab of the Power Properties dialog box (shown in Figure 22.5). From the scroll list, select the number of minutes desired.

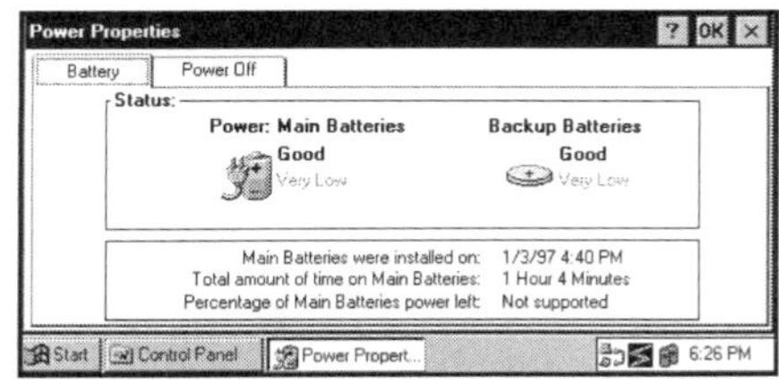

Figure 22.4.
The power status of the HPC.

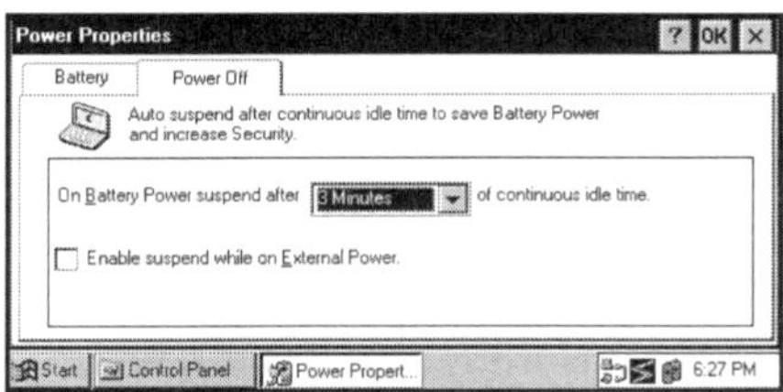

Figure 22.5.
Setting the auto suspend properties.

The following additional tips can help you extend battery life:

- Do not use battery power for communications.
- Use an AC adapter whenever possible.
- Limit the use of the backlit display if your HPC is so equipped.
- Do not use battery power for PC cards other than memory cards.

Removing Programs

Like Windows 95, Windows CE provides a method for cleanly removing programs and any associated files and registry settings. Because a registry editor isn't provided with Windows CE, it's particularly important to remove programs using only the steps below—don't just delete program files.

To remove a program from your HPC, follow these steps:

1. Select Settings from the Start menu.
2. Double-tap the Remove Programs icon.
3. Select the program that you want to remove.
4. Tap the Remove button.
5. Tap the OK button.

Note that programs such as Pocket Word and Pocket Excel are built-in to your HPC and therefore cannot be removed. Also, programs that you have manually installed cannot be removed through this procedure.

Summary

In this hour, you learned some of the most common tricks and traps of Windows CE. You learned how to adjust the memory allocation, how to resolve screen problems, and what to do if you forget your password. Additionally, you learned how to change volume and sound settings and play .wav files, how to remove programs, and ways to increase battery life.

Q&A

Q Will Windows CE give me a warning when battery life is about to run out?

A Yes. A message telling you so will appear on-screen.

Q Are there any small external lights that help with screen readability?

A Yes. Small battery-operated lights designed for book readers are available from most bookstores.

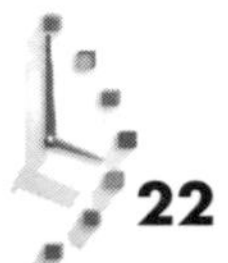

Hour 23

What to Look for in an HPC

When Windows CE was announced in November of 1996, it was embraced by many major hardware manufacturers such as Compaq, Hewlett Packard, Casio, Philips, NEC, Hitachi, and several others. Deciding between the numerous HPCs available can be a daunting experience. The following information presented during this hour should help you make a good choice:

- Factors to consider
- Comparison table of available HPCs

Factors to Consider

For most users, deciding on the right HPC depends what you are going to use it for. Considering the following factors that differ among HPCs may help you decide which brand best fits your needs:

- **Built-in software.** The software built-in to most HPCs is the same, with a few exceptions. The Cassiopeia comes standard with bFAX software, and the Compaq PC Companion includes River Run enhanced e-mail software and Dataviz Desktop-to-Go for enhanced support from other PIMs.

- **Built-in modem.** If you primarily want to use your HPC for communications, you may want to choose an HPC with a built-in modem, such as the Philips Velo 1 or some models of the Compaq PC Companion.
- **Screen clarity**. The Hewlett Packard provides a wider screen than the other HPCs.
- **Backlit display.** An HPC with a backlit display is preferable if you are using your HPC in poor lighting conditions.
- **Amount of standard memory.** The first HPCs came with 2M of memory, but the newer models come standard with at least 4M. Most HPCs provide some capability to upgrade the RAM internally.
- **PCMCIA slots.** Most HPCs come standard with a PCMCIA card slot; some, such as the Hewlett Packard, provide two. This extra slot can be important if your HPC does not have a built-in modem because you cannot use a flash memory card at the same time your modem is installed. Flash memory cards enable you to expand your storage space, but you cannot use them for program memory.
- **Upgradeable ROM.** Because Windows CE is built-in to a ROM chip, the primary way to upgrade the Windows CE programs is through a ROM upgrade. Some manufacturers provide this upgrade as an option. This capability can be an important consideration when selecting an HPC.
- **Accessories and unique features.** Some HPCs come standard with a docking cradle; others provide a cable with a docking station as an option. Some HPCs provide truly unique features, such as the voice recorder found on the Philips Velo 1.

Comparison Table of HPCs

Table 23.1 provides a comparison of the HPCs available at the time this book was published. Undoubtedly, other HPCs have been released since then, but this table provides a baseline comparison between HPCs.

Table 23.1. Comparison of HPCs.

Manufacturer	HPC name	Processor chip	Memory
Casio	Cassiopeia	Hitachi SH3	2M or 4M
Compaq	PC Companion	Hitachi SH3	2M or 4M
Philips	Velo1	MIPS	4M or 8M

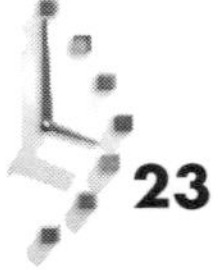

Summary

The first generation of HPCs provides a wide range of capabilities. You can expect a number of improvements in the area of screen clarity, keyboard improvements, increased memory, and standard communications features, but these current products offer impresssive functionality. When choosing the HPC that is right for you, consider factors such as display, keyboard, communications capabilities, and any other features that are important to you.

Q&A

Q Does Windows CE support color?

A No. Version 1.0 of Windows CE does not support color. Microsoft has indicated that they will support many other consumer electronic devices with Windows CE, so you can expect future versions of Windows CE to support color displays.

Q Can I run Windows 95 programs on my HPC?

A No. Only programs specifically designed for Windows CE will run on your HPC.

PART V

Hour 24

Third-party Products and Services

One of the main advantages of HPCs over electronic organizers is the wealth of third-party hardware, software, and services available for the Windows CE platform. Because Windows CE uses a subset of the same 32-bit API used by Microsoft Windows 95, software developers can adapt products from their Windows 95 software development projects.

This hour covers the following topics:

- Microsoft Pocket Automap Streets
- Other third-party software and hardware
- Windows CE Internet sites

Microsoft Pocket Automap Streets

Microsoft Pocket Automap Streets is the first mapping software for Windows CE. If you have enough storage space on your HPC, you can take street maps of up to 40 metropolitan U.S. cities with you. With Pocket Automap Streets, you locate a specific address quickly and zoom in and out to see more or less detail. You can also move around a virtual city by using the panning buttons in the toolbar.

One of the best things about Pocket Automap Streets is its price: It's free. You can download Pocket Automap Streets along with any of the cities you want from Microsoft's Web site. Pocket Automap Streets works with any HPC that has 2M of memory or more and a serial cable or docking station.

Installing Microsoft Pocket Automap Streets

To install Pocket Automap Streets, follow these steps:

1. Connect to the Microsoft Automap Web site from your desktop computer. The address is as follows:

   `http://www.microsoft.com/windowsce/hpc/software/automap.htm`

   Figure 24.1 shows the Web site.

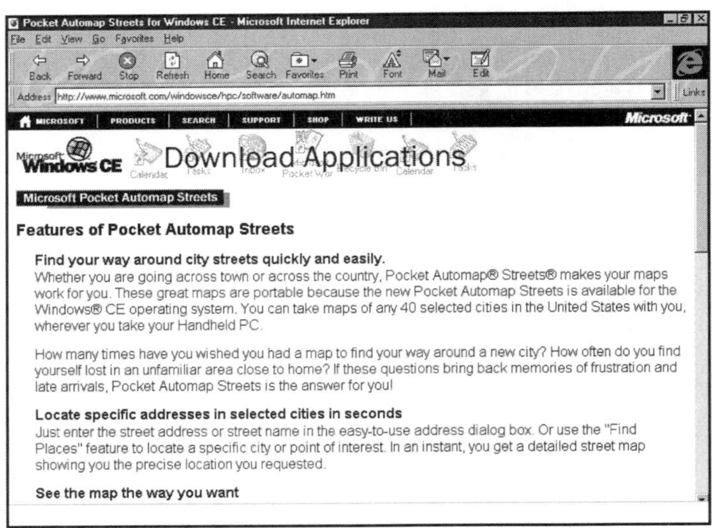

Figure 24.1.
Downloading Pocket Automap Streets from the Internet.

2. Click the `Download and install Pocket Automap Streets` text.
3. Find the download site nearest to you, and click the corresponding `pstreets.exe` (as shown in Figure 24.2) to download the main program.

Figure 24.2.
Choosing the closest download site.

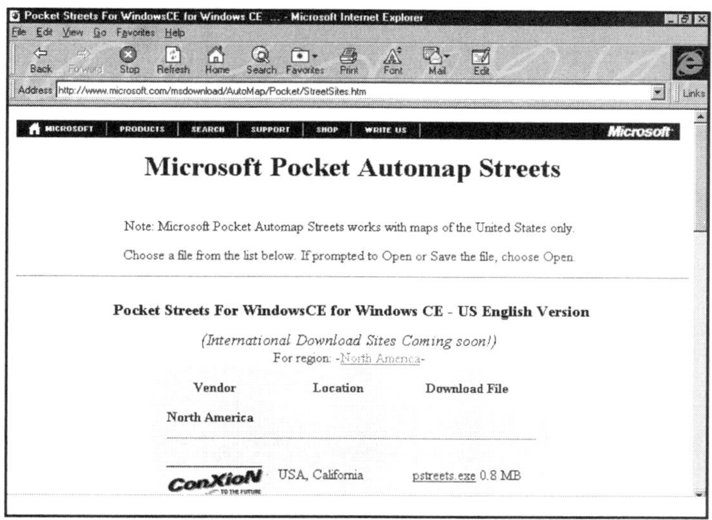

4. Download the maps you want by clicking the city you want. Currently, Microsoft supports the following cities, although new cities are being added:

Albuquerque, NM	Memphis, TN
Atlanta, GA	Miami, FL
Baltimore, MD	Milwaukee, WI
Birmingham, AL	Minneapolis, MN
Boston, MA	New Orleans, LA
Charlotte, NC	New York, NY
Chicago, IL	Orlando, FL
Cincinnati, OH	Philadelphia, PA
Cleveland, OH	Phoenix, AZ
Dallas, TX	Pittsburgh, PA
Denver, CO	Portland, OR
Detroit, MI	Salt Lake City, UT
Honolulu, HI	San Francisco, CA
Houston, TX	Seattle, WA
Indianapolis, IN	St. Louis, MO
Kansas City, MO	Tampa, FL
Las Vegas, NV	Washington, D.C.
Los Angeles, CA	

5. Double-click the Pstreets.exe icon on your desktop computer.
6. Read the license agreement, and then click the Yes button.
7. Click the Next button on the Pocket Automap Streets Setup screen (shown in Figure 24.3).

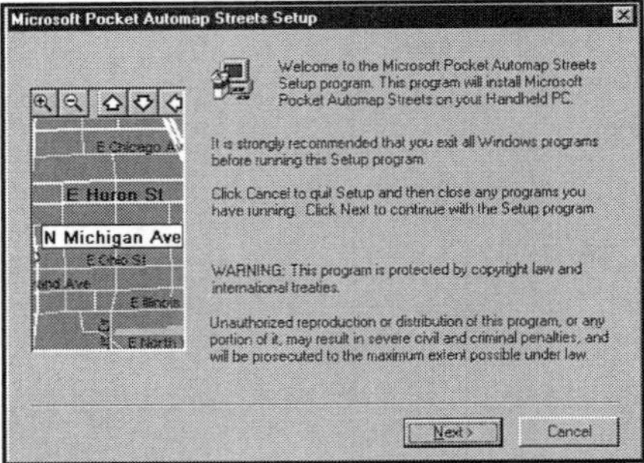

Figure 24.3.
Starting the setup process.

8. Click the Next and OK buttons until you reach the end of the setup process. Click the Finish button to complete the installation.
9. Use HPC Explorer to transfer maps to your HPC that have been downloaded to your desktop computer.

Running Pocket Automap Streets

To run Pocket Automap Streets, follow these steps:

1. Double-tap the Pocket Automap Streets icon on your HPC.
2. Select Other Maps from the View menu.
3. Navigate to the directory where you have installed the maps for the cities that you want to view. Once you have located the directory, you will see a list of available cities (refer to Figure 24.4).
4. Select the city that you want to view by double-tapping it. Your screen should look similar to Figure 24.5.

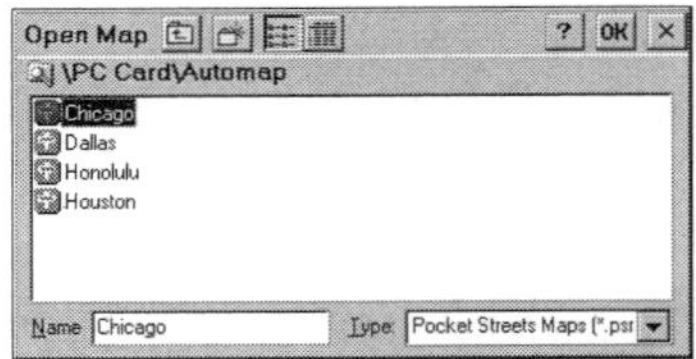

Figure 24.4.
Opening the correct city map.

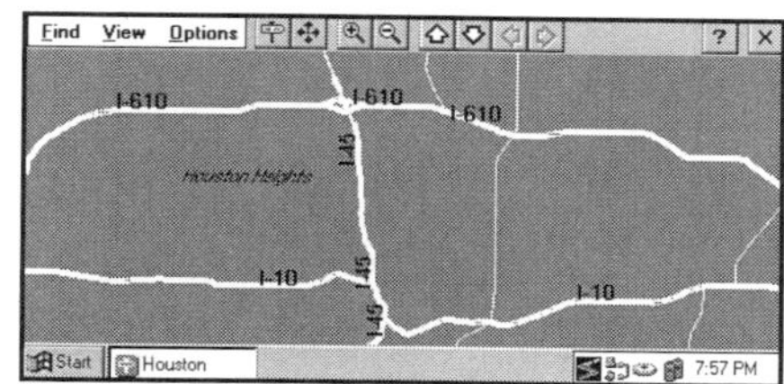

Figure 24.5.
Welcome to Houston.

As with most Windows CE programs, you can accesss Pocket Automap Streets help by tapping the Help button.

To quit Pocket Automap Streets, select Exit from the Options menu.

Finding an Address or Landmark

Pocket Automap Streets also enables you to locate a particular address or landmark. To find a particular place, such as a museum or restaurant, follow these steps:

1. From the Find menu, tap Find Places.
2. Type all or part of the name (such as museum) of the place you want to search for and press the Enter key (refer to Figure 24.6).

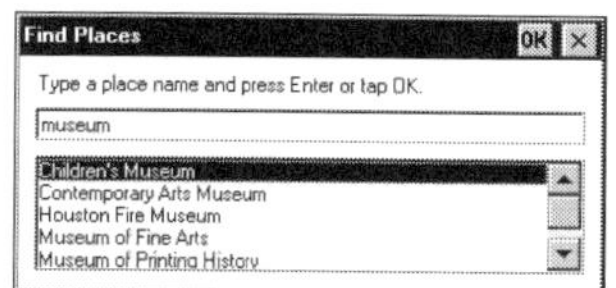

Figure 24.6.
Locating a specific place.

3. From the list of matches, tap the one you want, and then tap the OK button.

To find a particular address, follow these steps:

1. From the Find menu, tap Find Address.
2. Type the address you want to search for and press the Enter key (refer to Figure 24.7).

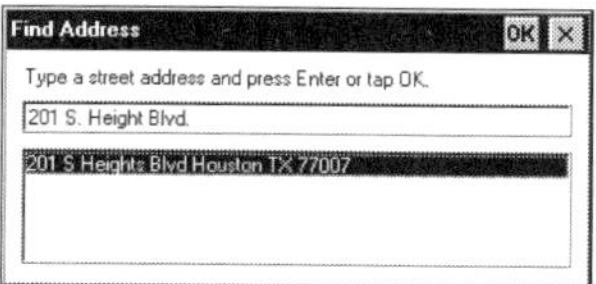

Figure 24.7.
Locating a specific address.

3. Tap the OK button to locate the selected address (as shown in Figure 24.8).

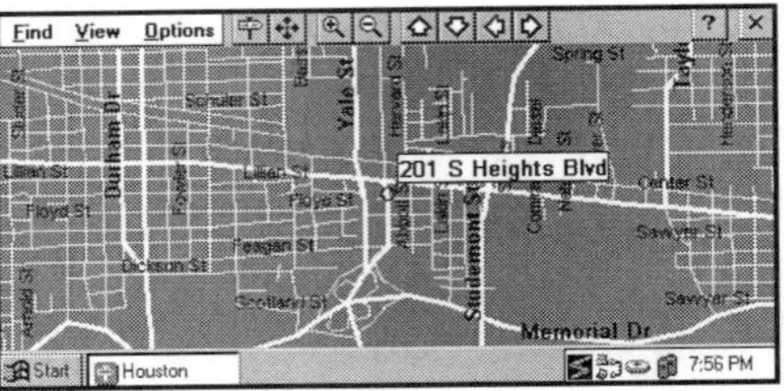

Figure 24.8.
Showing the found address.

Toolbar Icons and Keyboard Shortcuts

The toolbar of Pocket Automap Streets provides useful navigational icons. These icons allow you to zoom in and out and pan the map display. The arrows move the map a section at a time in the direction the arrow is pointing. The magnifying glass with the plus symbol zooms in, and the one with the minus symbol zooms out. The pointing sign icon is the toolbar shortcut for finding a place, and the four-directional arrows icon is the find address shortcut.

Pocket Automap Streets provides several keyboard shortcuts:

Key combination	*What it does*
Ctrl+A	Finds a particular address
Ctrl+P	Finds a particular place
+ sign	Zooms in
- sign	Zooms out
Arrow keys	Moves map display in direction of arrow

Customizing Maps

You can customize how the maps are displayed by selecting Map Styles from the Options menu (see Figure 24.9). You can display maps with a gray or white background. You can also define whether the program displays short names or the full street address when you tap on a street. To choose which points of interest are displayed, select Points of Interest from the Options menu. From the dialog box that appears (shown in Figure 24.10), select the check boxes for the points of interest you want to be displayed.

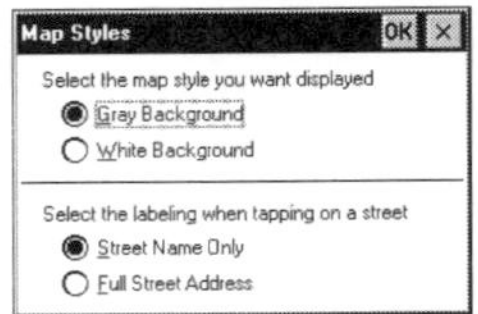

Figure 24.9.
Customizing your map.

Figure 24.10.
Selecting points of interest to view.

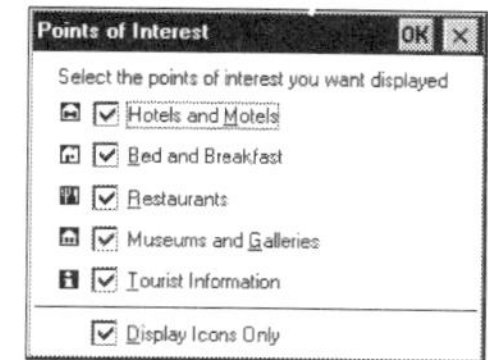

Other Third-party Software and Hardware

One of the most useful third-party communications programs available for your HPC is pcAnywhere CE. This program enables you to access, control, and transfer files from your desktop computer remotely. You can even run applications just as though you were in front of your desktop computer. Because your HPC's screen is much smaller than a traditional desktop or notebook computer screen, pcAnywhere CE provides several screen utilities such as ezZOOM, ezSCROLL, and ScreenScale to enhance readability and navigation.

To run pcAnywhere CE remotely, you will need a modem for your HPC and the desktop computer you are connecting to. Additionally, 4M of memory is recommended, but as long as you have at least 200K available for storage memory and 600K for program memory, pcAnywhere CE will operate. You need at least 16M of available hard disk space on your desktop computer. For additional information on pcAnywhere CE, contact Symantec Corporation at 1-800-441-7234.

Another useful Windows CE program is Dataviz's Desktop To Go. This utility, bundled with the Compaq PC Companion, adds synchronization and file transfer capabilities in addition to what comes standard with Windows CE. Desktop To Go supports Lotus 1-2-3, WordPerfect, Microsoft Works, Lotus Organizer, Microsoft Outlook, Internet Sidekick, ACT!, and several other desktop programs. You can reach Dataviz at 203-268-0030. Puma Technologies provides a similar program called Intellisync for Windows CE. You can reach Puma Technologies at 800-774-PUMA.

Windows CE Internet Sites

In addition to third-party hardware and software developers, several Internet sites provide useful information, freeware, and shareware. The following is a list of the most popular Windows CE sites on the Internet:

- Microsoft's Windows CE Web site: `www.microsoft.com/windowsce.com`
- Windows-4-CE Web site: `members.aol.com/Windows4ce/index.htm`

- Compaq PC Companion: www.compaq.com/us/common/prodinfo/handhelds
- Casio HPC Web site: www.casiohpc.com
- Hewlett Packard: www.hp.com/handheld
- Hitachi: www.hitachi.com
- LG Electronics: www.lge.co.kr
- NEC: www.nec.com
- Philips: www.velo1.com
- Windows CE Web site: www.windowsce.com

Summary

In this hour, you learned how to install, run, and use Microsoft Pocket Automap Streets. You also learned about several useful third-party software applications and popular Internet sites to help you get more out of your HPC.

Q&A

Q Can I run Pocket Automap Streets and store maps on a PC memory card?

A Yes, but Pocket Automap Streets will run much more slowly.

Q Can I use pcAnywhere while connected to a desktop computer?

A Yes.

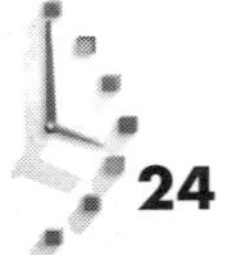

INDEX

A

B

C

D

E

F

G–H

O

P

Q–R

S

T

U–V

W–Z

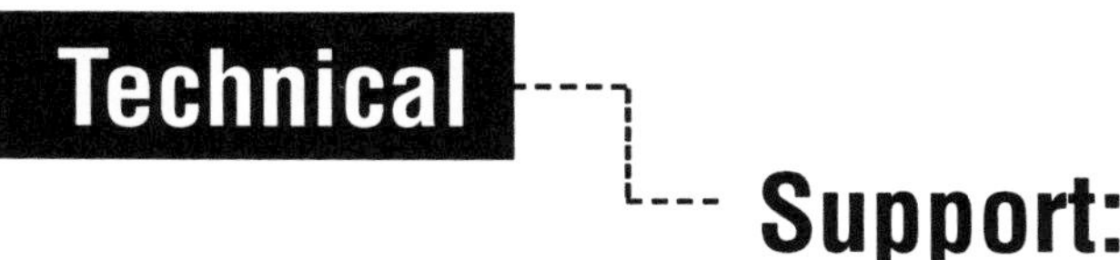

If you need assistance with the information in this book or with a CD/Disk accompanying the book, please access the Knowledge Base on our Web site at **http://www.superlibrary.com/general/support**. Our most Frequently Asked Questions are answered there. If you do not find the answer to your questions on our Web site, you may contact Macmillan Technical Support **(317) 581-3833** or e-mail us at **support@mcp.com**.

Teach Yourself Windows 95 in 24 Hours, Second Edition

Greg Perry

With learning broken down into twenty-four one-hour lessons, this easy-to-follow tutorial can be used by individuals, in seminars, in training sessions, and in classrooms. Whether users are just starting out or are migrating from previous versions of Windows, this must-have resource gets them up and running quickly and easily.

Loaded with "quick-start" chapters, "Do and Don't" tips, Question & Answer sections, quizzes, and exercises to help users master the concepts with ease.

$19.99 USA, $28.95 CDN

ISBN: 0-672-31006-6, 550 pages

Teach Yourself Microsoft Office 97 in 24 Hours

Greg Perry

An estimated 22 million people use Microsoft Office, and with the new features of Office 97, much of that market will want the upgrade. To address that market, Sams has published a mass-market version of its best-selling *Teach Yourself* series. *Teach Yourself Microsoft Office 97 in 24 Hours* shows readers how to use the most widely requested features of Office. This entry-level title includes many illustrations, screen shots, and a step-by-step plan to learning Office 97.

This book teaches readers how to use each Office product and how to use the products together. Readers also learn how to create documents in Word that include hypertext links to files created with the other Office products.

$19.99 USA, $28.95 CDN

ISBN: 0-672-31009-0, 450 pages

Teach Yourself Access 97 in 24 Hours

Timothy Buchanan, Craig Eddy, and Rob Newman

As organizations and end users continue to upgrade to NT Workstation and Windows 95, a surge in 32-bit productivity applications, including Microsoft Office 97, is expected. Using an easy-to-follow approach, this book teaches the fundamentals of a key component in the Microsoft Office 97 package, Access 97. Users will learn how to use and manipulate existing databases, create databases with wizards, and build databases from scratch in twenty-four one-hour lessons.

$19.99 USA, $28.95 CDN

ISBN: 0-672-31027-9, 400 pages

Teach Yourself Microsoft Outlook 97 in 24 Hours

Brian Proffitt & Kim Spilker

Microsoft Office is the leading productivity suite available, and in its current version, it provides Outlook as a personal information manager. Using step-by-step instructions and real-world examples, readers will explore the new features of Outlook and learn how to successfully integrate Outlook with other Office 97 applications. Each day focuses on working with Outlook as a single user as well as in a group setting.

$19.99 USA, $28.95 CDN

ISBN: 0-672-31044-9, 400 pages

Microsoft Office 97 Unleashed, Second Edition

Paul McFedries, et al.

Microsoft has brought the Web to its Office suite of products. Hyperlinking, Office Assistants, and Active Document Support let users publish documents to the Web or an intranet site. Office 97 also completely integrates with Microsoft FrontPage, making it possible to point-and-click a Web page into existence. This book details each of the Office products—Excel, Access, PowerPoint, Word, and Outlook—and shows the estimated 22 million registered users how to create presentations and Web documents.

This book shows how to extend Office to work on a network and describes the various Office Solution Kits and how to use them. The CD-ROM includes powerful utilities and two best-selling books in HTML format.

$39.99 USA, $56.95 CDN

ISBN: 0-672-31010-4, 1,200 pages

Teach Yourself Access 97 in 14 Days, Fourth Edition

Paul Cassel

Through the examples, workshop sessions, and Q&A sections in this book, users will master the most important features of Access. In just two weeks, they'll be able to develop their own databases and create stunning forms and reports.

This book has been updated for Access 97 and covers Wizards, tables, data types, validation, forms, queries, artificial fields, macros, and more! Readers learn how to program with Access Basic and Access lingo.

$29.99 USA, $42.95 CDN

ISBN: 0-672-30969-6, 700 pages

Peter Norton's Complete Guide to Windows 95, 1997 Edition

Peter Norton & John Mueller

Following the success of the best-selling *Peter Norton Premier* series, this complete reference provides users with detailed insights into this powerful operating system. Users will master all the tricks of the trade as well as learn how to create a Web page.

This book covers the new Internet Explorer interface, DSD, OEM Service Pack 2.1 enhancements, and more. It also provides advanced tips, optimization techniques, detailed architectural information, and extensive coverage of the Microsoft Plus! Pack. Peter's Principles, quick reference, and tear-out survival guide makes learning easy.

$35.00 USA, $49.95 CDN

ISBN: 0-672-31040-6, 1,224 pages

Teach Yourself Web Publishing with Microsoft Office 97 in a Week

Michael A. Larson

As the number-one selling office suite in the business world with over 22 million users, Microsoft Office is taking the market by storm. Using a clear, step-by-step approach and practical examples, users will learn how to effectively use components of Microsoft Office to publish attractive, well-designed documents for the World Wide Web or an intranet.

This book focuses on the Web publishing features of the latest versions of Microsoft Word, Excel, Access, and PowerPoint and explains the basics of Internet/intranet technology, the Microsoft Internet Explorer browser, and HTML.

The CD-ROM is loaded with Microsoft Internet Explorer 3.0 and an extensive selection of additional graphics, templates, scripts, ActiveX controls, and multimedia clips to enhance Web pages.

$39.99 USA, $56.95 CDN

ISBN: 1-57521-232-3, 464 pages

Book ISBN 0-672-31065-1